Getting Started in

Online
Brokers

T0334657

The Getting Started In Series

Getting Started in
Online
Brokers

Kristine DeForge
with
Loren Fleckenstein

John Wiley & Sons

New York • Chichester • Weinheim • Brisbane • Singapore • Toronto

This book is printed on acid-free paper. ∞

Copyright © 2001 by Kristine DeForge. All rights reserved.

Published by John Wiley & Sons, Inc.
Published simultaneously in Canada.

No part of this publication may be reproduced, stored in a retrieval system or transmitted in any
form or by any means, electronic, mechanical, photocopying, recording, scanning or otherwise,
except as permitted under Sections 107 or 108 of the 1976 United States Copyright Act, without
either the prior written permission of the Publisher, or authorization through payment of the
appropriate per-copy fee to the Copyright Clearance Center, 222 Rosewood Drive, Danvers, MA
01923, (978) 750-8400, fax (978) 750-4744. Requests to the Publisher for permission should be
addressed to the Permissions Department, John Wiley & Sons, Inc., 605 Third Avenue, New York,
NY 10158-0012, (212) 850-6011, fax (212) 850-6008, Email: PERMREQ@WILEY.COM.

This publication is designed to provide accurate and authoritative information in regard to the
subject matter covered. It is sold with the understanding that the publisher is not engaged in
rendering professional services. If professional advice or other expert assistance is required,
the services of a competent professional person should be sought.

DeForge, Kristine, 1970–
    Getting started in online brokers / Kristine DeForge with Loren Fleckenstein.
        p. cm.
    ISBN 0-471-39425-4 (pbk. : alk. paper)
    1. Online stockbrokers—United States—Directories.   2. Electronic trading of securities.
    I. Title.
    HG4907 .D44 2001
    025.06′332632—dc21   00-064914

10 9 8 7 6 5 4 3 2 1

To my parents, Pearley and Linda DeForge.
Thank you for a lifetime of unconditional love!
—Kristine DeForge

Acknowledgments

First and foremost, I wish to acknowledge and thank the person who inspired me to begin this project and who made me realize that anything is possible if you set your mind to it. Thank you, Dr. Ann E.G. Robinson, for your empowering spirit. I would also like to thank my fiancé, Mark Minervini, for his encouraging words to take on this project. Thank you, Mark, for standing behind me and for all your assistance—I love you. I would also like to thank my family for the encouragement and the wealth of support they have given me while writing this book. To all the brokerage firms that were of assistance to me in conducting the research thank you for your time and insight. Loren wishes to first thank Larry Connors, cofounder and CEO of TradingMarkets.com, for his support of this project. A number of people contributed invaluable ideas and criticism during the writing of this book. Among those whom Loren wishes to express his appreciation are James Angel, associate professor of finance at Georgetown University's McDonough School of Business and visiting scholar at Nasdaq; Bryan Brown, principal of Spectrum Equity Services; John Bollinger, president of EquityTrader.com; Douglas Gerlach, founder and editor in chief of Investorama.com and an authority on online investing; journalist Paul M. Krawzak of Copley News Service: Dave Landry, stock trader, columnist, and director of research for TradingMarkets.com; Jim Novakoff, expert on portfolio design and partner in the investment firm of Levitt, Novakoff; Fred Wynia, technical analyst and trader for NDB Capital Corp.; Kevin T. Reardon and Kerry Street, directors of technology integration at Medibuy.com; and Susan Woodward, chief economist at OffRoad Capital and former chief economist of the Securities and Exchange Commission. Finally, Loren wishes to thank Kathleen Desforges for her support and encouragement.

Kristine DeForge

Contents

Introduction

Congratulations! Since you're reading this book, it's safe to assume that you're preparing to open an online brokerage account to trade or invest in securities. You couldn't have arrived at a better time. The Internet has reshaped the investing landscape to your advantage. You will pay a fraction of the brokerage costs individuals paid just a few years ago, and you will possess at your disposal a treasure trove of information unthinkable in the days before the Web crashed the gates of the Wall Street elite.

Perhaps you have never bought a share of stock in your life. Maybe you're a seasoned point-and-click trader who seeks a brokerage with lower trading costs or more to offer. Perhaps you lie somewhere in between the novice and the veteran. Whatever your circumstances, some form of online account will probably serve you better than would conducting all your investing offline.

To help you choose the best option, this book surveys the trading costs and features of 117 brokers. Before diving into their individual offerings, you should first take stock of your own needs. Start by asking yourself three basic questions, and be honest with yourself.

KNOW THYSELF

1. How much *responsibility* are you prepared to take with your investments? Do you have the desire, acumen, and experience to go it alone? Or do you need or prefer outside help in your investment decisions and account management.

2. Are you a *trader* or an *investor*? Admittedly, the lines can blur between these two camps. Broadly speaking, traders seek to take advantage of relatively short moves in securities prices. They react quickly to market changes, buying and selling securities over time frames as short as a few weeks, days, or even minutes or seconds. Investors tend to buy

and hold stocks, bonds or mutual fund shares for months or years. They make far fewer transactions than do traders.

3. How do you plan to manage *risk?* You should never buy a security without understanding how you will prevent that investment from turning into a severe loss. Methods for reducing risk vary with investing and trading styles. Your choice of brokerage can help or hinder your ability to carry out your risk management plan and safeguard your hard-won capital.

Once you answer these questions, you can better determine the mix of costs and features that best suit you in a brokerage. We'll describe these and other considerations in greater detail.

THE NEW FRONTIER

The online revolution struck the brokerage industry like a tidal wave in the 1990s. The discount brokerage industry discovered the Internet, and an army of online brokerages sprung up almost overnight, offering point-and-click trading from the home for dirt-cheap commissions. At the same time, a multitude of websites emerged, scattering stock charts, analyst reports, stock-screening databases, portfolio trackers, and delayed and real-time quotes across cyberspace. Not long ago, such tools were reserved for Wall Street professionals and wealthy individuals. Not only did the online revolution make trading and investing affordable to just about anyone; it also democratized access to the most valuable asset of all—timely information.

For all its remarkable benefits, the new wave in investing had a frontier quality about it. The cyber prairie was pioneered by a band of gunslingers and homesteaders—aggressive traders and starstruck newcomers. Many people confused the point-and-click ease of entering orders from their personal computers with the serious, disciplined work of making money in the markets. The new frontier also had its outlaws. Cyber bandits found in the anonymity of the Internet ideal cover for classic fraud schemes on gullible investors. Meanwhile, just about anyone could open shop and sell online brokerage services—just hook up to the Internet, trumpet low commissions, and run commercials about customers striking it rich in the markets. A Gold Rush mentality set in, fueled both by get-rich-quick fantasies and by the reality of the raging bull markets of the 1990s.

Inevitably, some of these online prospectors went bust. Some blamed their losses on their brokers. The list of accusations aimed at the brokerage industry included lost or delayed order executions, website crashes, and backlogged call centers. All those failings occurred. Often, however, the do-it-yourselfers fell prey to their own lack of preparation.

Some failed to research the capabilities of their brokers before signing up. Some dived into the financial markets without a sound strategy. They bought stocks on half-baked hunches and tips and didn't base their choices on thorough homework. They bought with no thought to minimize the danger of incurring severe losses to their accounts. While you can call into question the lofty commissions levied by full-service brokerages, ignorance poses a greater threat to wealth than do trading costs. Even full-service brokers of mediocre talent would have recognized some of the obvious blunders that befell many in the go-it-alone crowd. In the Wild West, you're on your own.

THE SECOND WAVE

That's changing, and hopefully for the better. Trading costs will stay low and will continue downward. Meanwhile, discount brokerages are rolling out badly needed improvements, including personalized advice, better customer service, and faster, more reliable handling of orders. The brokerage industry isn't doing this out of the kindness of its heart. It must improve itself to attract new customers and retain existing customers.

In a recent study, Jaime Punishill, senior analyst at Forrester Research Inc., an online services research group, observed that the "aggressive affluent" traders and "get-rich-quick" investors who led the dash into online trading represented only 22 percent of the total investing population in the year 2000. As a source of new customers, that group is largely tapped out. Most active traders already trade over the Net, but analysts still predict explosive growth in accounts and assets moving online.

Who lies behind this growth? Mainstream investors.[1] Perhaps you count yourself among them. Mainstream investors recently displaced active traders as the largest source of new business in the brokerage industry (see Figure I.1). Punishill expects that gap to widen in the years ahead.

To capture this market, online brokers must address a different set of needs and tastes. Mainstream investors buy and hold over long periods and

[1] James P. Punishill, "Net Investing Goes Mainstream," The Forrester Report, March 1999.

	1997	1998	1999	2000	2001	2002	2003	2004	2005
Aggressive Affluent	43%	34%	29%	19%	11%	9%	8%	7%	8%
Get Rich Quick	31%	24%	5%	3%	1%	1%	1%	1%	1%
Portfolio Cruise Control	17%	27%	43%	52%	52%	38%	30%	28%	17%
Retirement By The Book	9%	15%	23%	26%	35%	52%	60%	65%	74%

FIGURE I.1   Percentage of New Online Investors
Source: Forrester Research Inc.

pursue conservative savings and investment plans. In the past, they have felt more anxiety than excitement at the prospect of entrusting their precious wealth to newfangled technology. Many prefer the security of mutual funds to the risk of betting on handpicked stocks. As a result, they didn't rush to log on when the online brokers cranked out their first advertising blitz.

Attitudes are changing, however, as the Internet becomes as much a part of our lives as the television and the telephone. Investors will want more than cheap trading costs and a convenient way to buy or sell securities. They'll need help with investment decisions, tax management, and estate planning in addition to the assistance provided by customer service departments that answer basic questions about using their online accounts.

A few years ago, if you wanted personalized advice, you signed up with a full-service broker and paid triple-digit commissions on every order to buy or sell stock. Online brokers offered little in the way of customer service or advice.

Discount brokers are starting to invade the full-service broker's turf of financial advice. Advances in technology, according to Punishill, will give rise to better interactive questionnaires that generate automated advice based on a customer's profile. This won't do away with the role of human advisors. Many investors will use online advice in collaboration with advisors.

The full-service brokers have fought back, and, again, the consumer is the winner. Our survey lists full-service brokerages that offer so-called wrap accounts for their online customers. For a flat yearly fee, a number of traditional brokerages will give you personal advice, as well as unlimited trading, online or offline.

This second wave will not forget the active trader. It's true that active traders represent a minority of total online accounts as well as a decreasing share of new account growth. However, they produce the lion's share of total trades handled by the brokerage industry. In a recent report for Bear, Stearns & Co., analyst Amy S. Butte observed that *self-directed asset managers*—in other words, investors—held 69 percent of an estimated 12.5

	Accounts (in thousands)	Daily Trades (in thousands)	Accounts (percent)	Daily Trades (percent)
Self-directed asset managers	8,611	56	68.9	3.0
Active traders	3,839	381	30.7	20.6
Semiprofessionals	50	1,413	0.4	76.4
Total	12,500	1,850	100.0	100.0

FIGURE I.2   Account and Daily Trades by Market Segment (Accounts and Trades in Thousands)
Source: Amy S. Butte, Bear, Sterns & Co.

million online accounts in the United States but made only 3 percent of daily average trades. As Figure I.2 shows, a disproportionate share of daily trades is generated by *active traders,* defined by Butte as traders who trade 25 to 50 times per year, and *semiprofessional traders,* who make 25 to 40 trades per day.[2]

It's not hard to see that the brokerage industry will go a long way to satisfy this small but influential group of account holders. They are demanding (and they are getting) smarter trading technology to obtain better pricing when buying and selling securities. Some of this improved capability, as Butte notes, appears destined to trickle down to mainstream investors.

This brings us to another important theme of the second wave of online trading and investing. As we enter the twenty-first century, brokers will remain under pressure to lower costs, but the most dramatic declines in trading costs appear to be behind us. The battle for your business is shifting to service levels and features as brokerage firms seek to differentiate themselves from their competitors.

As Kenneth Michal observed in *Computerized Investing,* an online newsletter of the American Association of Individual Investors,[3] the sharp

---

[2] Amy S. Butte, "Day Trading and Beyond," Bear, Sterns & Co., April 2000.
[3] The American Association of Individual Investors is a not-for-profit organization providing education in stock investing, mutual funds, portfolio management, and retirement planning. Membership is $49 a year, which includes full access to the AAII website, www.aaii.com, and a subscription to the monthly *AAII Journal.* You can contact AAII via the Web or their toll-free telephone number, 800-428-2244.

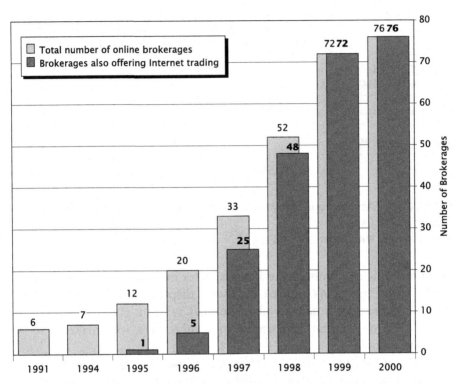

FIGURE I.3 Number of Online Brokers and Brokers also offering Internet trading
Source: American Association of Individual Investors, *Computerized Investing.*

decline in commission costs resulted largely from the explosive growth of competition in the brokerage industry in the 1990s. As the number of brokerage startups increased, the drop in commission rates sharpened as well. As the growth of added competition downshifted in 1998 and 1999, the drop in commissions slowed in turn.[4] This relationship stands out clearly in Figures I.3 and I.4. Analysts believe that the brokerage industry is shifting from an era of proliferation to one of consolidation. Weaker or smaller players will fall by the wayside or be bought out by the stronger, larger firms, which are hungry for more accounts, more assets, and the innovative trading technology demanded by their customers.

[4] Kenneth Michal, "On-Line Discount Brokers," *Computerized Investing,* American Association of Individual Investors, January/February 2000.

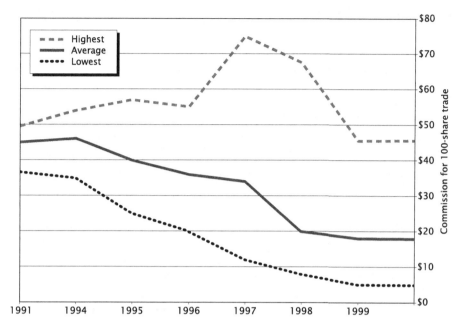

FIGURE I.4 Commission Costs for 100-Share Trade, 1991–1999
Source: American Association of Individual Investors, *Computerized Investing.*

WHY INVEST ONLINE?

Above all, you should be motivated by a desire to take personal charge of your money. No one has as great a stake in your financial future as you. Unlike human brokers, computer chips don't take vacations, go on golf trips, break for lunch, or keep your telephone call on hold while they give priority service to clients who generate more fee revenue. Once you've made a trade or investment decision, you log on to your account, click your mouse, and your order is entered and executed.

PERSONAL RESPONSIBILITY

With the power of an online account also comes responsibility. Do you have the time and commitment to learn a moneymaking strategy, perform your own research, and monitor your trades and investments? Do you possess the discipline to take emotions out of your decisions and act on objective rules, even during times when fear or euphoria is sweeping the financial markets?

If the answer is no, then do not trade or invest in individual stocks, let alone in the even more volatile securities such as options and futures. This does not, however, rule out some of the benefits of maintaining an online brokerage account.

Anyone with a long-term investing horizon should put part of his or her equity to work in stocks. Over the long term, stocks outperform all other major asset classes. For those who lack the time or commitment to deal with stocks in individual companies, stock mutual funds provide superb investment vehicles. If you invest in funds from different mutual fund families, an online account with access to a *mutual fund supermarket* may be just the ticket. A supermarket enables you to buy funds listed with the supermarket through a single brokerage account, which greatly simplifies record keeping and account management.

To take advantage of this revolution, you must adopt an approach to making money in securities that matches your time, temperament, and goals. Then you can find a brokerage that fits your style. This book will help you track down the right brokerage by listing 118 firms and detailing more than a score of criteria on each one to help you in your decision. Among other factors, you'll find information about trading costs and additional fees, availability of after-hours trading, products available to trade online, execution time, minimum deposit required, free services, banking services offered, and company background.

Before diving into the nitty-gritty details of individual brokerages, we'll explain the basics of opening an account and placing stock orders. Then we'll give you an overview of moneymaking strategies. Finally, we'll provide some advice on choosing computer equipment and an Internet connection for online trading and investing.

Nuts and Bolts

There's a lot more to trading securities than simply opening an account with a Web brokerage and reaching for your mouse. For starters, you must decide whether to open a cash account or a margin account. Then for each trade, you must choose the type of order instructing your broker how to handle that particular transaction. You must understand also how securities are priced. Finally, you should obtain timely order confirmation that your trade was executed.

CASH AND MARGIN ACCOUNTS

In a *cash account*, the account holder pays for all securities in full. Establishing a cash account is fairly clear-cut. You print out an account application from the broker's website, fill it out, and mail it in. The brokerage will have different forms, depending on whether you file for a standard individual or joint account or an Individual Retirement Account (IRA). You deposit the minimum equity required by the brokerage, and you're set.

The simplest way to establish an account balance is by depositing cash, by either check or wire transfer. You also can transfer assets from one brokerage to another. Your brokerage will provide you with forms needed to authorize the transfer. Most inter-brokerage account transfers are submitted through a regulated system called the Automated Customer Account Transfer Service, or ACATS.

Your brokerage also will have procedures for accepting securities certificates. Most people, incidentally, have their certificates held *in street name.* In other words, they leave their securities certificates in the physical possession of their brokers.

Once you've submitted your application and deposit, you should be able to check your account status by logging on to your brokerage's website or by contacting the broker by telephone. Your broker will notify you by regular mail once your account becomes active. Most brokers usually will arrange to notify you by email if you ask them to.

Once your deposit is credited to your account, your brokerage typically will park your cash in an interest-bearing account until you exchange money for securities such as stocks. Whenever you sell a security, your broker will sweep the proceeds back into the interest-bearing account. Brokerages often set a minimum balance—typically $1,000 to $2,000—for interest-bearing sweep accounts.

A *margin account* allows you to buy stock with money borrowed from a broker. (A margin account also is necessary for short-selling stock, a means of profiting from a price decline. Short-selling will be discussed in greater detail later.) Margin increases your buying power. It enables you to buy up to double the number of shares of stock as you could with only your own equity. As a result, margin will magnify your gains or losses beyond what would occur when buying stock on a cash basis.

A margin account works like a pre-approved credit line. When you draw on the credit line, your brokerage charges you interest and requires you to put up part of your own capital as collateral. This collateral is called *margin.* Under Regulation T set by the Federal Reserve Board, you can borrow no more than 50 percent of the value of cash and stocks in your account. This is called the initial margin requirement. Let's say you want to buy, on margin, $5,000 in stock. You would have to stake at least $2,500 of your own equity as collateral in the transaction.

After buying stock on margin, you become subject to the minimum maintenance level requirement of your brokerage. Under rules of the New York Stock Exchange and the National Association of Securities Dealers, you must maintain at least 25 percent equity in your margin account. Your brokerage may adopt this level or require still more margin, particularly when dealing with highly volatile stocks. If the value of your stock falls below the maintenance level, your broker will issue a margin call requiring you to deposit additional collateral—either cash or other marginable securities—to meet the maintenance minimum.

If you fail to meet the margin call by deadline, your broker will sell any assets in your margin account to collect the loan plus interest and commissions. In fact, your broker may not even bother issuing a margin call if losses threaten to mount too rapidly in a fast-moving market. The brokerage has the discretion to sell margin account assets without advance notice if the market turns badly against your holdings.

This may sound unfair, but remember that whenever you trade on margin, you're dealing with the broker's money. If you establish a margin account, be sure to read the credit agreement, which spells out the terms and conditions under which your broker extends credit in a margin account. Be aware that your broker may raise its house requirement, which sets the minimum level of equity required in margin accounts.

Inexperienced investors and traders should stay off margin and operate on a cash basis. Some of the worst financial misfortunes have occurred when the market turned against people who held heavily margined positions. Beware of letting the excitement of a raging bull market lead you into the reckless use of margin. When the crowd gets caught up in a buying mania and pulls out the stops on borrowed money, a severe downturn is usually right around the corner.

This happened recently in the Nasdaq bear market of 2000. In a memorable article for *Investors Business Daily,* staff writer Ed Carson told the stories of several people who gambled on margin and suffered disastrous losses. Carried away by a rally in technology stocks, many traders and investors went on a margin-financed buying binge. Margin debt swelled to a record $278.5 billion in March even as the market peaked. In the same month, a family physician mortgaged his home and went on margin to buy stock in a high-flying networking company. "As the market averages rolled over," Carson reported, "analysts questioned the company's future growth rate. The stock crashed 84% in three weeks, forcing a margin call from the doctor's broker who demanded repayment."[5]

The doctor later told Carson, "All of the money from the mortgage is totally gone. All of my savings account is totally gone. My whole life is turned upside down." The bear market did not spare professional traders either. The same article pointed out that the head of an online trading and data service made big margin bets and subsequently lost $45 million in the sell-off.

Everyone who trades or invests in stocks makes mistakes and suffers losses. The key to survival and prosperity lies in keeping those losses small

[5] Ed Carson, "Investors Learn Unforgiving Lesson: Margin and Bad Markets Don't Mix," *Investor's Business Daily,* May 22, 2000.

and giving your winning trades time to bear fruit and yourself time to learn a strategy. Even afterward, don't feel that you have to use margin. Many people build wealth in the stock market without pumping up their risk with borrowed money.

MARGIN MATH

Let's go over a few examples of how margin can boost returns and losses. To keep this illustration simple, these cases will ignore commission and interest costs.

For starters, take a simple cash transaction. You buy a round lot (100 shares) of stock at $50 a share, so you pay $5,000. We'll assume that $5,000 represents all the equity in your cash account. The stock subsequently appreciates $5, or five points, to $55 a share. You sell your shares for $5,500 and pocket a $500 profit. So you realize a 10 percent return on your equity.

With a margin account, you could have doubled your position in the same stock and reaped twice the return. In this scenario, you buy 200 shares at $50 a share. Half of your position is paid with your own cash. This satisfies the 50 percent margin requirement under Regulation T. The other half is borrowed from the broker. You now own $10,000 of the stock. The stock price rises five points to $55 a share. You sell your position for $11,000, pay back the $5,000 in loan principal, and pocket a $1,000 profit. That profit amounts to a 20 percent return on your equity.

Going on full margin, as the preceding example demonstrates, doubles the return of a winning trade. Full margin, however, is a double-edged sword. It multiplies the downside of a losing trade.

Let's look again at an ordinary cash trade. You buy 100 shares of stock at $50 a share. The stock declines five points to $45 a share, so the value of your position falls from $5,000 to $4,500. At this stage, you decide to cut your losses and sell the stock. The resulting $500 loss represents a 10 percent drawdown to your equity.

You would have fared worse if you had doubled your exposure by going on full margin. In this case, you put $5,000 of your own cash into the stock and borrow an equal amount from your broker, giving you a $10,000 stake. The share price subsequently falls five points to $45 a share. You sell your shares for $9,000, returning the full amount of the loan ($5,000) to your broker. You're left with $4,000—a $1,000 loss and a 20 percent bite out of your original equity.

QUOTES AND SPREADS

Whether the merchandise is kitchen appliances, commercial real estate, farm produce, or financial securities, buyers and sellers come together in a market for the same reason: to get the best possible price. Buyers want to pay the lowest price they can get for merchandise. Sellers seek the highest price they can get for their wares.

Stock markets quote both sides of the trade. When you decide to trade a stock or other security, you will find that it trades at not one but two prices: one for sellers and one for buyers. At any point in time, a security is quoted at the *bid,* the price buyers are willing to pay, and the *ask,* the price at which sellers are willing to sell. The ask also is referred to as the *offer.*

When you punch up a real-time quote using a conventional online brokerage during normal trading hours, you will see what is officially known as the *National Best Bid and Offer* (NBBO) at that point in time. The NBBO represents the combination of the best bid and the best ask (or offer). The best bid is simply the highest price that buyers are willing to pay for the stock. The best ask is the lowest price at which sellers are disposed to sell. The combination of the best bid and ask for a given security also is referred to as the inside market or the inside quote.

Table 1.1 displays the inside quotes for three stocks at a particular time. If you were to buy Intel shares at the market, you would pay the best ask, that being the most attractive price offered by sellers of the stock. You submit your buy order, which is executed, or filled, at $63^{11}\!/_{16}$ (assuming the price doesn't change before your order is filled). If you wanted to sell Intel at the market, your order would be filled at the bid, $63\frac{5}{8}$ (again, assuming the price doesn't move your fill).

The difference between the bid and the ask is called the *bid-ask spread.* Spreads vary with market conditions. In Table 1.1, Intel's spread was $\frac{1}{16}$ of a point, or 6¼ cents; Genzyme's, ¼ point, or 25 cents; and Kos Pharmaceuti-

TABLE 1.1 A Look at Three Quotes				
Company	*Ticker*	*Bid*	*Ask*	*Spread*
Intel	INTC	63⅝	63¹¹⁄₁₆	¹⁄₁₆ (6.25 cents)
Genzyme	GENZ	59¾	59¹³⁄₁₆	¼ (25 cents)
Kos Pharmaceuticals	KOSP	16⅜	16½	⅛ (12.5 cents)

cals', ⅛ point, or 12½ cents. Whenever an online trader or investor buys a stock, someone in the market profits from the spread in exchange for handling your order. Here's how it works.

Let's say a stock is quoted at 45 bid, 45⅛ ask. The spread is ⅛ point, or 12½ cents. You enter your buy order for 1,000 shares, buying at 45⅛ (assuming the ask price does not change between the entry of your order and its execution). If your brokerage deals in that stock, its trading desk will take the other side of the trade. If not, it will route your order to another brokerage or trading firm that makes a market in your stock. In any event, your order goes to a trading desk with direct access to the market. Unlike you, the trading desk buys at the bid, then turns around and sells at the ask. A professional trader acquires the 1,000 shares at 45 and sells them to you at 45⅛, pocketing $125 from the spread (1,000 shares × 12½ cents). This is called *making the spread.*

If you sell, the mechanism works in reverse. You enter an order to sell 1,000 shares at 45 a share. The trading desk buys your 1,000 shares at 45, then turns around and sells them at 45⅛, making the spread for a $125 profit.

TYPES OF TRADE ORDERS

You've logged on to your Web account, and you're ready to buy shares in that hot company. Perhaps you want to sell a stock that you already own. Or maybe you want to sell short. Don't click the "Submit Order" button just yet. You first must instruct your brokerage *how* to execute your trade.

You have a choice of four different trade orders: *market order, limit order, stop order,* and *stop-limit order.* You also can give your brokerage additional instructions in handling your trade. These choices will appear on your order entry ticket once you click on the button to initiate stock transactions. Figure 1.1 shows an example of discount brokerage Ameritrade's order entry screen.

A *market order* tells your brokerage to execute your trade immediately at the best price available at the moment. If you direct your broker to buy at the market, your order usually will be filled at or near the latest ask price at the time you submitted your order. If you sell at the market, your order usually will be filled at or near the best bid quoted when you submitted your order. Be aware that there's no guarantee that your brokerage will be able to fill your order at that price. In the time it takes the brokerage to execute your order, the price could move against you, which is called *execu-*

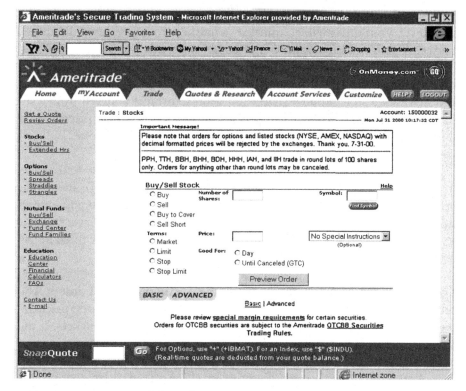

FIGURE 1.1 Ameritrade's Order Entry Screen
Source: Ameritrade Holding Corporation.

tion slippage, or in your favor. But you are assured that your order will be filled.

Many brokers restrict their cheapest commissions to market orders. The next order types that we'll discuss—limit, stop, and stop-limit—often carry higher commissions.

A *limit order* is an order to buy or sell at a specific price set by you. The brokerage will fill your order at your price or better if the stock moves to that level. For instance, you enter a limit order to purchase 100 shares of a stock at 40 a share. At the time, the market is 40¼ bid and 40⅝ ask. Your broker will fill your order if the ask falls to or below 40. You also can use limit orders to sell stocks. For example, you enter a limit order to sell if the stock hits 45 on the bid. Your stock will remain unsold until buyers bid the share price to 45 a share or higher.

You'll never pay more for a stock, or sell a stock for less, than you specify in a limit order. However, if the stock price never reaches your desired price level, your order will go unfilled. A market order ensures a fill but not a price. A limit order guarantees a price but not a fill.

A *stop order* instructs your brokerage to buy or sell a stock at the market if the price reaches or passes through a specific level. Let's say you buy 100 shares of a stock at 50 a share. You want to protect yourself from a severe loss in price. You place a stop-loss order setting the stop price at 47 a share. If the stock hits your stop price or falls lower, your broker will sell your shares to the highest bidder.

You also can use stop orders to buy stock. For instance, say a stock has traded at 50 or below for several months. You decide that a move above that price level would signal the start of a new advance in price. So you enter a stop order with a stop price of 51. If the stock reaches or surpasses that level, your stop order will become a market order and will be filled at the best ask.

Stop orders will not guarantee a fill at or near your stop level. Once activated, your order must compete with other incoming market orders. The probability that your trade will be executed at or close to your stop price decreases if you're dealing with volatile stocks or fast-moving markets. If the stock moves very fast, you could wind up paying too much for a new buy or selling for much less than your stop price.

A *stop-limit order* solves this problem. Like a stop order, a stop-limit order tells your brokerage to buy or sell once a stock hits the stop price. The stop-limit order also tells the brokerage not to pay more or sell for less than a specified price, called the limit price. This type of contingent order is not offered by all brokerages. If this type of order is important to you, be sure to check with your prospective brokerage firms about its availability.

Take the prior example of a stock that has traded at 50 or below. You want to buy if it breaks above that price, but you don't want to chase the stock too far up. You might enter an order to buy at "51 stop, 53 limit." This guarantees that you will not pay more than 53 a share if the stock hits your stop price.

You also can employ stop-limit orders on the sell side. For instance, let's say you buy a round lot at 50 a share. Then you can place an order to sell at "47 stop, 45 limit." That tells your brokerage to sell if the stock falls to or undercuts 47, but not to take less than 45.

There's the usual catch with any limit order. In a fast-moving market, a stock can blow past your limit before your order can be filled. This can prove costly if you relied on a stop-limit order for protection against a loss in one of your holdings. The order can go unfilled while the stock continues to head lower, increasing your paper losses.

SELLING SHORT

So far, we've only discussed trade orders to buy or sell stocks. When you buy a stock, you obviously hope that it will appreciate in price. If you're correct, you can later sell that stock for a profit. If you're wrong, you may end up selling the stock for a loss. Either way, your aim is to benefit from a rise in share price.

As odd as it may sound, there are ways to profit if a stock declines in price. One method is called *selling short,* or shorting. Shorting involves borrowing stock, so you must have a margin account in order to short.

Why short a stock? Markets, of course, don't always rise. They also decline. Bull markets, characterized by long-term advances in stock prices, give way to major declines called bear markets. Minor setbacks, called corrections, occur within bull markets. Furthermore, not all individual stocks share in the good times. Even when the market is advancing, as indicated by benchmarks like the Dow Jones Industrial Average and the Standard & Poor's 500 Index (S&P 500), there are always some stocks that hit the skids. Going short affords an opportunity to make money in these situations. (Going long, by the way, is trading lingo for buying a stock in hopes that it will rise in price.)

The mechanics of a short sale are pretty straightforward. Let's say you take a "bearish" view on the stock. You borrow shares from your brokerage and resell them, pocketing the proceeds of the sale. That's a short sale.

If you bet correctly, the stock falls in price. Then you cover your short, buying back the same number of shares that you had sold. In this hypothetical case, you made a winning trade. You "covered your short" at a lower price than that at which you sold, returning the borrowed stock to your brokerage and pocketing the difference minus margin interest and commissions.

What happens if you bet wrong and the stock rises in price? You lose money. Stocks can fall no lower than zero, but there is theoretically no limit on how much a stock can appreciate. As a practical matter, your broker will probably issue a margin call once the paper loss grows beyond the house limit and will liquidate your position if you fail to meet the margin call. By this time, of course, you will have suffered a severe loss. Just as with buying stocks, then, you should always have a plan for containing your losses in the event that a short sale turns against you.

Let's take an imaginary example of a successful short. You've formed a bearish opinion about Company XYZ. In other words, you believe its stock will drop in price. You borrow 100 XYZ shares from your broker and sell them at the market, receiving, say, 30 a share, or $3,000. To do this from your Internet account, you select "sell short" as your chosen transaction and enter the company's ticker symbol as well as the number of shares to be shorted into your online order entry ticket. The stock falls over the next few days. Then you cover your short by entering the ticker and number of shares and selecting "buy to cover" on your order entry ticket. Your order is filled at 25 a share. The round lot of XYZ stock is credited back to your broker, and you net a $500 profit, minus margin interest and commission costs.

Now look at the same scenario if you prove wrong. You short XYZ shares at 30. Contrary to your forecast, the stock *rises* in price. Imagine how you feel as you watch XYZ shares tick higher and higher—31, 32¾, 33⅛, 34. With each move up, you hope the stock will finally fall in line with your opinion, but, of course, the market doesn't care about your opinion! When the stock reaches 34⅝, you've had enough. You enter your "buy-to-cover" order, which is filled at 35 a share. You suffer a $500 loss on the trade, plus interest and commission costs, and the brokerage gets back its 100 shares.

Borrowing from your broker to short stock raises other complications that don't crop up when you deal strictly with your own cash and long trades. Shorting a stock makes you responsible for any dividends paid by the underlying company to the shareholder from whom you borrowed the stock. Your broker can call the stock at any point in time. You also pay margin interest on the borrowed stock.

OTHER ORDER INSTRUCTIONS

Good-till-canceled (GTC) orders remain in force until filled or lifted by the account holder or expire automatically under terms set by your brokerage. Most brokers set time limits on GTC orders. GTC orders typically stand for at least a month. *Day orders* expire if unfilled by the end of the trading day. You must reenter a day order if you wish it to be in effect the next trading session.

All-or-none (AON) instructions pertain to large orders. An AON instruction tells your broker to execute your trade only if sufficient shares are available to fill your trade in full. For example, let's say you entered a stop-limit order to buy 500 shares of ABC Corp. at 50, 51 limit, AON. This order instructs your broker to buy the stock if ABC rises to or above 50 a share, but not to pay more than 51 a share. Even if ABC meets both conditions, your order will go unfilled if fewer than 500 shares are available in that price range. *Fill-or-kill* (FOK) instructs the broker to fill the entire order at your limit price or better immediately—or not at all.

A *market-on-close* (MOC) instruction tells the broker to fill your order at the market as close to the end of regular trading hours as possible. Some day traders use MOC orders to switch back to cash by the end of the day. A *market-on-open* (MOO) instruction tells the broker to execute your trade as soon as the market opens.

TRADE CONFIRMATION

Your broker will send you a trade confirmation upon execution of your trade, either by on-screen display when you check your account or, if you request, by email. You also will receive a hard copy of your order confirmation by regular mail. This record will specify the stock bought, sold, or sold short; the price at which your order was filled; the number of shares; and the time and date when your order was executed.

ORDER ENTRY MISTAKES

The speed of online trading, combined with the excitement or fear that comes from standing to make or lose real money, can lead people to make basic errors in how they enter orders. Here are some common danger areas and pitfalls.

✔ **Ticker Symbol:** Before you trade, be sure you know the correct ticker symbol for the stock that you intend to transact. Some companies issue different classes of stock, each with a slightly different ticker symbol.

✔ **Order Size:** A single, unintentional tap on the keyboard can add another digit into the "Number of Shares" field of your order entry ticket, multiplying your order to ten times the intended size.

✔ **Market Orders:** Volatile stocks—stocks that tend to move very fast in price—can make real tracks between the time you submit an order and the time the order is executed. You can wind up paying far more or receiving far less for a stock than you intended. There are two ways to deal with this problem. A skilled trader with a brokerage account providing rapid order execution and confirmation might be able to act fast enough to deal in these risky issues. If you don't fall into this category, steer away from these stocks or rely on limit orders. Many investors get into trouble chasing stocks on the day of their initial public offering (IPO). The average stock opens about 15 percent above its offering price. In a hot industry, however, such as the Internet stocks in the late 1990s, some stocks would trade up to many times their offering or opening prices in a few minutes.

✔ **After-Hours Orders**: Many brokers give customers access to Electronic Communications Networks (ECNs) that offer stock trading between the close and open of the regular markets. Even relatively staid stocks can turn quite volatile in the after-hours market. If you transact stocks outside of the normal trading hours of the major exchanges and the Nasdaq, consider using limit orders to avoid chasing stocks too far.

✔ **Duplicate orders**: According to the Securities and Exchange Commission (SEC), one of the most common complaints of online investors pertains to delays in processing orders and confirming the receipt and execution of orders. A typical scenario involves an investor who submits a buy order and receives no indication, either on-screen or by email, that the trade has gone through. A few minutes later, the investor has a change of heart and sends an instruction directing the broker to cancel the order. Unbeknownst to the account holder, the trade already has taken place. Then a few minutes later, the investor changes his or her mind once more and enters a second order to buy the stock. The investor now owns twice as much stock as was originally intended.

Chapter

Strategy and Money Management

Perhaps the most dangerous market myth is that of the hot stock tip: All a person needs to do is bet big enough on that sleeper stock, then sit back and wait for those shares to lift off to the moon. This isn't investing; it's gambling. Playing around with your hard-won money in this manner is far more likely to expose you to severe losses than to fat returns.

Think about what makes up the stock market. Yes, we live in a time when more and more individuals are buying and selling stocks for their own accounts. But never forget who lies behind the bulk of daily transactions in the national markets—professionals. A New York Stock Exchange survey found that individuals accounted for only 6 percent of trading volume for a week in December 1999. The remaining 94 percent came from floor traders and other professionals, securities firms, and institutional investors like mutual funds, pension funds, and insurers.

Now give yourself a reality check. Up against thousands of pros trolling the market for prospective trades and investments, what is the likelihood that you'll luck across some undiscovered treasure chest by grace of a hot stock tip? In a word, slim.

Making money in the stock market rests on learning and practicing a sound strategy, not only for selecting individual stocks or mutual funds for purchase, but also for determining how long you will hold your investments. For instance, under what circumstances should you sell? To be effective, your strategy must also include a plan for dealing with *risk*, the potential of losing money on your trades or investments. This is called *money management*.

Within the world of stock trading and investing, you'll encounter a

21

Beware Internet Scams!

The Internet has given new life to age-old scams that prey upon people naïve enough to stake their cash on hot stock tips. Countless chat rooms have multiplied across the Web, filled with people trumpeting the next get-rich-quick stock. Some of these individuals have honest intentions. They may truly believe that they've discovered the next El Dorado. Others are out to commit fraud. One of their favorite schemes is called the *pump and dump.* The perpetrators will typically manipulate an obscure, low-priced stock that trades only a few hundred or a few thousand shares a day. They trade the stock back and forth among themselves. This rapid-fire action artificially "pumps" up the share price and creates the impression of a buying frenzy. At the same time, the scam artists fan out across the Web, masking their identities behind chat room pseudonyms, and hype the stock. Gullible tip hunters swallow the bait and snap up shares. This allows the fraudsters to "dump" the stock at inflated prices. Then they vanish from cyberspace with a fat profit. In the absence of their manipulation, the stock goes into freefall, leaving the buyer-victims with shares worth only pennies on their long-gone dollar.

What's the best defense against this fraud? Never risk your money based solely on a tip or other single source of information. If a tip sounds promising, check it out through careful research. Any number of free websites will provide you with the stock's trading history and other information on the company, such as earnings and sales figures, valuation ratios, and analyst recommendations. Read the company's press releases. Pull its legal filings with the SEC, available for free from the SEC's EDGAR database, which you can reach through the federal agency's website (www.sec.gov). Steer clear if the stock fails to meet the criteria of your strategy. Stocks that trade on average fewer than 300,000 shares a day pose additional risk due to a lack of liquidity. Stick to stocks that are listed on the NASDAQ national market, New York Stock Exchange, or American Stock Exchange. Stay away from stocks that trade on the over-the-counter bulletin board.

plethora of moneymaking strategies or styles. If you haven't decided upon a specific strategy, set aside the eternal debate about which strategy is "superior." The striking reality is that two traders or investors can pursue seemingly opposite styles and yet both succeed in the stock market. There are many valid, proven strategies. The key to success lies in finding and mastering the one that best fits your temperament, the amount of time you can commit to the market, and your tolerance for risk.

At times, one approach may indeed reward its practitioners with better returns than its "opposite." Then market conditions will shift, and the opposite style will outperform. This is the reason why so many investors, including professionals, produce poor results over the long run. A popular strategy enters a period of underperformance, wearing out its adherents and causing them to jump ship to another approach. This often occurs just as their original style was set to begin a new phase of superior performance.

Broadly speaking, the major approaches fall into four categories of opposite or complementary approaches: (1) *Income* and *Appreciation;* (2) *Growth* and *Value;* (3) *Passive* and *Active;* (4) *Technical* and *Fundamental;* and (5) *Momentum* and *Contrarian.* Some strategies combine elements from several of these categories. You can put these strategies to work either by trading individual stocks for your own account or by investing in mutual funds that follow your preferred approach.

INCOME AND APPRECIATION

Common stock represents a unit of ownership in a company. As a shareholder, you own in proportion to your stake in the company a portion of its *earnings,* the company's profit after it pays taxes to the government, interest to bondholders, and dividends to shareholders of preferred stock. You stand to reap a possible return on your investment in the form of dividend income or share-price appreciation.

Some companies pass on a portion of their profits to shareholders in the form of cash called *dividends,* usually paid on a quarterly basis. Stock selected because its underlying company has a history of paying dividends is called, naturally, an *income stock.* Of course, if you own income stocks in a taxable account, you will incur income tax on your dividends.

The second way a stock can benefit its shareholder is by *appreciating* in price—which allows you to sell your shares for more than you paid for them. Some companies don't pay dividends. Instead, they plow all their profits back into the business with the goal of making the company more profitable in the future. If the market perceives that is the case, your shares will rise in price accordingly. An advantage of owning such stocks is that you have no dividends on which to pay taxes. However, you will incur *capital gains tax* if and when you sell your stock for a profit (capital gain).

It should be noted that some stocks appreciate in price, for a time, even though their underlying companies show no earnings or earnings growth. When this occurs, the market often is anticipating the prospect of profitability or profit growth in the future. One example might be a business that recently became a publicly traded company in an IPO. The company has just raised capital by selling shares in the IPO. For a time, it will live off cash while attempting to establish a successful, profitable business. Another example is a company in a highly cyclical industry, or in other words, an industry that goes through boom and bust cycles. As a result, cyclical stocks will often appreciate rapidly from beaten-down levels before their companies report positive earnings as the market anticipates the turnaround. Likewise, after an extended run, cyclical stocks can sell off while earnings growth is still "on the table" as investors foresee the next bust phase.

GROWTH AND VALUE

Investing for share-price appreciation can be further divided into growth and value strategies. *Growth* investors invest in companies that are increasing their earnings at a faster-than-average clip. Such stocks often don't come cheap. They tend to exhibit higher-than-average *price-to-earnings (P/E) ratios*—a stock's share price divided by its earnings per share—because the market anticipates the higher profits in the future and has priced that expectation into the stock.

Value investors seek out stocks trading at low or depressed share prices relative to their earnings. They hope that other investors will come around to their view. If this happens, the stock price will rise as new buyers come to the stock. Value stocks typically trade at low P/E ratios. However, successful value investing requires more than simply snapping up low-priced shares. Many stocks with low P/E ratios represent struggling or failing companies that deserve their poor valuations. The key to successful value investing lies in spotting companies that enjoy sound business prospects missed by the market.

Some strategies—like growth at a reasonable cost, or GARP—blend elements of growth and value styles in an effort to find bargain-priced stocks in companies with rapid earnings growth.

PASSIVE AND ACTIVE

Active investing means taking the hands-on approach. You pick your own stocks, or you invest in an actively managed mutual fund, in effect hiring professional management to pick stocks for you. In either case, the investor attempts to one-up market returns by buying, selling, or short-selling securities according to a strategy.

Say it softly, but even professionals come up short for their clients when compared to the Standard & Poors 500 Index, which tracks the stocks of 500 of America's leading companies. Each year, approximately 80 percent of professional money managers fail to beat the S&P 500. So why not just buy a sampling of stocks that represent the market and hold?

That's the approach of *passive* index investing. In the past, index investing has meant buying shares in an index mutual fund or, more recently, an exchange-traded fund—a hybrid financial security that has diversified stock holdings like a mutual fund but trades throughout the day like individual stocks. The best-known index funds track the S&P 500, buying a representative sampling of index stocks, then periodically rebalancing those holdings to stay in sync with the chosen benchmark. Other index approaches follow strategies, such as growth or value, but remove human judgment by relegating buy and sell decisions to a mechanical set of selection criteria.

Technology now can enable online investors to create their own index portfolios without depending on mutual funds. The online broker Foliofn, for example, provides a variety of prepackaged portfolios based on different strategies and risk levels. The account holder can rebalance and customize portfolios for a fixed annual or monthly fee. For many index investors, this approach may prove less costly than incurring the annual capital gains distributions and paying the management fees and other expenses levied by mutual funds.

TECHNICAL AND FUNDAMENTAL

The terms *technical* and *fundamental* actually refer to ways traders and investors analyze stocks and companies rather than strategies per se. Technical analysis involves the study of a stock's past trading behavior—specifically, the changes in its price and trading volume—in hopes of finding clues about its future behavior. *Chartists* are technicians who use stock charts to identify bearish and bullish price-and-volume patterns to time buy and sell decisions. Fundamental analysis focuses on corporate earnings and sales, balance sheets, and other economic data in order to forecast stock price movements.

Some investors and traders rely exclusively on technical analysis, others on fundamental analysis. Some strategies combine both technical and fundamental analysis to pick stocks and investments and to time entries and exits.

MOMENTUM AND CONTRARIAN

Momentum investors and traders live by the Wall Street maxim, "Make the trend your friend." The idea is that a trend will likely persist in the same direction. Momentum can be technical and fundamental in nature, bullish and bearish. A number of studies have shown that high *relative strength stocks*—stocks that have appreciated more by percentage than the vast majority of their peers over a period of time—stand the best chance of outperforming the market in the future. Stocks caught in long-term price declines are odds-on favorites to fall further. A company with a track record of strong and improving earnings growth stands the best chance of its increasing profitability in the future. A company with weakening profits is likely to become less profitable.

Contrarian investing or trading is the flip side to momentum. Trends may persist, but they also can give way to excesses that end in violent reversals. Contrarians seek to trade off those extremes in crowd psychology. They sell or short-sell when excessive optimism sends share prices to unsustainably overpriced levels. Contrarians buy when panic selling marks shares down to bargain-basement prices.

For instance, an advancing group of stocks can become so obvious that a buying mania catches hold of the public, propelling share prices well beyond any reasonable valuation. At some point, the bubble bursts, and the downward price action can be quite swift and violent. The biotech sector stands as a good case in point. The American Stock Exchange (Amex) Biotech Index soared 240 percent from its low on October 18, 1999, to its peak on March 7, 2000. The subsequent markdown was nearly as breathtaking. The index of biotechnology stocks plunged 53 percent over the next six weeks. The reverse also holds true. Bear markets, for example, often end in climactic sell-offs. Fear gives way to outright panic. Shareholders throw away their stocks at fire-sale prices. At this juncture, astute contrarians will step in to profit as buyers.

Even successful momentum traders need some contrarian instincts to tell them when to get off the train. The great contrarian Humphrey Neill put it well when he wrote that "the public is right during the trends but wrong at both ends."[6]

MONEY MANAGEMENT

The first rule of making money in the stock market is to play a strong defense. Every person who trades or invests experiences losses. The key is to adopt and stick to a *money management plan* that prevents losses from becoming large enough to inflict serious damage to your precious capital. Over time, strong money management will enable the returns earned by practicing a valid trading or investing strategy to offset the inevitable losses.

Money management must address two forms of risk: *market risk* and *nonmarket risk*. Over the long term, the stock market has produced great returns for investors, outperforming all major asset classes. Of course, the market did not deliver those results in a straight, uninterrupted advance. As measured by major stock indexes like the Dow Jones industrial average and the S&P 500, the market undergoes major phases of rising share prices (bull markets) and major phases of declining share prices (bear markets). Within those cycles, stocks also go through lesser advances and declines called *rallies* and *corrections*. Market risk represents the risk of suffering a decline in the value of your account due to an adverse move in the general market.

All stocks and mutual funds do not share equally in the good and bad times. Within raging bull markets, stocks of certain companies and industries suffer steep losses. Likewise, some stocks resist the tug of bear markets and even rise in price. Nonmarket risk describes the risk unique to your portfolio, individual stocks, or groups of stocks.

TIME HORIZON

Money management starts with recognizing your personal goals and then determining a realistic length of time required to meet those goals. This is called

---

[6] Humphrey B. Neill, *The Art of Contrary Thinking* (Caldwell, Idaho: Caxton Press 1985).

your *time horizon.* Most people have multiple financial objectives, each with a different time horizon. The longer the time horizon for a given goal, the more market risk you can tolerate when investing for that goal. That's because your money has more time to appreciate and compound. If the market turns against you, your capital has more time to recoup your losses. The shorter the time frame, the less time your capital has to build or recuperate. As a result, a high degree of exposure to individual stocks or stock mutual funds may be appropriate for longer-term goals but not for shorter-term goals.

Imagine a 30-year-old person who saves money for two purposes: her retirement fund and a down payment on a home to be purchased within the next two years. Money for the down payment probably should not go into stocks or stock mutual funds. A correction or bear market could intervene, slashing the value of her investments before she hopes to buy her new home. Even if the decline were relatively brief, a subsequent rally or bull market might not fully restore the worth of her assets in time for her planned home purchase. She is probably better off putting that money in a federally insured interest-bearing savings account or, for a better rate of return, a money market account or certificate of deposit.

On the other hand, she faces far less market risk in her retirement account. Given her age, she doesn't expect to need those funds for the next 25 to 30 years or longer. Over that time, a number of bear markets will inevitably occur, but she can afford to remain invested in a properly diversified portfolio of stocks or mutual funds. Over time, successive bull markets should more than make up for the bear phases.

Jim Novakoff, a designer of portfolio models and a partner of Levitt, Novakoff, an investment firm based in Boca Raton, Florida, points out that your *evaluation horizon* should be consistent with your time horizon. "If you are investing for a 30-year period, for example, you should avoid evaluating performance based on daily trading patterns," Novakoff says. "Instead, while you should monitor your portfolio on an ongoing basis, you should pick intervals, say, once a year or once every other year, to evaluate your portfolio. This evaluation should compare your portfolio to similar portfolios or benchmarks. If you have a one-year time horizon, it is unwise to wait until the end of the year to evaluate your investments. Monthly assessments would be more appropriate."

BUY-AND-HOLD VERSUS MARKET TIMING

Buy-and-hold and market timing represent two contrasting approaches to the problem of market risk. A *buy-and-hold* approach, using stock funds or a diversified portfolio of individual stocks, can compound into outstanding returns over the long run. Some buyers and hold investors use a technique called *dollar-cost averaging* or *dollar averaging*. Through up and down markets, buy-and-hold investors continue to buy shares in fixed increments of equal dollar amounts. During bear markets, they acquire shares at depressed prices. During bull markets, they buy shares at higher prices. Over time, their cost basis averages out, which cancels out much of the risk of bear markets. This approach is well suited to long-term investors who have little time or inclination to track the market.

Market timing is a much trickier proposition. Active investors and traders who market time try to anticipate bull and bear markets, or rallies and corrections. They use a variety of fundamental, technical, and sentimental techniques to spot these turns. Market timers buy stocks, mutual funds, or exchange-traded funds when they believe bulls and rallies are at hand. They sell and run to cash, or short-sell, when they conclude that bears or corrections are emerging.

DIVERSIFICATION

Diversification entails building a portfolio that spreads your risk among many different securities of the same type (like stocks) or among different *asset classes* (for example, stocks, bonds, real estate, precious metals, and cash). Investors with shorter-term horizons may invest in a mix of money market instruments and long-term bonds as well as stocks. Bonds, for example, tend to hold their value or to appreciate when stocks decline. This sort of asset allocation reduces market risk (although it also can reduce returns compared to an all-stock portfolio during a strong stock market).

Studies of long-term returns, notably by Professor Jeremy Siegel of the University of Pennsylvania's Wharton School, show that stocks outperform all major asset classes, and that allocating assets outside equities reduces returns with no appreciable reduction in risk. What's the upshot of this reality? An all-stock portfolio can produce greater returns with no significant sacrifice in risk than can a mixed portfolio of stocks, bonds, and other asset classes—over the long term. The long-term investor should begin to shift assets out of stocks as his or her time horizon approaches.

While a long-term time horizon reduces market risk, the all-stock trader or investor still must contend with nonmarket risk. Imagine placing all your investment capital into the stock of a single company. The market could stand at the threshold of a powerful bull cycle, but if trouble strikes your company, your stock could plunge in value. You can reduce this risk if you deploy your money among stocks in a variety of companies from different industries.

However, the benefit of diversification comes up against a law of diminishing returns. The more stocks you add to a portfolio, the less diversification you obtain from each additional position. Let's say you've used all the money in your account to buy shares in a single company. You reconsider your decision and split your money between stocks in two separate companies. You've just slashed your exposure to any single company in half; your company-specific exposure falls 50 percent. Later you diversify further, spreading your equity in equal portions among three different stocks. Now your company-specific exposure falls to 33 percent of your total portfolio. That's a change of 12 percent. With each new stock, you obtain smaller and smaller amounts of additional diversification.

As a result, once you go beyond 10 or 15 stocks, additional gains in reducing your portfolio's volatility due to problems in individual stocks come only with large numbers of additional stocks. This shows up clearly in Figure 2.1.

A study by Gerald Newbould and Percy Poon, two finance professors at the University of Nevada at Las Vegas, suggests one might need to diver-

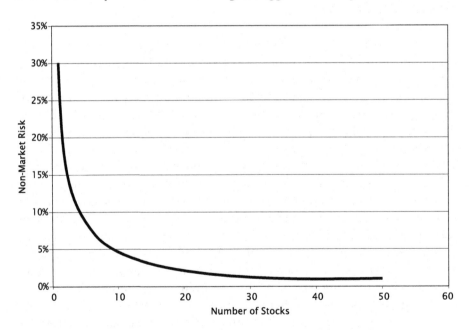

FIGURE 2.1 Nonmarket Risk versus Number of Portfolio Stocks

Note: Nonmarket risk equals percentage standard deviation of portfolio minus standard deviation of 1000 stock portfolio.

Source: www.foliofn.com.

sify among up to 40 stocks to obtain the full, practical benefit of diversification. Holding 40 stocks is manageable for a passive index investor, assuming that your trading fees or commissions don't bury you in transaction costs. And, of course, mutual funds and exchange-traded funds often hold even more than that number of stocks. If you select individual stocks according to an active strategy, however, a portfolio of 40 stocks, or even half that number, may exceed your ability to monitor your holdings.

Diversification also means more than simply splitting one's capital among many stocks. An investor must select stocks of companies that are not closely related to each other; a fully diversified portfolio would contain shares representing a wide cross section of industries. Let's go back to our investor who splits a one-stock portfolio into two stocks. The investor gains little risk reduction by owning stocks in, say, two Internet companies. If trouble hits Internet or technology stocks, chances are that shares in both companies will take a hit. On the other hand, imagine that the investor buys shares in an Internet company, and, say, a pharmaceutical company. The share price of one stock is far less likely to be affected by troubles affecting the share price of the other.

"It's important when diversifying that you understand what you are diversifying into," Jim Novakoff notes. "Buying 40 banks is different diversification than buying the S&P 500. Buying 40 value stocks is different than buying 20 value and 20 growth stocks."

PROTECTIVE STOPS AND POSITION SIZING

Even with diversification, you may consider additional approaches to curtailing risk. One possible approach is to put part of your money to work in mutual funds and to invest a smaller portion of your capital in a few stocks that you know well and can monitor.

Another method is to rely on loss-cutting tactics. Many traders and investors limit the amount of money they will risk in any single stock by setting an initial price floor at some percentage below their cost. This is called an *initial protective stop*. Let's say you set your initial protective stop at 5 percent below cost, and you buy stock of XYZ Company at $30 a share. You would sell if the stock fell to 28½ a share or lower. The art to this kind of risk control is to give stocks enough room to allow for normal bouncing around, or volatility, without giving them so much room that you expose yourself to a big loss. Inevitably, some stocks will fall just far enough to trip your initial protective stop, only to recover and head on to higher price levels. This leads some investors or traders to cheat on their stops, allowing stocks to fall further in price in hope that the stock will rebound and prove them right. Sooner or later, they regret relaxing their rules when a deteriorating investment snowballs into a huge loss.

You face a different sort of problem when you pick a winner. When do you sell once a stock advances well beyond your purchase price? Many traders and investors use elaborate systems of sell rules to time exits from profitable trades. One technique is the *trailing stop*. As the name suggests, you raise your protective stop behind your stock as it advances.

Protective stops work in reverse when short-selling stocks. The short-seller places the stop at some level above the point where he or she sold the stock short. If the stock advances far enough to tag the stop, the short-seller buys back the shares and covers the short.

No single form of risk control eliminates all risk. For example, let's say some out-of-the-blue disaster strikes a company in which you own shares. The stock could plunge to a fraction of your cost before you could sell at your desired stop level. For this reason, you should limit the size of your position in any one stock.

Many professional traders limit the dollar size of their positions in individual stocks to a percentage of the total dollar value of their accounts. A good rule of thumb is never to risk more than 2 percent of your total capital on any single trade. Some pros set that limit at 1 percent. Understand that the percentage does not represent the size of your position—it indicates the maximum loss allowed under your initial protective stop.

To illustrate, imagine a trader who uses a 5 percent initial protective stop and has a trading account worth $100,000. The trader also chooses to confine all losses to 1 percent of the total value of her trading account, so a 5 percent decline in a single position must not exceed $1,000 (1 percent of $100,000). That's the maximum allowable loss per trade.

So how much can the trader invest in the stock of a given company? Divide the maximum allowable loss per trade (in this case, $1,000) by the stop-loss percentage (0.05). That yields a maximum position size of $20,000.

In conclusion, your strategy should include a complete approach to controlling risk. If you are interested in learning more about strategies and money management from the trader's viewpoint, you'll find extensive lessons on the subject in the education sections of the TradingMarkets.com website (www.tradingmarkets.com),[7] for which Loren Fleckenstein serves as stocks editor. If you're in the investor camp, two superb online education sources are the American Association of Individual Investors (www.aaii.com) and the Motley Fool (www.fool.com).

[7] Loren Fleckenstein serves as stocks editor of TradingMarkets.com.

Chapter

The Right Broker for You

Before you start comparison shopping among the scores of brokerage firms competing for your business, ask yourself three basic questions:

1. How much help do you need with trading and investing decisions? Will you need someone to pick individual stocks and other investments for you? Do you plan to take matters into your own hands, buying and selling financial securities according to your own strategy and homework? Or will you take a middle path, placing part of your portfolio in the hands of a professional while making some decisions on your own?

2. Do you feel confident placing orders and tracking your account on your own? Or do you want the security of access to a live person to help you sort out the nuts and bolts of using your account?

3. How much speed do you need? Do you require streaming stock quotes along with rapid order execution and confirmation? Generally speaking, this applies to traders and active investors who must move quickly to take advantage of short-lived opportunities or who use price-triggered protective stops to exit positions. Or do you use dollar-cost averaging or buy-and-hold approaches that largely remove the need to react quickly to changes in the markets?

We'll use these three questions to help put you on the right track as you sort through the considerations that go into picking the right broker.

Then we'll give you some further pointers to help you choose among brokers based on their features and costs.

FULL-SERVICE BROKERS

Brokerages come in two flavors: full-service and discount. A *full-service brokerage* sets you up with a live broker who will offer you one-on-one advice, including estate and tax planning and a host of other personal financial services.

The key distinction of the full-service broker is that he or she has passed an exam to receive a Series 7 license. Among other things, this authorizes the broker to give you specific stock recommendations. Formerly, brokers were aided by their exclusive access to the recommendations and reports of professional analysts employed by their firms. If empowered by you, a full-service broker could also take over management of your account, buying and selling securities on your behalf.

For their services, full-service brokers charged through the nose. Full service, as you might guess, also meant full price. The full-service brokers levied commissions well into the triple digits. Discount brokers appeared about 20 years ago, followed by the online investing revolution in the 1990s. Discount brokers slashed commissions to a fraction of full-service fees. Although discount brokers did not offer specific stock recommendations, the gusher of information unleashed by the Internet caused many investors to dump their expensive full-service brokers and to take matters into their own hands.

Some had predicted the online investing revolution would all but do away with the traditional full-service broker, but a funny thing happened on the way to the revolution. Old-fashioned brokers like Merrill Lynch, Morgan Stanley Dean Witter, Paine Webber, Prudential Securities, and Salomon Smith Barney rolled out their own online offerings along with an alternative to commission-based trades. Instead of dinging your account with every transaction, these and other full-service houses offer *wrap accounts,* which allow unlimited trading for a flat fee based on a percentage of your assets under management. Brokers who receive income from trading commissions have an obvious financial incentive to push trades, whether or not they are in the interest of the client. A wrap account eliminates this long-standing conflict of interest. It may even encourage better client service because the broker has a direct stake in building the value of the client's portfolio.

The advantage is the convenience of online trading with the benefits of advice, specific recommendations, and, in times of confusion or anxiety, hand-holding from your personal broker. If you simply don't have time to watch the market or your portfolio, or you still want a live person to cross-check your decisions before you buy or sell, a full-service firm may be the ticket.

There are obvious drawbacks: cost and account size. Account minimums for wrap accounts typically range between $50,000 and $100,000, with asset-based fees running from about 0.125 percent to 1.5 percent per year.

DISCOUNT BROKERS

There was a time when establishing an account with a discount online broker meant cheap trades for the customer but little else in the bargain. You were pretty much left on your own to pick stocks, figure out your portfolio allocation, and make other big decisions. That is no longer the case. Even if you can't afford a full-service broker, you can still find a discount broker to match your level of independence.

At the upper end in terms of personal advice are discount brokerages that offer extensive tools to guide you in allocation and investment selection decisions and referrals to live financial advisors and consultants. Among these firms are Charles Schwab and Fidelity Investments. Even deep discounters are getting into the act. E*TRADE, for instance, has teamed up with Ernst & Young to provide tax and financial planning to its account holders.

What if the cost of personal advice still exceeds your pocketbook, and you still lack the time or inclination to pick your own stocks and keep close tabs on your holdings and the market? Online brokerages offer several solutions.

MUTUAL FUNDS AND MUTUAL FUND SUPERMARKETS

Not everyone is cut out to invest in individual stocks. You must perform thorough research on publicly traded companies. You must learn a strategy and possess the discipline to make decisions according to that strategy. You must not deviate your strategy because of tempting tips or emotions. Then you must track your portfolio holdings on a regular basis and practice sound money management.

If that sounds like too much to tackle, don't worry. Even if you can't afford the services of a full-service broker or upper-end discount broker, you can still afford to hire some of the best financial pros in the business by investing in mutual funds. Mutual funds also work well as a supplementary investment vehicle for stock pickers. For instance, you may choose to put a limited portion of your capital to work in a handful of individually selected stocks. Meanwhile, you could invest the remainder of your assets in mutual funds.

Stock mutual funds enable you to invest in equities with the competence of professional management and diversification. In the case of managed funds, highly trained fund managers and analysts take over the responsibility of selecting which stocks to hold on behalf of their shareholders. In the case of index funds, management simply invests in samplings of stocks aimed at tracking the market as benchmarked by a major index, such as the S&P 500. In either case, your dollars are spread across scores or even hundreds of publicly traded companies. This significantly reduces the risk of suffering a catastrophic loss. If your asset allocation profile includes bonds and other assets as well as stocks, you will find mutual funds to suit that mix as well.

Many online brokerages enable you to pick and choose among thousands of mutual funds through mutual fund supermarkets. A *supermarket* allows you to buy shares in mutual funds from many different fund families, all under your brokerage account. Of course, you can also buy shares in mutual funds directly from the fund families themselves, bypassing the broker. This scatters your holdings among different fund family accounts, however. What if you decide later to sell shares in the fund of one family and move the proceeds into the fund of a different house? Dealing directly with multiple fund families can become a major headache because every transfer of assets among your separate accounts entails substantial paperwork. A supermarket consolidates your activities into one brokerage account. A single order entered from your computer or by telephone does the trick.

Another potential advantage is cost. A growing number of discount brokers not only waive commissions for mutual fund activity but also have arranged with participating fund houses to waive *loads,* sales fees associated with buying shares in a load mutual fund. *No-load funds* do not charge a sales fee. Depending on your brokerage, you may be able to buy shares even in load funds without paying the load.

There are disadvantages to supermarkets. Not all funds participate in supermarkets. You should also be aware that the brokerage firms that offer mutual funds get a cut of the yearly fees that the funds extract from shareholder assets for their services. The brokers typically collect around 30 basis points (three-tenths of 1 percent) of assets. This is why some of the lowest-cost funds do not participate in supermarkets. A great source of information on mutual fund supermarkets is the nonprofit American Association of Individual Investors (AAII). Each September, AAII releases a survey of mutual fund supermarkets to its members. The survey details how many mutual funds are traded in each supermarket, with and without transaction fees, and reports whether supermarkets offer switching between fund families. The survey details which online services and features are available through supermarkets.

EXCHANGE-TRADED FUNDS

Exchange-traded funds (ETFs) have emerged as a relatively new alternative to mutual funds. Like mutual funds, ETFs spread your invested dollar among the stocks of many different publicly traded companies. Some ETFs track broad market indexes, making them suitable for dollar-cost averaging strategies. Others target industries and sectors.

True to their name, exchange-traded funds trade throughout the day on major exchanges, and their share prices fluctuate throughout the day, just like stocks. This differs from the vast majority of mutual funds. When you buy shares in an *open-end mutual fund,* you acquire your shares from the fund family. When you sell, the family redeems your shares. Because open-end fund shares do not trade on a market, they are priced only once a day. At the end of each market day, the mutual fund houses recalculate the *Net Asset Value* of their fund shares based on the closing prices of those funds' holdings, minus fund expenses.

The vast majority of exchange-traded funds are listed on the American Stock Exchange, so if you plan to make ETFs part of your portfolio, you'll need access to Amex-listed securities through your brokerage. If your brokerage charges commissions on stock transactions, you will also pay a commission whenever you buy or sell shares in an ETF.

Exchange-traded funds offer certain tax advantages compared to mutual funds: ETFs and mutual funds operate under the same tax rules, but the ETFs have figured out a way to avoid distributing capital gains. This differs from mutual funds, which must distribute capital gains once a year, causing shareholders to incur capital gains taxes. You incur capital-gains taxes on your ETFs only when you sell your shares (assuming you do so at a profit). Like mutual funds, ETFs distribute cash dividends paid on their component stocks. Those distributions are taxable.

BE YOUR OWN MUTUAL FUND

Nothing comes for free on Wall Street—least of all professional management! Both mutual funds and exchange funds come with management and other expenses. Mutual funds have the added problem of annual capital gains distributions. This differs from individual stocks. You realize a capital gain only when you sell your stock at a profit. Until you sell, you have no capital gain on which to pay capital gains tax.

According to Morningstar Inc., the online mutual fund education and rating service (www.morningstar.com), the average domestic stock mutual fund takes a yearly bite of 1.4 percent from assets under management. Although that may sound small, it can take a big toll in the long run. Each dollar subtracted from your account means less equity to grow and compound in the years ahead.

Take $50,000 invested in stocks for 20 years, and assume an annual return of 12 percent. At the end of 20 years, your $50,000 investment would have mushroomed to $482,315. Now factor in a yearly cost of 1.4 percent, reducing your annual return to 10.6 percent. In 20 years, the same $50,000 investment would have grown to $375,036. In other words, a loss of 1.4 percent per year pares your final return by $107,279, or 22 percent!

What if you could run your own diversified portfolio and fire your expensive mutual fund management? With the right online broker, you can! Online discount brokerage Foliofn (www.foliofn.com) has pioneered personalized stock portfolios for its customers. Investors can choose among scores of different portfolios tailored to suit different risk and return goals, investing styles, and other variables. The portfolios typically invest in about 25 stocks but can run up to twice that number, so you can achieve the same practical level of diversification afforded by a mutual fund or exchange-traded fund.

You simply choose a portfolio, then click. The brokerage buys all the portfolio stocks for your account. It's a snap when the time comes to rebalance your portfolio. With a single click, the brokerage evens up your holdings so that no one stock or group of stock represents an outsized share of your capital or departs from your chosen stock-selection criteria. You can also customize portfolios, subtracting computer-selected stocks to make room for your own choices. You can also create your own portfolios from scratch using Foliofn's stock-selection tools.

The broker charges a fixed annual or monthly fee. You incur no commission costs, no matter how many stocks you buy or sell or how frequently you trade. The key is that your account should be large enough to make the percentage cost of the annual fee competitive with the percentage cost of putting the same amount of money in a mutual fund.

This approach to investing has important tax advantages over mutual funds. Because you own individual stocks, you avoid the annual, taxable capital gains distributions encountered when you own mutual fund shares. You can also reduce your taxes by selling losing stocks at the end of the year. Foliofn provides tax tools that track each purchase and identify the positions that correspond to an investor's tax goals.

Foliofn will soon face competition. James P. O'Shaughnessy, an authority on quantitative investing and former chairman of O'Shaugnessy Capital Management, has taken his firm out of the mutual fund business and has founded Netfolio Inc. (www.netfolio.com). Netfolio, a registered investment adviser, has teamed up with brokerage Bear, Stearns to offer its own personalized portfolio service to investors. Customers take an online quiz to determine their goals and risk tolerance. Then Netfolio creates a customized portfolio of stocks tailored to the investor. Because Netfolio is a registered investment adviser, it can give clients specific investment advice.

E*TRADE, the second largest online broker after Schwab, has teamed up with eInvesting, another personalized portfolio pioneer. They will offer eInvesting's "Build Your Own Fund" product as part of E*TRADE's extensive offerings. Like Foliofn, Netfolio and E*TRADE/eInvesting allow you to create portfolios and rebalance for a flat annual fee. All three rely on dollar-dominated, rather than share-denominated, investing, so you have no odd-dollar amounts left in cash.

"You get all the advantages of owning individual stocks with all the advantages of a diversified portfolio," notes James Angel, associate professor of finance at Georgetown University's McDonough School of Business and visiting scholar at Nasdaq. "I think that's where the wave of online investing is going. You no longer need to hire a really expensive person to manage your money. It's now cost effective for individuals to be their own fund managers.

It's now possible for an individual to hold a big diversified portfolio of sound investments for virtually pennies. That's my vision of the future."

ALLOCATION TOOLS

Whether you invest in mutual or exchange-traded funds or in individual stocks, you still must make allocation decisions to deal with market risk. Some discount brokers, such as Charles Schwab and Fidelity Investments, can refer you to advisers to help with allocation decisions based on your personal profile, including the time horizons of your various goals and risk tolerance. A number of brokerages also offer automated allocation planners online. The online magazine SmartMoney.com (www.smartmoney.com) offers an interactive worksheet that will calculate your asset mix based on your age, income, net worth, spending needs, risk tolerance, and expectations about the future. You can find the application on the Web at http://university.smartmoney.com/Departments/TakingAction/AssetAllocation/.

CUSTOMER SERVICE

If you are new to trading or investing, you should give added weight to brokerages that are highly rated for customer service. How long will you have to wait before a live person takes your telephone call or responds to your email? Are customer service personnel knowledgeable about online transactions and order handling? A number of Web-based publications and organizations provide up-to-date surveys that rank brokerage firms by a host of factors, including customer service and their fitness for different trading or investing styles.

The leader in this field is Gomez Advisors (www.gomez.com). In particular, zero in on those brokers receiving high ratings for "consumer confidence." According to Gomez, the leaders in this category scored well in website availability and phone response time, had large, well-trained customer service staffs, and disclosed "key information about trading rules and executions to their customers." Other reputable providers of broker rankings include Forrester Research Inc. (www.forrester.com), SmartMoney.com (www.smartmoney.com) and the American Association of Individual Investors (www.aaii.com). Another valuable survey is compiled by Don Johnson (www.sonic.net/donaldj).

DISCOUNT BROKERAGES FOR DO-IT-YOURSELF STOCK PICKERS

If you plan to invest or trade in individual stocks, your major decisions in choosing a broker boil down to speed and reliability of order execution and trade confirmation, access to tools and research, trading costs, and access to your account. The proper mix of these factors will vary according to your style of investing or trading.

Increasingly, brokerages offer research, educational courses, and interactive tools, such as databases that enable you to screen for stocks meeting your strategy criteria. Before you give any weight to these offerings, find out what's already available for free or for subscription on the Web.

One of the best places to start is Investorama (www.investorama.com). Investorama provides a superb service by gathering together links to the best investing and personal finance sites on the Web as well as offering its own original educational content. In particular, check out Investorama's "Stock PowerSearch." When the user enters a ticker symbol, Investorama creates a page with scores of links to sources of information on that particular stock and company. For stock-screening sites, check out Hoover's Online (www.hoovers.com) and Market Guide (www.marketguide.com). Traders and active investors who use technical analysis in trade selection and timing should try out TradingMarkets's "StockScanner" and explore the site's other screens, indicators, commentaries, and lessons (www.tradingmarkets.com).

"Most of the research you'll find on online broker sites is something you can get for free elsewhere," notes Douglas Gerlach, founder and editor in chief of Investorama and an authority on online investing. "Sometimes, you do get some extra information that might be premium information, but it's not unique to a particular firm."

If you follow a buy-and-hold approach or use a system that does not require fast response to market movements, there's no reason to pay up for premium features like real-time streaming quotes and rapid order execution and confirmation. Just hunt down the broker offering the lowest commissions for the level of customer support and mix of features that you require. Make sure, though, that your brokerage offers portfolio tracking and issues clear, readable account statements.

Susan Woodward, chief economist at OffRoad Capital, an Internet-based investment bank, and former chief economist of the Securities and Exchange Commission, points out that speed of order execution makes little difference to the buy-and-hold retail investor. "Some brokers will execute it in a few seconds, others in a few minutes. Delay is just as likely to work in your favor as your detriment," Woodward says. "So it doesn't make much difference. Your market order has to be executed at the reigning National Best Bid or Offer, also known as the inside quote—assuming your order is sufficiently small, that it's not so large that it has to be put aside."

How large is too large? Most major brokerages will guarantee execution of market orders of up to 5,000 shares, well beyond the requirements of the vast majority of retail investors.

Not everyone practices a buy-and-hold or buy-and-rebalance strategy. Traders and some investors time their buy and sell decisions in response to moves in share prices, changes in market indexes and indicators, or other signals. If you're in this category, you'll need a brokerage that provides fast, reliable order execution, trade confirmation, and account updating. Some brokerages, such as Datek Online and MyTrack, specialize in serving the needs of traders and active investors. Mainstream brokerages like Schwab and E*TRADE have trotted out premium services of their own for active traders and investors.

The one-time snapshot quotes offered by many brokers these days may not be enough for active investors and definitely fall short of the needs of traders. If you fit into this group, you may also require a source of streaming quotes to keep you continuously informed of the prices at which your holdings and target stocks are trading. Some brokerages offer streaming quotes as part of their packages for active traders. If this is important to you, shop around and compare the cost of using a broker account with streaming quotes versus buying your quotes separately from a data vendor.

DIRECT-ACCESS BROKERS

Direct-access brokers cater to day traders and other highly active traders. Their software enables traders to scan all the available price quotes for a given stock before routing their orders to the sellers or buyers offering the best terms in just seconds. At present, the complexity and cost of direct-access trading systems exceed the skills and pocketbooks of most retail investors. However, the "smart" order-routing technology of direct access is becoming better, more automated, and easier to use all the time. It seems inevitable that the technology will make its way into mainstream brokerages in the future. In early 2000, Schwab acquired CyBerCorp and its direct-access software platform, CyBerTrader. Schwab is expected to introduce parts of the system to its clients. Other big online brokers are reportedly shopping for direct-access firms instead of risking the loss of their most active traders to brokerages that offer the technology.

At present, most mainstream brokers route their customers' orders to outside trading firms. These trading firms turn a profit on this order flow by making the spread. In return, the trading firms kick back a part of their revenue to the brokerages under a controversial arrangement called *payment for order flow.* We'll discuss this practice in greater detail later. In a nutshell, the customer's order is executed less efficiently than would be the case if the trade were carried out over a direct-access system.

WEIGHING TRADING COSTS

There's no free lunch on Wall Street. You can easily find brokers offering commissions as low as $8 a trade or lower. That's incredibly cheap compared to what prevailed just a few years ago. As recently as 1995, discount commissions averaged around $25 a trade, according to the American Association of Individual Investors. Some online brokerages have cut commissions to the lowest level possible—zero!

But watch out. Choosing a broker solely on commissions could expose you to hidden costs. The speed with which your broker fills your orders can affect the price you get when buying or selling securities. Depending on how you invest or trade, slow execution may cost you more than what you save on commissions.

You also should realize that those rock-bottom commissions advertised by brokers often don't tell the whole story about commission costs. Many Web brokers have established tiered commission structures. The lowest advertised rate typically refers to the cost of an Internet-entered market order. The same account holder can wind up paying more for an Internet limit order. Phoned-in, broker-assisted trades can run you still more. Some Web brokers reserve the cheapest commissions to orders of a certain size or to stocks listed on exchanges. Some brokers reserve their lowest rates to their most active traders.

This does not mean that everyone should sign up with brokerages offering premium order execution in exchange for higher commissions. The answer lies in striking the right balance between service and commission, based on how you trade or invest.

COMMISSION COSTS

Your total cost under a given commission structure depends on two factors: your trading frequency and the size of your typical order. All other things being equal, the more you trade, the more your total commission cost will mount. The smaller your typical order, the larger your trading costs per trade.

Let's look at a hypothetical example of two people who pay the same commission per trade. Joe Trader and Jane Investor have online accounts with a brokerage firm that charges a commission of $30 per order. They pay 30 bucks in commission every time they buy or sell.

Over the course of a year, Joe enters 200 buy or sell orders. His average trade involves $3,000 worth of stock, so his average commission cost equals 1 percent per order. Of course, a complete trade, or *round trip,* means selling as well as buying the same stock. Joe's cost per complete trade comes to 2 percent, so right off the bat, Joe enters every trade with a 2 percent loss. On average, his trades must make up that amount and then some for Joe to clear a profit. The cumulative effect is costly as well. Two hundred trades at 30 bucks a pop add up to $6,000 in trading costs for the year.

Jane Investor buys or sells stock only 30 times a year. However, she takes larger positions. Her average trade involves $20,000 worth of stock. As a result, Jane reckons her trading costs in mere tenths or hundredths of a percent. On average, she pays 0.15 of 1 percent per order or 0.3 of 1 percent per round trip. She also pays far less than Joe does for the year. Jane paid $900 in commissions for the year—a fraction of Joe's bill.

By the way, this example was worked out so that each trader turned over the same amount of money in a year's time. Jane entered 30 buy or sell orders averaging $20,000 per trade. Joe traded 200 times with an average order of $3,000. Each traded $600,000 in stock for the year, yet they fared far differently in terms of trading costs.

Clearly, Joe is paying too much in commissions, whereas Jane's commission costs appear negligible. Given Joe's rapid turnover rate, we can assume he's a short-term trader, holding positions for a few days to a few weeks. That's not much time for a stock to move very far in price. The best short-term traders and day-traders reap profits amounting to a few percentage points per trade. If your average trade produces, say, a 5 percent profit before commissions, you obviously can't afford commissions totaling 2 percent per round trip. That's 40 percent of your profit!

Traders or investors who buy and hold stocks for months or even years at a time have less to worry about. Assuming this approach gives their avcrage winning stocks time to generate double-digit percentage returns or better, and commission costs become less of a factor.

All things being equal, you should try to get the lowest commission possible. However, all things are never equal, even when it comes to calculating trading costs. There's also the issue of the price at which you buy or sell stock. As we will see, how your broker handles your order can make a difference of an eighth of a point (12½ cents) per share or more.

EXECUTION SLIPPAGE

Stock prices don't have to stand still between the time you enter your order and the point at which it is filled by your brokerage. In fast-moving markets, stocks can swing far and wide while your order awaits execution. Backlogs can also form during times of high trading volume, further delaying executions. In the meantime, stock prices don't stand still. While your order sits unfilled, the stock that you are buying could move higher in price. The stock you're selling could move lower.

This is called *execution slippage*. Execution slippage represents the degree a stock price slips or moves against you between the time you enter your order and the order is filled. Slippage causes the buyer to pay more for a stock. The seller winds up selling for less. In fact, market orders to buy or sell a stock can take minutes to fill, and there is no federal requirement that your order be executed within a minimum amount of time.

Professional stock trader Dave Landry recounted an experience that illustrates how speed of execution can affect a trader's overall trading costs. "Today there's more competition in the brokerage area, so you're probably likely to get better fills than used to be the case. But ten years ago," Landry recalled, "a friend of mine and I both happened to buy a thousand shares of the same stock at the same time. I had an account with a major discount brokerage. He was with one of the newer, lower-cost brokers. If memory serves, my commissions were twice what he paid. We submitted our orders at virtually the same time, but he ended up paying a quarter point more per share. So he wound up paying $250 more for the stock than I did. Even after commissions, that trade ended up costing him more than it did me."

To a short-term trader who's out to scalp small gains over many trades, execution slippage can prove very expensive as the lost fractions of a point add up over time. If you're a short-termer, you should focus on brokerages that provide rapid order execution and confirmation. Slippage also should be a consideration for longer-term traders and investors who use price signals to time buy and sell decisions. However, if you invest in stocks with the intention of holding over several months or longer, and you don't buy or sell off specific price points, then slippage may not be a concern. A stock could as likely move in your favor as to your disadvantage while you await your fill.

PAYMENT FOR ORDER FLOW

The purpose of any market is to match buyers with sellers and vice versa. For example, Nasdaq relies on a system of market makers to make sure there's someone to buy your stock when you sell and sell stock to you when you wish to buy. A market maker is a dealer who commits to buy or sell a given stock at its publicly quoted price. Often a number of market makers from different broker-dealers will compete to fill orders in the same security. Making a market can be a lucrative business. Most online investors buy stock at the offer price and sell at the bid price. The market maker buys at the bid, then can turn around and sell at the offer, pocketing the spread. He works the same advantage in reverse on sales.

Most retail investors buy or sell stocks *at the market,* meaning they will take the best prevailing price at the time their orders are transacted. If you enter a market order for a stock, and your brokerage makes a market in that stock, the firm will handle the order in house, making the spread.

In most cases, though, the broker will not make a market in your

TABLE 3.1 Brokerage Net Revenues for Calendar Year 1999		
	Margin Interest *(percent)*	*Payment for Order Flow* *(percent)*
Ameritrade	26	8
E*TRADE	19	6
DLJ*direct*	16	6
TD Waterhouse	19	5
Schwab	18	N/A

Source: Amy S. Butte, Bear, Stearns & Co. Inc. company reports.
Note: Commissions exclude estimated/reported order flow. Schwab commission percentage represent a calculation prior to the pro forma combination with U.S. Trust. Ameritrade percentage represent commissions and clearing fees per the financial statements. TD Waterhouse percentage represent commissions and fees per the financial statements for fiscal year.

stock. Under a prior arrangement, then, the broker will pass your trade to an outside market maker who deals in the security. The market maker transacts your order and pockets the spread. In return, the market maker makes a payment back to the referring brokerage.

This arrangement is called *payment for order flow.* Critics claim it amounts to a legal kickback from the market maker to the broker. The country's top market cop, SEC Chairman Arthur Levitt Jr., has stated that some brokers appear to route orders not to the market makers offering the best price but to market makers providing payment for order flow. At the very least, payment for order flow creates a potential disincentive for market makers to compete for orders by offering the best prices. Why should they compete if they're already guaranteed a stream of orders? In fairness to the brokerage industry, brokers have to make a profit some way. If they don't make it in commissions, they will find another to pay the bills. The key for you is to recognize all the factors bearing on your trading costs. Then choose the brokerage with the mix of order handling and trading costs that best fits your profile.

MARGIN INTEREST

Another revenue source for brokerages is *margin interest,* the amount of money brokerages charge for extending credit whenever you use margin to buy or short-sell securities. Professional traders use margin sparingly, going on margin to increase their exposure only when they detect unusually favorable market conditions. Thus, margin interest does not generally represent a significant recurring cost to the investor or trader. However, as you can see in Table 3.1, margin interest and payment for order flow do provide substantial sources of revenue to brokerages.[8]

[8] Amy S. Butte, "Day Trading and Beyond," Bear, Sterns & Co., April 2000.

Chapter

4

Your Online Lifeline

The Internet is a technological marvel, but it has a long way to go before it achieves the reliability of the telephone system. If you trade via the Web, never forget that this is your lifeline. As an investor or trader, you will depend on a reliable, speedy connection to the Internet both to enter your buy and sell orders and to obtain timely information, including research, breaking news, and stock price quotes.

Breakdowns in data service can quickly result in backlogged or lost orders, tardy trade executions and confirmations, and delayed or interrupted quotes and alerts from real-time quote vendors. You can miss out on opportune trades. Even worse, you may fail to get out of deteriorating trades or investments in time to avert severe losses to your account.

Fortunately, you can minimize these hazards by taking the following steps from the outset to safeguard your vital online lifeline.

ONLINE SURVIVAL TIPS

Buy a computer with a big brain

An online trader can run a multitude of software programs at once on the same personal computer. You have programs to process real-time quotes, track portfolios, create charts, and screen databases for securities that meet your trading criteria. You'll run one or more Web browsers to access your online account as well as pull down research from other websites. Toss in email and spreadsheet programs for good measure.

That kind of heavy lifting can easily slow program running speeds to a snail's pace or crash a PC with limited chip speed and memory. Purchase a computer with enough memory to run multiple programs and a microprocessor that's fast enough to process all that information. In other words, you want a computer that can think fast and remember a lot!

How much speed and memory are enough? That will vary with the user; and, of course, the demands we put on our computers increase over time as programs become fatter and more packed with features. For starters, here's a good rule of thumb: Check the product line of a reputable manufacturer or vendor, and buy somewhere between the supplier's fastest and slowest shipping microprocessor.

Microprocessor speed is measured in megahertz, or MHz. The higher the number, the faster the microprocessor. As of early 2001, a safe minimum for an active trader would be 400 MHz. An investor whose strategy does not require immediate reaction to market developments can get by with a 233 MHz microprocessor. If you use the Windows operating system, you may want a microprocessor with more horsepower if you move up from Windows 95 or 98 to Windows ME (Millennium Edition) or Windows 2000.

Memory capacity is measured in megabytes of Random Access Memory, or RAM. If you don't have to stay on top of the market minute by minute, you can get along fine with 64 megabytes (MB) of memory. A more active investor or trader can probably get along with this minimum, too, but 128 to 256 megabytes of RAM would be preferred. Sometimes, adding RAM can make a computer run faster than paying up for more microprocessor speed. In fact, RAM is probably your single most effective upgrade for the money. In most situations, you'd obtain a bigger bang for the buck by forgoing 100 to 200 MHz of microprocessor speed for an additional 64 MB to 128 MB of RAM.

Be ready to fall back on the telephone

Many brokerages will honor phoned-in orders at their online commission rate when high market trading volume or technical problems interfere with customer access to their websites. Keep at hand a record of your holdings, your online account number and password, your broker's telephone number, and any other information needed to access your account by phone.

Consider resorting to stop-loss orders

If you use protective stops and you lose online access to your account or quote service, consider using stop-loss orders. Most successful traders prefer to execute their own stops with market orders rather than relying on brokers, but you can take action only when receiving timely quotes. If your quote service fails, you're flying blind. Telephone your data vendor right away. If the vendor doesn't provide assurance of a swift remedy, consider instructing your broker to enter stop-loss orders on your standing positions. This is not a substitute for acting on your own stop-loss rules yourself. In fast-moving markets, many investors who relied on standing stop-loss orders with their online broker have found to their dismay that their orders were filled at levels far from their targeted stop-loss price.

Choosing Your Internet Service Provider

Sign up with an Internet Service Provider (ISP) with a track record for reliable service and customer support. If you travel and wish to access your online broker or other services from a portable computer, a national service is the ticket. If this is not a consideration, you might consider a local ISP, but watch out. Although some local ISPs provide excellent service, smaller companies often lack the depth of staffing and infrastructure of major providers. A few of the biggies include America Online and its subsidiary CompuServe, EarthLink, Microsoft Network, and AT&T. All offer unlimited access for a flat fee averaging $20 a month. For more information on ISPs, check out "The List" at www.thelist.com. The List provides an up-to-date, worldwide survey of ISPs, including their costs and features. You can search for ISPs by area code or country. It's also a good idea to check with friends, neighbors, and coworkers for their experiences with their Internet providers. If you use an ordinary analog telephone modem, confirm with your local operator that the ISP's access telephone number is a toll-free call. You don't want to share your investment gains with the phone company!

Think of a dependable Internet connection as an insurance policy against the losses and missed opportunities that can come with service failures. Buying a cut-rate insurance policy from a fly-by-night insurer can leave you stuck with inadequate coverage when disaster strikes. Marginal Internet service can leave you financially exposed as well. You run the risk of busy signals when you dial up, connection disruptions, and service slowdowns due to hardware and software failures at the ISP or heavy traffic that overwhelms the ISP's capacity.

If you require constant, uninterrupted access to your account and quote service, sign up with two separate ISPs. If one ISP fouls up, you'll have a backup. Ideally, both will be well-established providers. If the expense of maintaining two accounts bothers you, check out one of the free or limited-access services as your backup. Weigh the cost of the second service against the danger of missed order executions or sitting blind without streaming real-time quotes. A second ISP is overkill if your strategy and money management plan don't require continuous market vigilance.

Making the Right Connection

You can buy a computer with state-of-the-art chip speed and plenty of memory. You can sign up with a top-notch ISP, a premium online broker, and a real-time quote service to track your positions throughout the market day. All these bells and whistles will be worthless, however, if your data jams in the narrow "pipe" afforded by using an ordinary modem to dial up to your ISP over the standard "Plain Old Telephone Service" (POTS).

Dialing up by phone modems offers the cheapest way to log on to the Internet. But POTS is too slow and too unreliable for active traders who live or die by real-time market information and immediate execution and confirmation of trading orders. Moreover, analog modems appear to have hit the upper limit in terms of access speeds. You can buy modems that advertise speeds of up to 56,000 bits per second, or 56 kilobits per second (Kbps). In actuality, these modems tend to top out at 30 to 40 Kbps because of the limitations of standard telephone lines.

If you're willing to pay extra, your solution is a *high bandwidth,* or *broadband,* connection to the Net. Bandwidth refers to the range, or band, of frequencies available to your connection. The conventional telephone service to your home accommodates a relatively narrow range of frequencies. This works fine for ordinary phone conversations or for sending email and text files. Now the Web floods our computers with graphics and streaming audio and video—more data than can be pushed truly through this "thin pipe."

Think of broadband as a "fat pipe." Broadband technologies open up a wider range of frequencies, vastly increasing the amount of information that can be delivered to and from your computer. Connection speeds run into the millions of bits of data per second. Also, broadband access is "always on." The link between your computer and your ISP stays active and does not necessitate a dial-up.

A broadband link is close to essential for the active trader who requires streaming quotes and near-instantaneous order execution. The higher price—upwards of $40 a month—may be worth it even if you're a long-term investor. If you do a lot of research online, how much time do you want to spend waiting for your Web browser to open pages? Your Web pages will update instantly with a broadband connection.

The first broadband technology to reach the mass market was the *integrated services digital network* (ISDN). This technology uses existing copper wire but shoots data to and from your computer at 128 Kpbs. That's about four times faster than practical dial-up speeds. Two other broadband technologies—digital subscriber line and digital cable—have since superseded ISDN.

Like ISDN, *digital subscriber line* (DSL) runs across copper phone lines. Digital subscriber line usually means asymmetrical digital subscriber line (ADSL). A DSL-connected computer retrieves, or downloads, data at a faster rate than it sends, or uploads. For the purposes of a trader or investor, this is a distinction without much practical difference. Your only time-critical uploads are order entries, which amount to small packets of information. The heavy traffic of market information is on the higher-bandwidth download end. Most DSL services currently offered to the home user deliver data to your computer in the range of 128 Kbps to 1.5 Mbps (that's *megabits,* or million bits, per second).

Digital cable funnels data traffic through the coaxial cable used by your cable television service instead of old-fashioned copper wires. This "fatter pipe" can shuttle information at even faster speeds than DSL—for outgoing as well as incoming data traffic. Access speeds can run as high as 5 megabits. That's 5 million bits per second. If offered by your local cable company, pricing usually is in the same ballpark as DSL.

There is a drawback. Everyone who uses digital cable in your neighborhood connects to the service at the same point. As more people log on to digital cable in your neighborhood, the available bandwidth splits among the different users, slowing performance. Some digital cable providers pledge to maintain minimum speeds that still exceed DSL.

Online brokers have trotted out a third way to hook up to your account: wireless access. TD Waterhouse Group and Fidelity Investments were among the first to offer stock trading on cell phones. In June 2000, Charles Schwab announced that it would start offering customers trading over handheld computers and cell phones. At present, you probably should regard wireless as a backup feature, keeping you in touch with your account when you are away from your personal computer. The displays on cell phones and palm-type computers are too small for performing in-depth analysis. Access is less reliable than it is with DSL or cable. You can also wind up paying additional fees for wireless service as well as footing the cost of the gadgets themselves.

DIAGNOSING CONNECTION PROBLEMS

The Internet is a pieced-together network of competing computer networks linked together by switching machines called routers. Whenever you send information over the Internet, as when you transmit a buy order, transfer a file, or send an email, your computer converts this information into little packets of digital information. These *Internet Protocol packets,* or IP packets, span numerous routers and make multiple "hops" before reaching their intended destination. The same goes for any information sent back to your computer.

The path your data takes to reach a given destination can vary. This fact stems from the Internet's Cold War–era origins. Today's Internet evolved from a Pentagon-sponsored network called Arpanet, which was designed to keep computers connected with each other even during the extreme outages that could occur in war. If any computer in the network becomes disabled or unavailable, the network will look for alternate routes to deliver your data.

Delays and breakdowns can occur at any link along this complex electronic chain. Don't assume the problem lies with the website that you are trying to contact if you experience a slowdown in the flow of data between your computer and the websites. There are two common causes of trouble. One is traffic. Just like a motorist during rush hour, you're more likely to run into congestion during peak use hours than during times when fewer people are online. Any link in the route between your computer and destination website can become overwhelmed with competing traffic, delaying or losing your data in the process. The other source of delay is the number of hops. Think of the difference between driving across city surface streets versus taking a highway. The fewer hops encountered along the way, the sooner information arrives at its intended destination.

Fortunately, you'll find a number of useful tools on board your computer and available on the Web to test your connection, pinpoint trouble spots, and check the speed of your broker's website.

TOOLS ON YOUR COMPUTER

The Microsoft Windows operating system has two handy diagnostic utilities called *Ping* and *Tracert.* You operate both from the MS-DOS Prompt window, which you'll find by clicking on the Windows "Start" button, then the programs menu.

Ping stands for *Packet InterNet Gropper.* The word also borrows from

Navy sonar terminology. Submarines and surface ships can measure distances to other craft by sending out bursts of sound called "pings" and timing the returning echoes. The Ping program works in a similar fashion. Ping dispatches an IP packet to a chosen website and measures the time it takes to get a response in milliseconds. The program also tells you the percentage of any data lost in the process. To use Ping, just type the command "ping" and the site's server name at the DOS prompt, then press the enter key on your keyboard. For example, to ping the Investorama website, you would type *ping www.investorama.com* and press enter.

Ping tells you the speed of a connection to a given destination. In the event of a slow connection, however, Ping won't pinpoint the source of the problem. For that diagnosis, there's Tracert, which stands for *Trace Route*. The speed of a connection depends on all the hops over which your data travels. A slow connection with your broker's website may stem from trouble at the broker's server, the connection between your computer and your ISP, or one of the routers in between. Tracert tells you which link in the chain is slacking off.

Tracert reads out the site name or address of all the hops along the path to a given destination and reports the response time of each. Tracert also will inform you of data lost at any of the hops, printing an asterisk (*) next to the bad hop. If Tracert reports four "Request timed out" responses, you probably have come across a router that refuses Tracert requests. Sometimes, Tracert will keep pinging away at an unresponsive router. If this occurs, you can quit the Tracert program by holding down the *Control* key on your keyboard while pressing the *C* key.

To use Tracert, type the command "tracert" and the site's server name at the DOS prompt, then tap the enter key. Let's say you want to trace a route to the website of the American Association of Individual Investors. You would type *tracert www.aaii.com* and press enter.

The Macintosh equivalent to Tracert is WhatRoute, a shareware program that lists the names of all routers relaying IP packets from your Macintosh to a given destination computer. Like Tracert, WhatRoute measures the round-trip times at each hop and flags unresponsive links. You can find WhatRoute, from CNET's download site, at http://download.cnet.com.

WEB TOOLS

Microsoft's MSN website provides a *Bandwidth Speed Test* that will measure the connection speed between your computer and the MSN site. The Bandwidth Speed Test's Internet address is http://computingcentral.msn.com/topics/bandwidth/speedtest.asp.

Another useful tool is the Smart Money *Broker Meter.* SmartMoney.com (www.smartmoney.com), the Web-based magazine of personal finance, teamed up with Keynote Systems to provide a Web-based application that compares the speeds of dozens of brokerage websites. The Broker Meter updates daily and allows you to compare the response times of prospective brokers' websites on different days. You can find the Broker Meter by going to the magazine's home page, then clicking the "Tools" tab and looking under "Stock Tools". Or you can type the URL, www.smartmoney.com/si/brokermeter/, in your Web browser's address field and then press enter.

Chapter 5

Brokerage Profiles

CRITERIA

Brokerage Type: One of three types. Full service brokers provide a wide range of advice and services, including specific stock recommendations. Discount brokers provide lower-cost trades. Some discounters provide general financial guidance, but they don't give stock recommendations. Direct access brokers, mainly of use to highly active traders, enable customers to route their orders directly to buyers and sellers through Electronic Communications Networks (ECNs) and other routes such as Nasdaq's SelectNet and Small Order Execution Systems.

Commission Charges: Fees charged by a broker to buy or sell a stock or other security. Most online brokers have tiered commission schedules. Fees can vary with the choice of orders, such as market or limit; type of security, such as stock, bond or option, listed stocks or Bulletin Board stocks, U.S. or foreign stocks; method of accessing the broker, whether Internet, telephone, or in person with a representative of the brokerage; or other variables. Commission trades are listed separately for market orders, limit orders, option trades, telephone trading, and after-hours trading.

Market Orders: Orders to buy or sell a security at the best price available on the market. See Table 5.1 and Figure 5.1.

TABLE 5.1 Ranking of Market Order Commission Costs

Company	Market Order (dollars)	Profile Page Number
American Express Brokerage (account balance $25,000 and up)	0.00	79
FreeTrade	0.00	129
The Financialcafe.com	0.00	207
Tradescape	1.50	214
Buy and Hold.com	2.99	94
US Rica	4.95	224
Brown & Company	5.00	89
RJT.com	5.00	187
Trend Trader (Easy Trader)	5.00	218
Empire Financial	6.95	112
Firstrade	6.95	122
Scottrade	7.00	192
Inves Trade	7.95	143
Suretrade	7.95	201
Wyse Securities	7.95	244
Ameritrade	8.00	83
Wang Investments	8.00	234
Computel Securities	9.00	101
A.B. Watley (Watley Trader)	9.95	72
American First Trader	9.95	80
Direct Access Trader	9.95	106
InvestIn.com	9.95	142
Most Actives	9.95	158
RT Trader	9.95	190
Stoxnow	9.95	197
Trade Cast Securities	9.95	210
Trading Direct	9.95	217
Your Trade	9.95	245
Datek	9.99	104
JPR Capital	10.00	146
Trend Trader (Order Routing System)	10.00	218
On-Site Trading Inc.	10.95	173
Terra Nova Trading	11.95	204
Bidwell & Company	12.00	87

(continued)

		Profile
	Market Order	Page
Company	(dollars)	Number

TABLE 5.1 (Continued)

Company	Market Order (dollars)	Profile Page Number
My Discount Broker.com	12.00	162
Patagon.com	12.00	177
TD Waterhouse Group	12.00	202
Tru Trade	12.95	220
Harris Investorline	13.00	135
Invest Express Online	13.95	141
Internet Trading.com	14.00	138
Net Vest	14.00	169
JB Oxford & Company	14.50	144
Livestreet.com	14.50	149
1st Discount Brokerage	14.75	108
National Discount Brokers	14.75	164
Access Broker.com	14.95	74
American Express Brokerage (account balance less than $25,000)	14.95	79
Cybercorp.com Inc. (CyberX & CyberX2)	14.95	103
Equity Trading	14.95	114
E*TRADE	14.95	116
FBR.com	14.95	119
Fidelity Investments	14.95	120
Foliofn	14.95	123
Freeman Welwood	14.95	128
Gay Financial Network	14.95	131
MB Trading	14.95	152
Mr. Stock	14.95	159
Muriel Siebert	14.95	160
Polar Trading.com	14.95	180
Quick & Reilly	14.95	185
RML Trading, Inc.	14.95	188
Trade Pros	14.95	213
Unified Management Corporation	14.95	222
Vision Trade	14.95	227
Web St. Securities	14.95	236
INTLTRADER.com	14.99	139
Cales Investment Corporation	15.00	95
Dreyfus Brokerage Services, Inc.	15.00	111

	TABLE 5.1 (Continued)	
Company	Market Order (dollars)	Profile Page Number
Freedom Investments	15.00	126
Preferred Trade	15.00	182
Wilshire Capital Management	15.00	238
Sunlogic Securities Inc.	15.99	198
Cybercorp.com Inc. (Cyber Trader)	17.95	103
Franklin Ross, Inc.	17.95	125
Gro Trader	17.95	133
Peremel Online (Direct Account)	18.00	178
Stockwalk.com	18.95	195
The Executioner	18.95	205
Bull & Bear Securities, Inc.	19.95	91
Castle Securities Corporation	19.95	96
Citicorp Investment Services	19.95	100
Far Sight Financial Services, LP	19.95	117
Leighbaldwin.com	19.95	148
Main Street Market.com	19.95	151
One Invest.com	19.95	170
Pacific On-Line Trading and Securities	19.95	174
Smart Vest	19.95	194
The Net Investor	19.95	209
Trade 4 Less	19.95	212
Trade-Well Discount Investing, LLC.	19.95	216
Wachovia	19.95	228
Wall Street Discount Corporation	19.95	232
Wingspan Investment Services	19.95	240
WR Hambrecht	19.95	242
Netfolio.com	19.95	166
DLJ Direct	20.00	109
Vanguard Brokerage Services	20.00	225
A.B. Watley (Ultimate Trader)	23.95	72
American Century	24.95	81
Online Trading	24.95	171
Wall Street Electronica	24.95	233
All-Tech Direct	25.00	77
Bush Burns Securities	25.00	92
Net Bank	25.00	165

(continued)

TABLE 5.1 (Continued)

Company	Market Order (dollars)	Profile Page Number
US Bancorp Investing	25.00	223
Wall St. Access	25.00	230
Benjamin & Jerold Discount Brokerage	29.00	86
Frontier Futures, Inc.	29.00	130
World Trade Financial	29.00	241
Accutrade	29.95	76
Charles Schwab	29.95	98
Merrill Lynch Direct	29.95	154
Morgan Stanley Dean Witter	29.95	156
Sun Trust Securities	29.95	200
Atlantic Financial	35.00	85
Peremel Online (Personal Account)	38.00	178
Average	15.75	
Flat fee or percentage of assets–based		
Interactive Brokerage LLC	$0.01 per share	137
PaineWebber	Asset-based fee	176
Prudential Securities	Asset-based fee	183
Salomon Smith Barney	Asset-based fee	191
Net Stock	Dollar-based investing	168

Limit Order: An order to buy or sell a security at a specified price or better. For instance, if you enter an order to buy a stock at $30 a share, your broker will not buy that stock unless the price reaches $30 a share or lower. On a limit order to sell a stock at $30 a share, your broker will not sell your shares unless the price rises to $30 or higher. See Table 5.2 and Figure 5.2.

Option Trades: Automated and broker-assisted commissions on options trades.

Telephone Trading: Ability to enter orders by telephone and commission cost.

After-Hours Trading: Ability to trade stocks outside normal market

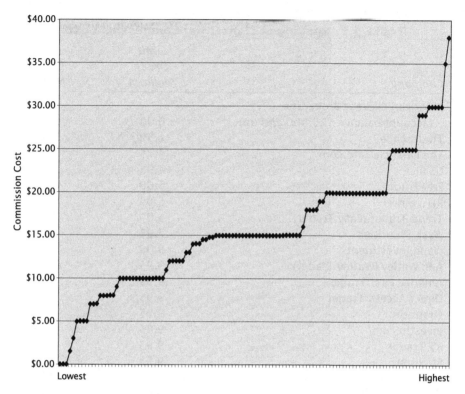

FIGURE 5.1 Market Order Commission Costs

trading hours, which run from 9:30 A.M. to 4:00 P.M. EST. Monday through Friday, except for holidays recognized by the national markets. After-hours trading is conducted over ECNs.

Products Available to Trade Online: Types of securities that a broker will enable its customers to trade. Examples are stocks, options, mutual funds, and bonds.

Average Execution Time: Average time to execute a market order once received by the brokerage firm. Information provided by the brokerage firm.

Minimum Deposit Required: The minimum dollar balance required to open an account with a brokerage. See Table 5.3 and Figure 5.3.

Additional Fees: Fees other than commissions charged by the brokerage. Examples include fees for account inactivity, extra account statements, exercising warrants, and check-writing.

TABLE 5.2   Ranking of Limit Order Commission Costs

Company	Limit Order (dollars)	Profile Page Number
American Express Brokerage (account balance $25,000 and up)	0.00	79
Tradescape	1.50	214
The Financialcafe.com	4.75	207
US Rica	4.95	224
FreeTrade	5.00	129
RJT.com	5.00	187
Trend Trader (Easy Trader)	5.00	218
Wyse Securities	7.95	244
Wang Investments	8.00	234
A.B. Watley (Watley Trader)	9.95	72
America First Trader	9.95	80
Direct Access Trader	9.95	106
Firstrade	9.95	122
InvestIn.com	9.95	142
RT Trader	9.95	190
Stoxnow	9.95	197
Suretrade	9.95	201
Trade Cast Securities	9.95	210
Trading Direct	9.95	217
Your Trade	9.95	245
Datek	9.99	104
Brown & Company	10.00	89
JPR Capital	10.00	146
Trend Trader (Order Routing System)	10.00	218
On-Site Trading Inc.	10.95	123
Empire Financial	11.95	112
Inves Trade	11.95	143
Terra Nova Trading	11.95	204
My Discount Broker.com	12.00	162
Patagon.com	12.00	177
Scottrade	12.00	192
TD Waterhouse Group	12.00	202
Ameritrade	13.00	83
Internet Trading.com	14.00	138
Livestreet.com	14.50	149

	Limit Order (dollars)	Profile Page Number
TABLE 5.2 (Continued)		
Company		
1st Discount Brokerage	14.75	108
Access Broker.com	14.95	74
American Express Brokerage (account balance less than $25,000)	14.95	79
Cybercorp.com Inc. (CyberX & CyberX2)	14.95	103
Equity Trading	14.95	114
FBR.com	14.95	119
Foliofn	14.95	123
MB Trading	14.95	152
Most Actives	14.95	158
Muriel Siebert	14.95	160
Polar Trading.com	14.95	180
RML Trading, Inc.	14.95	188
Trade Pros	14.95	213
Unified Management Corporation	14.95	222
Vision Trade	14.95	227
Web St. Securities	14.95	236
Bidwell & Company	15.00	87
Cales Investment Corporation	15.00	95
Dreyfus Brokerage Services, Inc.	15.00	111
Freedom Investments	15.00	126
Preferred Trade	15.00	182
Wilshire Capital Management	15.00	238
Mr. Stock	16.00	159
Cybercorp.com Inc. (Cyber Trader)	17.95	103
Franklin Ross, Inc.	17.95	125
Gro Trader	17.95	133
Invest Express Online	17.95	141
Tru Trade	17.95	220
Harris Investorline	18.00	135
The Executioner	18.95	205
Computel Securities	19.00	101
Net Vest	19.00	169
JB Oxford & Company	19.50	144
National Discount Brokers	19.75	164
Bull & Bear Securities, Inc.	19.95	91

(continued)

TABLE 5.2 (Continued)

Company	Limit Order (dollars)	Profile Page Number
Castle Securities Corporation	19.95	96
Citicorp Investment Services	19.95	100
E*TRADE	19.95	116
Far Sight Financial Services, LP	19.95	117
Fidelity Investments	19.95	120
Freeman Welwood	19.95	128
Gay Financial Network	19.95	131
Main Street Market.com	19.95	151
One Invest.com	19.95	170
Pacific On-Line Trading and Securities	19.95	174
Quick & Reilly	19.95	185
The Net Investor	19.95	209
Trade 4 Less	19.95	212
Trade-Well Discount Investing, LLC.	19.95	216
Wachovia	19.95	228
Wall Street Discount Corporation	19.95	232
Wingspan Investment Services	19.95	240
WR Hambrecht	19.95	242
Netfolio	19.95	166
INTLTRADER.com	19.99	139
DLJ Direct	20.00	109
Peremel Online (Direct Account)	20.00	178
Vanguard Brokerage Services	20.00	225
A.B. Watley (Ultimate Trader)	23.95	72
American Century	24.95	81
Leighbaldwin.com	24.95	148
Online Trading	24.95	171
Smart Vest	24.95	194
All-Tech Direct	25.00	77
Bush Burns Securities	25.00	92
Net Bank	25.00	165
Stockwalk.com	25.00	195
US Bancorp Investing	25.00	223
Wall St. Access	25.00	230
Benjamin & Jerold Discount Brokerage	29.00	86
Frontier Futures, Inc.	29.00	130
World Trade Financial	29.00	241

	Limit Order (dollars)	Profile Page Number
TABLE 5.2 (Continued)		
Company		
Accutrade	29.95	76
Charles Schwab	29.95	98
Merrill Lynch Direct	29.95	154
Morgan Stanley Dean Witter	29.95	156
Sun Trust Securities	29.95	200
Wall Street Electronica	29.95	233
Sunlogic Securities	32.00	198
Atlantic Financial	35.00	178
Peremel Online (Personal Account)	38.00	94
Buy and Hold.com	Limit order trading not available	
Average	$17.19	
Flat fee or percentage of assets-based		
Interactive Brokerage LLC	$0.01 per share	137
PaineWebber	Asset-based fee	176
Prudential Securities	Asset-based fee	183
Salomon Smith Barney	Asset-based fee	191
Net Stock	Dollar-based investing	168

Free Services and Financial Links: Research tools and reports, earnings estimates, and other information that brokerages may offer.

Real-Time Quotes: Availability of stock quotes at current market prices (as opposed to delayed quotes). This criterion identifies whether snapshot quotes, which require you to reenter a ticker to refresh the quote, and/or streaming quotes, which continually update for your chosen stocks, are available.

States Registered In: Whether the brokerage registered to do business with customers legally resides in your state.

Mutual Funds Offered: Number of mutual funds made available for purchase and redemption via the brokerage.

Payment for Order Flow: An arrangement under which a brokerage

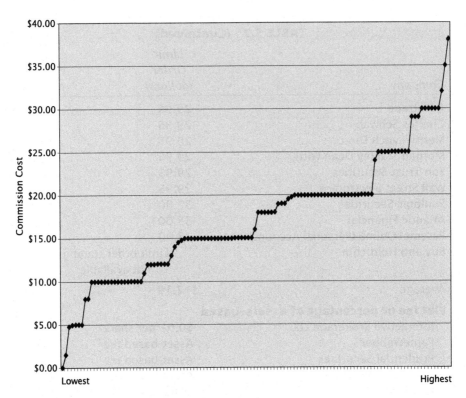

FIGURE 5.2   Limit Order Commission Costs

sends customers' orders to an outside trading firm for execution. In exchange, the brokerage receives a fee from the trading firm.

Banking Services Offered: Whether the brokerage offers banking services such as online bill payment, check-writing, and debit cards.

Company Background: A brief history of the brokerage.

Customer Service Rating: An assessment based on the author's direct experience with the brokerage. Ratings range from Excellent to Average to Poor. The rating was based on three factors: length of time to reach a customer service representative, courtesy and helpfulness of the representative, and the representative's depth of knowledge about the brokerage.

Gomez and Forrester Ratings: An assessment available for brokerages surveyed by these organizations. Gomez is a leading Internet measurement and benchmarking firm for customers and businesses.

TABLE 5.3   Minimum Deposit Required to Open a New Account

Company	Minimum Deposit Required (dollars)	Profile Page Number
1st Discount Brokerage	0	108
America First Trader	0	80
American Express Brokerage (account balance less than $25,000)	0	79
American Express Brokerage (account balance $25,000 and up)	0	79
Bidwell & Company	0	87
Citicorp Investment Services	0	100
Datek	0	104
DLJ Direct	0	109
Dreyfus Brokerage Services, Inc.	0	111
Firstrade	0	122
Foliofn	0	123
Freeman Welwood	0	128
Gay Financial Network	0	131
Harris Investorline	0	135
Invest Express Online	0	141
Main Street Market.com	0	151
Muriel Siebert	0	160
My Discount Broker.com	0	162
National Discount Brokers	0	164
Net Stock	0	168
One Invest.com	0	170
Patagon.com	0	177
Quick & Reilly	0	185
Sun Trust Securities	0	200
Suretrade	0	201
The Financialcafe.com	0	207
The Net Investor	0	209
Trading Direct	0	217
Unified Management Corporation	0	222
US Rica	0	224
Vision Trade	0	227
Wall Street Discount Corporation	0	232

(continued)

	TABLE 5.3 (Continued)	
Company	Minimum Deposit Required (dollars)	Profile Page Number
Wang Investments	0	234
Web St. Securities	0	236
Buy and Hold.com	20	94
Most Actives	100	158
Ameritrade	500	83
Net Bank	500	165
Scottrade	500	192
Trade-Well Discount Investing, LLC	500	216
Empire Financial	1,000	112
E*TRADE	1,000	116
InvestIn.com	1,000	142
Stockwalk.com	1,000	195
TD Waterhouse Group	1,000	202
Trade Cast Securities	1,000	210
US Bancorp Investing	1,000	223
Computel Securities	2,000	101
FBR.com	2,000	119
Freedom Investments	2,000	126
Interactive Brokerage, LLC	2,000	137
INTLTRADER.com	2,000	139
Inves Trade	2,000	143
JB Oxford & Company	2,000	144
Leighbaldwin.com	2,000	148
Merrill Lynch Direct	2,000	154
Morgan Stanley Dean Witter	2,000	156
Mr. Stock	2,000	159
Net Vest	2,000	169
Peremel Online (Direct Account)	2,000	178
Peremel Online (Personal Account)	2,000	178
RJT.com	2,000	187
Sunlogic Securities Inc.	2,000	198
Trade 4 Less	2,000	212
Wingspan Investment Services	2,000	240
WR Hambrecht	2,000	242
Wyse Securities	2,000	244
American Century	2,500	81

Company	Minimum Deposit Required (dollars)	Profile Page Number
TABLE 5.3 (Continued)		
Far Sight Financial Services, LP	2,500	117
Fidelity Investments	2,500	120
Smart Vest	2,500	194
Wall Street Electronica	2,500	233
World Trade Financial	2,500	241
A.B. Watley (Watley Trader)	3,000	72
Vanguard Brokerage Services	3,000	225
Access Broker.com (Millennium Investor Account)	5,000	74
Accutrade	5,000	76
Benjamin & Jerold Discount Brokerage	5,000	86
Bull & Bear Securities, Inc.	5,000	91
Bush Burns Securities	5,000	92
Cales Investment Corporation	5,000	95
Castle Securities Corporation	5,000	96
Charles Schwab (Schwab Account)	5,000	98
FreeTrade	5,000	129
Frontier Futures, Inc.	5,000	130
Pacific On-Line Trading and Securities	5,000	174
Preferred Trade	5,000	182
Trend Trader (Easy Trader)	5,000	218
Tru Trade	5,000	220
Netfolio.com	5,000	166
A.B. Watley (Ultimate Trader)	10,000	72
Atlantic Financial	10,000	85
Charles Schwab (Schwab One Account)	10,000	98
Cybercorp.com Inc. (Cyber Trader)	10,000	103
Cybercorp.com Inc. (CyberX & CyberX2)	10,000	103
Direct Access Trader (Margin Account Only)	10,000	106
Equity Trading	10,000	114
Franklin Ross, Inc.	10,000	125
Internet Trading.com	10,000	138
JPR Capital	10,000	146
Livestreet.com	10,000	149
MB Trading (Margin Account Only)	10,000	152

(continued)

	TABLE 5.3 (Continued)	
Company	Minimum Deposit Required (dollars)	Profile Page Number
Online Trading	10,000	171
Polar Trading.com	10,000	180
RML Trading, Inc.	10,000	188
RT Trader	10,000	190
Stoxnow	10,000	197
Terra Nova Trading	10,000	204
The Executioner	10,000	205
Trade Pros	10,000	213
Tradescape	10,000	214
Wachovia	10,000	228
Wall St. Access	10,000	230
Wilshire Capital Management	10,000	238
Your Trade (Margin Account Only)	10,000	245
Brown & Company (Margin Account Only)	15,000	89
Trend Trader (Order Routing System)	15,000	218
Access Broker.com (Millennium Trader Account)	25,000	74
All-Tech Direct	25,000	77
Gro Trader	25,000	133
On-Site Trading Inc.	25,000	173
PaineWebber	50,000	176
Prudential Securities	50,000	183
Salomon Smith Barney	100,000	191
Average	5,801.00	

Following the Gomez Rating, some firms will have a Forrester PowerRankings™. Forrester is a leading, independent research firm that ranks the brokerage firms that it considers to be the top 10, giving scores ranging from 0 to 100. The six categories they chose to rank were advice and market information, customer service, features and content, transacting, usability, and value.

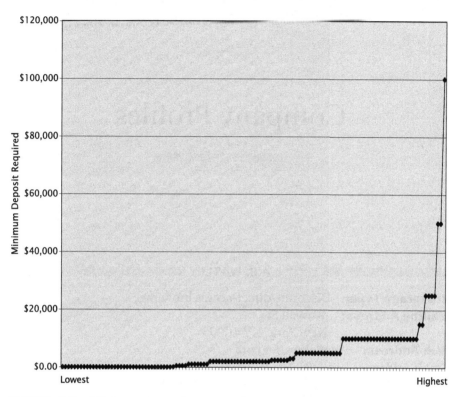

FIGURE 5.3 Minimum Deposit Required to Open a New Account

Company Profiles

Brokerage Type: Discount/direct-access brokerage
Mailing Address: 40 Wall St.
New York, NY 10005
Web Address: www.abwatley.com
Email Address: sales@abwatley.com
Telephone Number: 888-229-2853
Fax Number: 212-422-1624
Market Orders: Watley Trader Account: Web-based, $9.95 per trade, up to 5,000 shares, and additional $0.01 per share thereafter; bulletin board stocks $1.00 and under, $23.95 per trade plus 2.75% of principal; bulletin board stocks over $1.00, are $23.95 plus $0.015 cents per share. Ultimate Trader Account: Direct Access, $23.95 per trade, up to 10,000 Nasdaq shares and $23.95 per trade, up to 2,000 listed shares for first nine trades, goes down with future trades placed; bulletin board stocks $1.00 and under, $23.95 per trade plus 2.75% of principal; bulletin board stocks over $1.00, $23.95 per trade and additional $0.015 per share.
Limit Orders: Same as market orders.
Option Trades: Watley & Ultimate Trader Accounts, $30.00 plus $1.75 per contract, minimum $35.00.
Telephone Trading: $14.00 additional surcharge.
After-Hours Trading: 8:00 A.M. to 9:30 A.M. and 4:00 P.M. to 8:00 P.M. EST. Watley Trader Account: $9.95 per trade over the Internet plus ad-

ditional $14.00 to call a trade into a broker. Ultimate Trader Account: $23.95 per trade (retroactive based on trading volume).

Products Available to Trade Online: Stocks, options, mutual funds, and bonds.

Average Execution Time: Market order: Watley Trader Account, 15–45 seconds; Ultimate Trader Account, 2–6 seconds.

Minimum Deposit Required: Watley Trader Account: $3,000. Ultimate Trader Account: $10,000.

Additional Fees: Additional $0.015 per share for all ECN pass-through fees, excluding Island/Optional fees for Ultimate Trader Pro: Dow Jones Newswires, $95.00 per month; Turbo Options, $50.00 per month. Returned check fee, $25.00; stop payment, $15.00; late payment, $15.00; IRA annual fee, $30.00; IRA termination fee, $50.00; delivery of ACAT and DTC, $25.00; outgoing wire, $15.00; legal transfer, $25.00; foreign security transfer, $50.00; non-U.S. wire transfer, $50.00; registry and delivery of physical certificate, $15.00; non-mandatory reorganization, $35.00; posting and handling, $2.00; buy in/sell out (margin calls), $15.00; extra statement copies, $7.50.

Free Services and Financial Links: Briefing.com, Stock Finder, Industries Tracker, Market Guide, Research Reports from Wall Street on Demand including Standard & Poor's Stock Reports, Industry Reports, and News Reports, First Call Earning Estimates, Argus Reports, Ford Value Graph, Historical Price Charts, Business Wire Press Release, Renaissance IPO Research Reports, Vickers, and Wall Street Whispers. Watley Trader customers who have $10,000 or more in assets have access to Nasdaq level II quote services.

Real-Time Quotes: Watley Trader: not streaming. Ultimate Trader: streaming.

States Registered In: All U.S. states.

Mutual Funds Offered: None.

Payment for Order Flow: Yes, with the Watley Trader account.

Banking Services Offered: Clients have access to banking services through a money market account. The requirement is account balance of $50,000 for Ultimate Trader and $10,000 for Watley Trader.

Company Background: Brokerage/dealer A.B. Watley, Inc., is a NASD member insured by Securities Investor Protection Corporation (SIPC) that was founded originally in 1958 as a securities firm. Online trading with A.B. Watley began in May 1996. The A.B. Watley Group Inc. Institutional Sales and Trading Division specializes in the execution of complex and sensitive large-block equity transactions for institutions, major investment managers, insurance companies, banks, and high net worth individuals. A.B. Watley Group Inc. is small in size compared to other online brokers, averaging about 5,000 online clients as of November 1999, but plans to double in size by next year. A.B. Watley's current online clients trade between 2.5 and four times per day on average. The Watley Trader Account is engineered for a trader who can use such services as free real-time quotes and a broad range of other free services. The Ultimate Trader Account is engineered for active traders who depend on institutional quality real-time data. Clients have access to SOES and multiple ECNs with the Ultimate Trader Account, such as Instinet, Island, Redi, Terra Nova, Attain, and Bloomberg. A.B. Watley utilizes Penson Financial Service, Inc., as their clearing agent. Clients' accounts are protected up to $500,000, of which $100,000 is for cash coverage. Additional coverage up to $24.5 million is provided by a private insurance company.

Customer Service Rating: ★★★ Excellent
Gomez Rating: 6.68

ACCESSBROKER.COM

Brokerage Type: Direct-access brokerage
Mailing Address: 3400 Waterview Pkwy, Suite 101
Richardson, TX 75080
Web Address: www.accessbroker.com
Email Address: customerservice@accessbroker.com
Telephone Number: 800-TRADING, 972-818-9400
Fax Number: 972-818-1580
Market Orders: Millennium Investor: $14.95 per trade. Millennium Trader: $22.95 per trade (1–19 trades per month), $21.95 per trade (20–49 trades per month), $19.95 per trade (50–99 trades per month), $18.95 per trade (100–199 trades per month), $17.95 per trade (200–399 trades per month), $15.95 per trade (400–699 trades per month), $14.95 per trade, (700 or more trades per month). Trades for Millennium Trader based on 2,000 shares and additional $0.01 per share thereafter. Bulletin board trades $29.95 per 1,000 shares.
Limit Orders: Same as market orders.
Option Trades: $21.00 per trade plus $2.50 per contract; minimum $30.00.
Telephone Trading: Additional $10.00 surcharge. Orders placed

through Instinet will be billed at $0.04 per share, with a $35.00 minimum.

After-Hours Trading: 8:00 A.M. to 9:30 A.M. and 4:00 P.M. to 8:00 P.M. EST. Same commissions as online schedule.

Products Available to Trade Online: Stocks and options.

Average Execution Time: Market order: 4–5 seconds.

Minimum Deposit Required: Millennium Investor Account: $5,000. Millennium Trader Account: $25,000.

Additional Fees: Millennium Trader Platinum software fee: $299.00 per month (fee waived upon placing 50 or more trades per month). Millennium Trader Gold software fee: $225.00 per month (fee waived upon placing 50 or more trades per month). Additional ECN fees: Millennium Trader Account: ISI listed stocks (NYSE & Amex), $0.01 per share; Archipelago (ARCA) listed, $0.0075 per share; ARCA Nasdaq, $0.004 per share; Instinet (INCA), $0.004 per share; Bloomberg (BTRD), $0.004 per share; SelectNet (SNET), $0.004 per share; Attain System (ATTN), $0.004 per share. Millennium Investor Account: listed stocks (NYSE & Amex), $0.01 per share; INCA, $0.015 per share; BTRD, $0.015 per share; REDI, $0.02 per share; ARCA, $0.05 per share; ATTN, $1.00 per trade; SNET, $2.50 per trade. Optional fees for Millennium Trader Gold: Comstock News, $25.00 per month; Futures exchange data, $65.00 per month; Turbo Option Quotes, $8.00 per month. Regulation T extension: $5.00. mailgrams: $15.00. wiring funds: $20.00. overnight mail: $15.00. reorganization items: $5.00. Outgoing account transfers: $25.00. transfer fee: $15.00 per certificate. legal transfers: $25.00. returned checks: $40.00.

Free Services and Financial Links: Live events, free training, research, news.

Real-Time Quotes: Access to streaming real-time quotes with software package.

States Registered In: All U.S. states.

Mutual Funds Offered: Over 4,000.

Payment for Order Flow: No.

Banking Services Offered: None.

Company Background: AccessBroker.com was founded in October 1997 and is a licensed NASD brokerage/dealer. AccessBroker.com offers their clients a professional-level Internet-based, non-browser order entry platform, consisting of SOES, Island, and Archipelago for Nasdaq securities and the SuperDot system for NYSE and Amex securities. Clients' accounts are protected up to $25 million per account. The

SIPC provides up to $500,000, of which $100,000 is for cash coverage, and Pension Financial provides the additional $24.5 million.

Customer Service Rating: ★★★ Excellent

ACCUTRADE

Brokerage Type: Discount brokerage

Mailing Address: 4211 South 102nd St.
Omaha, NE 68127-1031

Web Address: www.accutrade.com

Email Address: info@accutrade.com

Telephone Number: 800-882-4887

Fax Number: 800-821-0743

Market Orders: $29.95 per trade, up to 1,000 shares, and additional $0.02 per share thereafter.

Limit Orders: Same as market orders.

Option Trades: Premium under $2.00: 1–10 contracts, $3.00 per contract; 11–30 contracts, $2.00 per contract; 31 or more contracts, $1.50 per contract. Premium $2.00–3.875: 1–10 contracts, $4.50 per contract; 11–30 contracts, $2.50 per contract; 31 or more contracts, $2.00 per contract. Premium $4.00–7.875: 1–10 contracts, $6.50 per contract; 11–30 contracts, $3.50 per contract; 31 or more contracts, $3.00 per contract. Premium $8.00 and over: 1–10 contracts, $8.00 per contract; 11–30 contracts, $6.00 per contract; 31 or more contracts, $5.00 per contract. Minimum option commission: $35.00.

Telephone Trading: $28.00 per trade plus $0.02 per share.

After-Hours Trading: 4:15 P.M. to 6:30 P.M. EST. Broker-assisted and limit orders only. $28.00 per trade plus $0.02 per share.

Products Available to Trade Online: Stocks, options, mutual funds, and bonds.

Average Execution Time: Market order: within seconds.

Minimum Deposit Required: $5,000.

Additional Fees: Special registration: $15.00 per issue. Funds wired: $15.00. Late statement: $0.35 per day per $1,000 (principal from settlement date). Legal item: $25.00 per issue. Overnight courier: billed at cost. Regulation T extension: $25.00. Nonmandatory reorganization: $25.00. Returned check: $25.00 plus $0.35 per day per $1,000 (principal from settlement date). Rule 144 stock: $50.00. Stop payments: $15.00. Transfer of accounts (outbound): $25.00.

Free Services and Financial Links: Financial news, stock news and quotes, Market Monitor, company screening, mutual fund screening, company reports, Standard & Poor's services, stock alerts, municipal bond guide, Bob Gabele's Insider Trading Watch, The Friday Report, Morningstar Reports, fund alerts, Mutual Fund Monitor, option chains, Dow Jones News, free IRA, free certificate delivery, free mandatory re-organization, free transfer of accounts (in bound).

Real-Time Quotes: Upon opening an account each client receives 100 real-time quotes, and with every trade placed they will receive 100 more, although they are not streaming and must be refreshed. Clients can also receive unlimited real-time quotes for $20.00 per month. Clients have access to free unlimited 15-minute delayed quotes.

States Registered In: All U.S. states.

Mutual Fund Offered: Over 8,000.

Payment for Order Flow: Yes, on select orders.

Banking Services Offered: Check writing and debit card.

Company Background: Accutrade was founded in 1975 and went on-line in December 1994. Accutrade clientele is primarily made up of individuals. Clients' accounts are protected up to $26 million ($25 million in stocks and $1 million in cash protection). Accutrade is a member of the National Association of Securities Dealers (NASD) and is registered with the SEC.

Customer Service Rating: ★★★ Excellent

Gomez Rating: 5.29

ALL-TECH DIRECT

Brokerage Type: Direct-access brokerage

Mailing Address: 160 Summit Ave.
Montvale, NJ 07645

Web Address: www.attain.com

Email Address: trade@attain.com

Telephone Number: 888-328-8246, sales 877-528-8246

Fax Number: 201-782-9090

Market Orders: $25.00 per trade, up to 4,000 shares if stock is under $25.00, and up to 2,000 shares if stock is over $25.00. May be lowered for active traders.

Limit Orders: Same as market orders.

Option Trades: Starting at $2.00 per contract.

Telephone Trading: None.

After-Hours Trading: 4:00 P.M. to 6:30 P.M. EST, online trading only, $25.00 per trade.

Products Available to Trade Online: Stocks and options.

Average Execution Time: Market order: 2 seconds, varying with market volatility and routing of your order.

Minimum Deposit Required: Casual day-trading account guidelines: recommended deposit, $100,000; minimum deposit, $25,000.

Additional Fees: Cost of quotes and execution system: $250.00 per month (waived upon 100 transactions per month). Wire transfer fee: $15.00. Exercising stock options: $35.00. Bond fees: handling fee on buy in/sell outs, $5.00; T-bills, $15.00; T-notes, T-bonds, and GNMA's and other government instruments, $15.00. Returned check: $15.00. Courtesy transfer: $25.00 on all securities when no buy ins or sell outs take place. SEC fee: $.01 per $300.00 value on the sell side of all listed securities, including options. Customer transfer to another dealer: $50.00.

Free Services and Financial Links: Charts and quotes.

Real-Time Quotes: With Level II system, included in $250.00 software fee (waived upon 100 transactions per month).

States Registered In: All U.S. states.

Mutual Funds Offered: Approximately 200 mutual funds.

Payment for Order Flow: No.

Banking Services Offered: Check writing.

Company Background: All-Tech Direct clients are offered three different service packages: ATTAIN Pro, ATTAIN Plus, and ATTAIN Online. ATTAIN Pro offers a customized trading platform, multiple real-time Level II quotes and charts, and point-and-click order entry. The fee is $250.00 per month, which is waived upon executing 100 or more trades per month. The minimum account balance is $25,000. ATTAIN Plus is a direct access trading system that caters to the active trader. ATTAIN Plus offers the technology and features of a professional trading system as well as free real-time Level II quotes. Charts and information delivered in a high-tech fixed-screen format using two market maker windows, two chart windows, and one market minder. The fee is free with a minimum account balance of $10,000 ($25,000 for day trading). ATTAIN Online is a browser-based system for obtaining quotes and executing trades online. The minimum account balance is $5,000. All-Tech's clientele base includes individuals trading their own accounts, brokers and dealers, institutions and hedge funds. In February 1998 All-Tech Investment Group, Inc., unveiled its own ECN on Nasdaq, the

ATTAIN ECN. All-Tech is a member of SIPC, which provides protection for client accounts up to $500,000, subject to limitation of $100,000 for cash balances.

Customer Service Rating: ★ Poor

AMERICAN EXPRESS BROKERAGE

Brokerage Type: Discount brokerage
Mailing Address: 70400 AXP Financial Center
Minneapolis, MN 55474
Web Address: www.americanexpress.com/trade
Email Address: contactus@aexp.com
Telephone Number: 800-297-5300
Fax Number: None.
Market Orders: Account balance less than $25,000: $14.95 per trade, up to 3,000 shares. Account balance $25,000 to $99,999: free, up to 3,000 shares. Account balance $100,000 or more: free unlimited shares.
Limit Orders: Same as market orders.
Option Trades: $40.00 per trade plus $2.00 per contract and additional $5.00 for limit orders. Trades placed through live broker only.
Telephone Trading: $44.95 per trade and additional $5.00 for limit or stop orders.
After-Hours Trading: None.
Products Available to Trade Online: Stocks, mutual funds, annuities, investment management accounts, CDs, IRAs, and bonds.
Average Execution Time: Market order: within 9 seconds.
Minimum Deposit Required: None, but sufficient funds are needed to place first trade.
Additional Fees: $5.00 per month banking fee if account balance is less than $5,000. Overnight delivery: $15.00. Check copy: $2.50 per check. Research: $25.00 per hour. Legal process: $40.00 per hour. Stop payment or reissue: $20.00. NSF check or NSF payment: $20.00. Wire transfer out: $50.00. Returned check or ACH: $15.00. Legal transfer: $20.00. Certificate delivery: $15.00. Transfer out: $50.00. Limited partnership transfer: $45.00 per issue. Private placement: $75.00 annual per account. Nonstandard custody safekeeping: $25.00. Voluntary physical reorganization: $35.00. Late trade settlement: $15.00 ($30.00 maximum client charge per settlement date). Options exercise and assignments: $44.95.
Free Services and Financial Links: Standard and Poor's fundamentals,

historical price charts, quick facts, company reports, stock screening, news, American Express financial advisors commentary, Dow Jones commentary, Smart Money commentary, TheStreet.com commentary.

Real-Time Quotes: New clients receive 500 free real-time quotes and an additional 100 free with every trade placed, although they are not streaming and must be refreshed.

States Registered In: All U.S. states.

Mutual Funds Offered: Over 2,000.

Payment for Order Flow: Yes.

Banking Services Offered: Account balance of $5,000 or more: check writing, online bill paying, and ATM debit card. Account balance of $25,000 or more: American Express Gold Card. Account balance of $100,000 or more: American Express Platinum Card.

Company Background: American Express Brokerage was founded in October 1999, and its clientele base is comprised mostly of individuals. An online WRAP account is offered in which clients can have an unlimited number of stocks in an account but pay a percentage of the entire account to an advisor, not a per trade charge. American Express Brokerage protects securities in accounts up to $500,000; there is coverage up to $24.5 million for securities in accounts held by American Enterprise Investment Services, Inc.

Customer Service Rating: ★★★ Excellent

AMERICA FIRST TRADER

Brokerage Type: Discount brokerage
Mailing Address: 60 East 56th St. 6th. Fl.
New York, NY 10022
Web Address: www.aftrader.com
Email Address: support@aftrader.com
Telephone Number: 888-OTC-NYSE, 212-644-8520
Fax Number: 212-644-3515
Market Orders: $9.95 per trade, unlimited shares.
Limit Orders: Same as market orders.
Option Trades: $25.00 per trade plus $1.75 per contract.
Telephone Trading: Stock trades: $30.00 per trade. Option trades: $50.00 per trade plus $1.75 per contract.
After-Hours Trading: None.
Products Available to Trade Online: Stocks, options, and mutual funds.
Average Execution Time: Market order: within 1 minute.

Minimum Deposit Required: Cash account: none. Margin account: $2,000.

Additional Fees: Wire Transfer out: $15.00. Extensions: $5.00. Sell out/Buy in telegram: $5.00. Legal transfer: $15.00. IRA termination: $50.00. IRA transfer: $50.00. E-signal Level II quotes: equity, $59.00 per month; Equity, futures, and options, $130.00 per month.

Free Services and Financial Links: Market summary, major market indices, news headlines, Stockfinder, Stockfinder pro, Market Snapshot, company news, intraday charts, economic calendar, options quotes, price history, IPO information, hot stock list, currency rates.

Real-Time Quotes: Free unlimited real-time quotes, although they are not streaming and must be refreshed.

States Registered In: All U.S. states excluding Maine.

Mutual Funds Offered: Over 2,500.

Payment for Order Flow: Yes.

Banking Services Offered: None.

Company Background: America First Trader was founded in 1995 and launched online trading in 1998. America First Trader serves individual traders. The website for America First Trader is offered in Chinese as well as English. Aftrader.com utilizes U.S. Clearing as its clearing firm. Clients are protected up to $100 million per account. SIPC provides $500,000, of which $100,000 is for cash protection, and the remaining $99.5 million is provided by Guaranty Insurance Co.

Customer Service Rating: ★★★ Excellent

Gomez Rating: 5.83

AMERICAN CENTURY

Brokerage Type: Discount brokerage

Mailing Address: American Century Brokerage, Inc.
P.O. Box 419146
Kansas City, MO 64141-6146

Web Address: www.americancentury.com

Email Address: Available through website.

Telephone Number: 888-345-2071, 888-345-2091

Fax Number: 816-340-2539

Market Orders: $24.95 per trade, up to 1,000 shares, and additional $0.02 per share thereafter.

Limit Orders: Same as market orders.

Option Trades: 25% discount off regular commissions.

Telephone Trading: Stock trades: $25.00 per trade plus 1.20% of principal ($0–$2,500); $40.00 per trade plus 0.60% of principal ($2,501–$5,000); $50.00 per trade plus 0.40% of principal ($5,001–$15,000); $80.00 per trade plus 0.02% of principal ($15,001–$50,000); $155.00 per trade plus 0.005% of principal ($50,001–$250,000); $180.00 per trade plus 0.004% of principal ($250,001–$500,000). Minimum charge: $35.00 per trade or $0.04 per share, whichever is greater. Maximum charge: $0.48 per share. Under $1.00 per share: 3% of transaction amount plus $35.00. Option trades: $30.00 per trade plus 1.50% of principal ($0–$2,500); $48.00 per trade plus 0.80% of principal ($2,501–$10,000); $90.00 per trade plus 0.30% of principal, ($10,001 or more). Minimum charge: $4.00 per contract on first 20 contracts, $2.00 per contract thereafter. Maximum charge: $35.00 per contract on first 2 contracts, $4.00 per contract thereafter.

After-Hours Trading: None.

Products Available to Trade Online: Stocks, options, and mutual funds.

Average Execution Time: Market order: 1 minute depending on conditions and funds in account.

Minimum Deposit Required: $2,500 for cash or margin account.

Additional Fees: Annual IRA maintenance: $30.00 per account (waived if account is more than $10,000). IRA termination: $30.00. Non-IRA outgoing transfer: $30.00 per account. Annual inactive account: $30.00 per account. Annual access account: $60.00 per account (waived if balance is more than $25,000). ATM transaction: $.75 per transaction. Access account check re-order: $15.00 for 200 checks, no per check minimum. Returned check fee: $20.00 per item. Stop payment: $10.00 per item. Copy of check or MasterCard debit: $2.50 per item. Wired funds: $20.00 per wire transfer, $1,000 minimum. Voluntary reorganization: $20.00 per item. Mandatory in-account reorganization: $5.00 per item. Mandatory physical: $40.00 per item. Transfers (register and ship): $15.00 per item. Legal transfer: $25.00 per item. GNMA transfer and ship: $40.00 per transfer. Foreign receive and deliver fees: Eurobond clearance, $50.00 per item; all other foreign securities, $75.00 per item. DK items: $10.00 per item. Customer name safekeeping: $2.00 per account per position per month. Mutual fund certificate: $50.00 per item. Margin extensions: $20.00 per item.

Free Services and Financial Links: Quotes and news, model portfolio, market headlines, economic indicators, Market Watch, investment ideas, S&P snapshot reports, Lipper profiles, FundScan, winners and losers, reports, research headlines, alerts, earnings, research services, earnings forecast, JP Morgan results research, Wall Street on Demand, investment glossary.

Real-Time Quotes: 100 real-time quotes upon opening account and 100 more with each trade executed.

States Registered In: All U.S. states.

Mutual Funds Offered: Over 9,000.

Payment for Order Flow: No.

Banking Services Offered: Unlimited check writing with no per check minimum, Gold Master Card, ATM and debit card with more than 250,000 ATMs available worldwide, overdraft protection, and telephone bill payment service. Clients must make a $10,000 minimum deposit to open this account. Clients have access to check writing privileges through a Standard Account with a $100.00 per check minimum.

Company Background: American Century Investment was founded in 1958 and launched its online investing in June 1995. Clients' accounts are protected up to $500,000, of which $100,000 is for cash coverage, provided by SIPC.

Customer Service Rating: ★★★ Excellent

Gomez Rating: 4.97

AMERITRADE

Brokerage Type: Discount brokerage

Mailing Address: Ameritrade, Inc.
P.O. Box 2760
Omaha, NE 68103-2760

Web Address: www.ameritrade.com

Email Address: starting@ameritrade.com

Telephone Number: 800-454-9272, 800-276-8746

Fax Number: 402-970-5529

Market Orders: $8.00 per trade, unlimited shares.

Limit Orders: $13.00 per trade, unlimited shares.

Option Trades: $25.00 per trade plus $1.75 per contract. Internet trades receive a 10% discount.

Telephone Trading: Stock trades: $18.00 per trade. Limit and stop orders: $23.00 per trade. Option trades: $25.00 per trade plus $1.75 per contract. Minimum $29.00.

After-Hours Trading: 4:15 P.M. to 6:30 P.M. EST. $13.00 per trade over the Internet, $23.00 to call a trade into a broker.

Products Available to Trade Online: Stocks, options, mutual funds, and bonds.

Average Execution Time: Market order: 2–3 seconds, depending on market volatility.

Minimum Deposit Required: $2,000 for cash or margin account.

Additional Fees: $20.00 per month for Zaurus plus $0.25 per minute with two minutes free for each executed trade. Returned check: $25.00. Research fee: $60.00 per hour. Stop payment: $25.00. Legal item: $25.00 per issue. Special registration: $15.00. Certificate delivery: $15.00. Foreign securities: up to $100,000 per certificate. Funds wired (outgoing): $15.00. Funds wired (international): $25.00. ACH transactions: $5.00. ACH return: $25.00. Early payments fee: $25.00 plus $0.35 per $1,000. Late payments fees: $0.35 per day. Transaction processing fee: $100.00. Custody holding fee: $100.00. Subscription fee: $100.00. Overnight courrier: billed at cost. T-extensions: $25.00. Mandatory reorganizations: $15.00. Nonmandatory and tenders: $25.00. Replacement statements, confirmations, and verifications of deposit: $10.00 per copy, 3 or more $5.00 each. Rule 144 stock: $50.00.

Free Services and Financial Links: Quick facts report, electronic trade confirmations by email, TheStreet.com, Big Charts, Stock Quest, Market Guide, Briefing.com, Zacks.

Real-Time Quotes: 100 real-time quotes with new account and 100 more real-time quotes for each Internet order filled, although they are not streaming and must be refreshed. Clients can receive unlimited real-time quotes for $20.00 per month.

States Registered In: All U.S. states.

Mutual Funds Offered: Over 8,000.

Payment for Order Flow: Yes.

Banking Services Offered: Account balance of $1,000 or more: check writing services. Account balance of $5,000 or more: money market account, which offers check writing services and a VISA debit card.

Company Background: Ameritrade was founded in 1975 and has grown to over 11.6 million secure trades a year. The majority of Ameritrade clients are independent investors. All Ameritrade accounts have private, secure access, and all account information and transactions are maintained with an extremely high level of security. Ameritrade offers email trade confirmations. Ameritrade customer assets are protected by SIPC up to $500,000.

Customer Service Rating: ★★ Average
Gomez Rating: 6.44
Forrester PowerRankings: 49.74

ATLANTIC FINANCIAL

Brokerage Type: Full-service brokerage
Mailing Address: Atlantic Financial Inc.
555 Washington Street, Suite #1
Wellesley, MA 02482
Web Address: www.atlanticfinancial.com
Email Address: service@atlanticfinancial.com
Telephone Number: 800-559-2900, 781-235-5777
Fax Number: 781-235-9222
Market Orders: NYSE trades: $35.00 per trade plus $0.02 per share. OTC and NASDAQ trades: $35.00.
Limit Orders: Same as market orders.
Option Trades: $40.00 per trade plus $3.50 per contract.
Telephone Trading: Stock trades: $59.00 flat rate (1–100 shares); $85.00 per trade plus $0.14 per share (101–500 shares); $100.00 per trade plus $0.11 per share (501–1,000 shares); $120.00 per trade plus $0.09 per share (1,001–2,000 shares); $140.00 per trade plus $0.075 per share (2,001 or more shares). Option trades: $40.00 per trade plus $3.50 per contract.
After-Hours Trading: None.
Products Available to Trade Online: Stocks, options, and mutual funds.
Average Execution Time: Market order: within 20 seconds.
Minimum Deposit Required: $10,000, but waivers given in special circumstances.
Additional Fees: Postage and handling: $3.50 per trade. Wire transfer: $20.00 (may be waived dependent upon account size). IRA maintenance: $30.00 annual fee (may be waived dependent on account size). IRA termination: $50.00. Returned check fee: $20.00
Free Services and Financial Links: Newsletters, financial dictionary, articles, investment forums, bookstore, charts, reports, opinions, and company profiles.
Real-Time Quotes: Unlimited streaming real-time quotes for $20.00 per month.
States Registered In: All U.S. states.
Mutual Funds Offered: Over 9,000.

Payment for Order Flow: No.

Banking Services Offered: Check writing with a $500.00 minimum check amount for each check written through a Brokerage Access Account. Unlimited check writing privileges and a VISA debit card for $95.00 a month through a VIP Account. Automatic bill payment is offered to clients for no charge and is compatible with several third party systems.

Company Background: Atlantic Financial is an independent firm that was founded in 1994. Clientele at Atlantic Financial consists of companies and individuals, and Atlantic offers free advice and financial planning to qualified accounts. Atlantic Financial also specializes in 401K plans and has extensive ties to mutual fund companies, money management firms, and trust companies, which gives its clients a large selection of investments to choose from. Securities are offered through Cantella & Co., and clients' accounts are protected up to $500,000, of which $100,000 is for cash coverage, provided by SIPC.

Customer Service Rating: ★★★ Excellent

BENJAMIN & JEROLD DISCOUNT BROKERAGE

Brokerage Type: Discount brokerage

Mailing Address: 141 West Jackson Blvd. Suite 3550
                       Chicago, IL 60604

Web Address: www.stockoptions.com

Email Address: info@stockoptions.com, kopf@earthlink.net

Telephone Number: 800-446-5112, 312-554-0202

Fax Number: 312-554-0268

Market Orders: Up to 1,000 shares: $36.00 per trade. Up to 5,000 shares: $29.00 per trade.

Limit Orders: Same as market orders.

Option Trades: 1–6 contracts: $36.00 minimum. 10 contracts: $45.00. 20 contracts: $80.00.

Telephone Trading: Stock trades: $40.00 minimum for 1–200 shares; $70.00 per trade for 500 shares; $66.00 per trade for 2,000 shares. Options trades: $40.00 minimum for 1–6 contracts, market orders only; $50.00 minimum for 1–8 contracts, limit, stop, contingency, and cancel/replace orders.

After-Hours Trading: None.

Products Available to Trade Online: Stocks and options.

Average Execution Time: Market order: Less than 2 minutes.

Minimum Deposit Required: $5,000 for cash or margin account.

Additional Fees: Ticket charge: postage and handling, $2.00. Stock certificate: $20.00. Options exercise and assignment: $4.00 per contract, $40.00 minimum.

Free Services and Financial Links: Stock options guide, net picks stock options advisory system (two-week free trial), McMillan analysis corporation, option wizard.

Real-Time Quotes: Real-time quotes are available free of charge, although they are not streaming and will need to be refreshed.

States Registered In: All U.S. states except HI, NE, ND, PR, SD, VT.

Mutual Funds Offered: None.

Payment for Order Flow: Stock trades: yes. Option trades: no.

Banking Services Offered: None.

Company Background: Benjamin & Jerold Discount Brokerage is a stock and options boutique that was founded in January 1992 and launched online trading in 1999. The founders, Benjamin Stevens and Jerold Kopf, are both registered options principals (ROPs), and the firm is registered with NASD and SEC. Clients' trades are cleared through Investec-Ernst & Co. Account protection at Benjamin & Jerold is provided by SIPC up to $500,000, of which $100,000 is for cash coverage. Investec-Ernst & Co. maintains additional coverage of $49.5 million through a private insurer. A specialty at Benjamin & Jerold is that clients can trade options, including spreads in their IRAs, and the brokerage will accept virtually all index and stock option trades in your IRA (Roth, SEP, Rollover). Benjamin & Jerold also accepts GTC stop or contingent orders. The clientele base at Benjamin & Jerold is primarily made up of individuals.

Customer Service Rating: ★★★ Excellent

BIDWELL & COMPANY

Brokerage Type: Discount brokerage

Mailing Address: 209 SW Oak Street
Portland, OR 97204-2791

Web Address: www.bidwell.com

Email Address: info@bidwell.com

Telephone Number: 800-547-6337

Fax Number: 503-222-1055

Market Orders: $12.00 per trade, up to 1,500 shares, and additional $0.01 per share on entire order thereafter.

Limit Orders: $15.00 per trade, up to 1,500 shares, and additional $0.01 per share on entire order thereafter.

Option Trades: $27.00 per trade plus $3.00 per contract.

Telephone Trading: Price per share, 0–10: $20.00 plus $0.05 per share, up to 500 shares, $0.03 per share thereafter. Price per share, 10⅛–20: $20.00 plus $0.06 per share, up to 500 shares, $0.03 per share thereafter. Price per share, 20⅛–30: $20.00 plus $0.07 per share, up to 500 shares, $0.03 per share thereafter. Price per share, 30⅛ or more: $20.00 plus $0.08 per share, up to 500 shares, $0.03 per share thereafter. OTC Securities under $1.00: 5% of the dollar amount, subject to a $20.00 minimum commission.

After-Hours Trading: None.

Products Available to Trade Online: Stocks, options, and mutual funds.

Average Execution Time: Market order: a few seconds, under normal market conditions.

Minimum Deposit Required: Cash account: none. Margin account: $3,000.

Additional Fees: Confirmation, statement, and 1099 replacement: one free, each additional $5.00. Early trade payment: $25.00 or interest. Foreign securities transfer: varies. IRA annual fee: $25.00. Insurance of third party checks: $5.00. Late payment: $5.00 plus interest. Late receipt of securities sold: $5.00. Legal transfer fee: $25.00. Limited partnership transfer: varies. Mailgram margin notices: $25.00. Overnight delivery: $15.00. Registered delivery of certificate: $10.00. Reorganization: $25.00. Restricted stock transfer: $50.00. Returned checks for NSF: $25.00 plus interest. Stop payment on check: $20.00. Wire transfer domestic and foreign: $15.00 and $25.00. Postage and handling fee: $1.25.

Free Services and Financial Links: Standard & Poor's, Value Line, Morningstar mutual fund reports, Zacks, Lipper mutual fund reports, AP online, PR newswire, business wire.

Real-Time Quotes: 100 free real-time quotes with new account and 100 more with each trade placed. Quotes are not streaming and must be refreshed.

States Registered In: All U.S. states.

Mutual Funds Offered: Over 700 through Bidwell Fund Source.

Payment for Order Flow: No.

Banking Services Offered: Check writing and ATM debit withdrawals.

Company Background: Bidwell & Company was founded in early 1982 and currently offers online trading. Bidwell & Company is a self-clearing firm. Clients' accounts are protected up to $150 million. SIPC provides up to $500,000, of which $100,000 is for cash coverage. Additional protection of up to $149,500,000 is also available at no charge to the client.

Customer Service Rating: ★★★ Excellent

Gomez Rating: 5.43

BROWN & COMPANY

Brokerage Type: Discount brokerage

Mailing Address: One Beacon St.
Boston MA 02108

Web Address: www.brownco.com

Email Address: Available through website.

Telephone Number: 800-225-6707

Fax Number: 617-426-8241

Market Orders: $5.00 per trade, up to 5,000 shares, and additional $0.01 per share thereafter. A rebate will be given for any month when commissions exceed $350.00. The rebate will be 10% of the total amount of those commissions.

Limit Orders: $10.00 per trade, up to 5,000 shares, and additional $0.01 per share thereafter. A rebate will be given for any month when commissions exceed $350.00. The rebate will be 10% of the total amount of those commissions.

Option Trades: Market orders: up to and including 30 contracts, $15.00 plus $1.50 per contract; over 30 contracts, $15.00 plus $1.75 per contract. Limit orders: $15.00 plus $1.75 per contract; minimum, $25.00.

Telephone Trading: Additional surcharge of $7.00 per trade. Market orders: up to 5,000 shares, $12.00; over 5,000 shares, $12.00 plus $0.01 per share. Limit orders: up to 5,000 shares, $17.00; over 5,000 shares, $17.00 plus $0.01 per share.

After-Hours Trading: None.

Products Available to Trade Online: Stocks, options, mutual funds, treasury bills, and Notes and Bonds.

Average Execution Time: Not divulged.

Minimum Deposit Required: $15,000 for a margin account. Clients must open a margin account to trade online.

Additional Fees: Conversions-bonds, preferred stock: $25.00. Exercising warrants: $25.00. Merger, money for stock: $12.50. Merger, voluntary cash election: $12.50. Bond maturities: $25.00. Warrants, preferred stock and bond redemptions: $30.00. Liquidations: $12.50. Voluntary reorganizations: $50.00. Exchange offers: $25.00. Exercising rights and warrants: $25.00. Tender offers: $25.00. Unit separations and combines: $25.00. Check writing fees: monthly fee, $0.99; returned check fee, $20.00; stop payment fee, $20.00; copy of cancelled check, $5.00; duplicate statements (per month), $5.00; duplicate 1099, $10.00; annual statement, $25.00. Transfer certificate into customer name: $20.00. Receiving securities in corporate name: $10.00. Excessive (over 5) changes to order: $10.00. Regulation T extensions: $25.00. Mailgrams: $5.00. Telegrams: $50.00. Outgoing funds wired: $15.00. Treasury bill rollover: $10.00. IRA recharacterization: $100.00. Deposit of recognized securities: $40.00. Odd lot purchase offers: $25.00. Odd lot tender offers: $12.50. Option assignment and exercise: $19.00.

Free Services and Financial Links: Brown & Company provides financial links to many free services, but they do not endorse, monitor, investigate, or verify them. Some include CBS Marketwatch, the Motley Fool, Quicken.com, SmartMoney.com, Yahoo finance, and ZD Interactive Investor.

Real-Time Quotes: Clients receive 100 free real-time quotes upon opening an account and 100 more with every trade placed, although these quotes are not streaming and must be refreshed. Clients can purchase additional quotes for $10.00 per 500 quotes.

States Registered In: All U.S. states.

Mutual Funds Offered: Some.

Payment for Order Flow: Yes.

Banking Services Offered: Check writing is available, although each check must be written for $500.00 or more.

Company Background: Brown & Company acts as a discount broker for qualified clients who make their own investment decisions. Clients' accounts are protected up to $100 million, of which $1,000,000 is for cash coverage. Established in 1960, Brown & Company is a member of the New York Stock Exchange, the American Stock Exchange, the

Boston Stock Exchange, the Chicago Stock Exchange, the Philadelphia Stock Exchange, and the National Association of Securities Dealers. It is a member of SIPC and a subsidiary of the Chase Manhattan Corporation. Brown & Company does not provide investment advice and guidance to its clientele. Clients must have 5 years investment experience, an annual income of $40,000, and a net worth of $50,000 to open an online account.

Customer Service Rating: ★★ Average
Gomez Rating: 3.76

BULL & BEAR SECURITIES, INC.

Brokerage Type: Discount brokerage
Mailing Address: One Liberty Plaza, 5th Floor
New York, NY 10006
Web Address: www.bullbear.com
Email Address: info@bullbear.com
Telephone Number: 800-262-5800
Fax Number: 212-428-6961
Market Orders: $19.95 per trade, up to 5,000 shares and additional $0.01 per share thereafter.
Limit Orders: Same as market orders.
Option Trades: Clients will receive 20% discount off the broker-assisted schedule for Internet trades.
Telephone Trading: Stock trades: $29.95, up to 5,000 shares, and additional $0.01 per share thereafter. Option trades for options selling at $0.50 or under: 0–49 contracts, $1.80 per contract plus 1.5% of the principal; 50–149 contracts, $1.10 per contract plus 1.8% of principal; 150–499 contracts, $0.75 per contract plus 2.0% of the principal; 500–1,499 contracts, $0.60 per contract plus 2.0% of the principal; over 1,500 contracts, $0.60 per contract plus 1.5% of the principal. Overriding minimum: $39.00 per trade. Option trades for options selling at greater than $0.50: $0–2,499 principal amount, $29.00 plus 1.6% of the principal; $2,500–9,999 principal amount, $49.00 plus 0.8% of the principal; $10,000 or more principal amount, $99.00 plus 0.3% of the principal. Overriding minimum: $37.25 plus $1.75 per contract. Maximum charge: $40.00 per contract on first 2 contracts plus $4.00 per contract thereafter.
After-Hours Trading: None.

Products Available to Trade Online: Stocks, options, and mutual funds.

Average Execution Time: Market order: 2–3 seconds.

Minimum Deposit Required: $5,000 for cash or margin account.

Additional Fees: None available.

Free Services and Financial Links: Clients receive American Airline AAdvantage miles by opening an account, transferring an account, or referring a friend; also market commentary, current reports, stock pick list, company news, intraday graphs, Java Charts, Zacks earning estimates, Standard & Poor's investment information, Reuters, no-fee IRA.

Real-Time Quotes: Real-time quotes offered free of charge, although they are not streaming and must be refreshed.

States Registered In: All U.S. states.

Mutual Funds Offered: Over 5,000.

Payment for Order Flow: Yes.

Banking Services Offered: None.

Company Background: Bull & Bear Securities is a member of Royal Bank Financial Group and NASD/SIPC. Clients' accounts at Bull & Bear Securities are insured up to $50 million.

Customer Service Rating: ★★★ Excellent

Gomez Rating: 5.11

BUSH BURNS SECURITIES

Brokerage Type: Discount brokerage

Mailing Address: Attn. Customer Service
4111-W Andover Road
Bloomfield Hills, MI 48302

Web Address: www.bushburns.com

Email Address: service@bushburns.com

Telephone Number: 810-540-2968

Fax Number: 810-540-2968

Market Orders: $25.00 per trade, up to 5,000 shares, and additional $0.015 per share to entire order thereafter. Listed stocks below $2.00 add $0.015 per share to entire order unless executed in third market.

Limit Orders: Same as market orders.

Option Trades: Options priced below $1.00: $15.00 per trade plus $3.00 per contract. Options priced $1.00 and over: $15.00 per trade plus $4.00 per contract. Minimum commission: $35.00.

Telephone Trading: Stock trades: $35.00 per trade, up to 5,000 shares, and additional $0.015 per share to entire order thereafter. Listed stocks below $2.00 per share add $0.015 per share to entire order unless executed in third market. Option trades: options priced below $1.00, $15.00 per trade plus $3.00 per contract; options priced $1.00 and over, $15.00 per trade plus $5.00 per contract. Minimum $35.00.

After-Hours Trading: None.

Products Available to Trade Online: Stocks, options, mutual funds, and Bonds.

Average Execution Time: Market order: within seconds.

Minimum Deposit Required: $5,000 for cash or margin account.

Additional Fees: Change in certificate name: $25.00. Copies of back-confirms and statements: $5.00 per item. Extensions: $25.00. Foreign securities: ADRs, stock commission applies; Canadian stocks (online), $35.00, (broker assisted), $45.00. Inactive account fee: $50.00 annual fee may apply if no activity for 12 months. IRA accounts: $25.00 fee to maintain. Legal item: $25.00 per item, includes 144 Stock. Shipment of certificate: $25.00. Option exercise and assignment: $35.00. Overnight courier: $15.00. Postage and processing fee: $3.00 per executed trade. Tender and reorganization (voluntary): $25.00. Wire funds out: $20.00. Returned check fee: $25.00.

Free Services and Financial Links: Option chains, Symbol Guide, tutorial, Message Center, Stockmaster, Data Broadcasting Corp (DBC) Online, Quote.com, Inter Quote, research, Reuters, Finance Watch, net worth, the Financial Center, INO Global Markets, world stock exchanges, Wall Street Journal Online, Investors Business Daily, Edgar, Disclosure Inc., Investor Protection Trust.

Real-Time Quotes: Real-time quotes for $30.00 a month, although they are not streaming and must be refreshed. Free delayed quotes are also available.

States Registered In: All U.S. states except TN and MA.

Mutual Funds Offered: Some.

Online Banking Services: Check writing through Federated.

Company Background: Bush Burns Securities was originally founded in 1992 and launched its online trading in 1996. Its clientele ranges from investment advisors, institutions, and retail traders, and it gears its services to high wealth individuals. Bush Burns wrote and developed all of its own programs and has been very successful in doing so. The firm is on the smaller size and feels this keeps customer service at its best. Clients' accounts are protected up to $25 million. SIPC protects up to $500,000, of which $100,000 is for cash, and Aetna Casualty protects the remaining $24.5 million. Bush Burns utilizes Herzog, Heine, Geduld Inc. as their clearing firm.

Customer Service Rating: ★ Poor

BUY AND HOLD.COM

Brokerage Type: Discount brokerage
Mailing Address: Buy and Hold.com Securities Corporation
110 Wall St. 11th Floor
New York, NY 10005
Web Address: www.buyandhold.com
Email Address: bizdev@buyandhold.com
Telephone Number: 800-646-8212
Fax Number: 212-425-3481, attn. Dominic
Market Orders: $2.99 per trade.
Limit Orders: No limit order trading available.
Option Trades: None.
Telephone Trading: None.
After-Hours Trading: None.
Products Available to Trade Online: Stocks.
Average Execution Time: 15 to 20 minutes; Buy and Hold.com executes trades twice a day.
Minimum Deposit Required: $20.00 minimum deposit required, although sufficient funds are required to place first trade.
Additional Fees: Securities transfer, out to transfer agent: $30.00. Certificate insurance and delivery: $30.00. Funds wired in: $15.00. Funds wired out: $15.00. Legal item: $35.00. Overnight courier: $25.00. Returned check: $25.00. Returned ACH: $25.00. Rule 144 stock: $35.00. Stop payment, check: $30.00. Stop payment, ACH: $30.00. Paper confirmations: $3.00. Paper statement: $5.00. Previous statement copies: $10.00.
Free Services and Financial Links: Bizfinity.com, Dow Theory Forecast and Charles B. Carlson, Financenter, Hardware St., the Motley Fool, Relia Quote.com, Quicken Loans, Software Street, Stocksandnews.com, B&H Bank link, Easyvest, E-chat.
Real-Time Quotes: None, although 20-minute delayed quotes are offered free of charge.
States Registered In: All U.S. states.
Mutual Funds Offered: None.
Payment for Order Flow: No.
Banking Services Offered: None.

Company Background: Buy and Hold.com was founded in November 1998, and online trading began November 26, 1999. Buy and Hold.com appeals to the long-term investor and shares the belief that a long-term investment horizon is the most accurate strategy—hence the company name. Clients' accounts at Buy and Hold.com are protected up to $500,000 per account ($400,000 in securities and $100,000 in cash) through SIPC. Buy and Hold.com executes orders only twice a day in order to keep their commissions as low as possible. The morning session is from 10:30 A.M. to 11:30 A.M. EST, and the afternoon session is from 2:30 P.M. to 3:30 P.M. EST. Clients can choose the amount of money they want to invest in a particular stock—$20, $50, $100 or more—and Buy and Hold will buy exactly that much stock (minus the $2.99 transaction fee). Buy and Hold.com has approximately 100,000 registered users; 60,000 are online individuals.

Customer Service Rating: ★★★ Excellent

CALES INVESTMENT, INC.

Brokerage Type: Full-service/discount brokerage
Mailing Address: 300 N. Lincoln Street
　　　　　　　　　　Denver, CO 80203
Web Address: www.calesinvestments.com
Email Address: contact@calesinvestments.com
Telephone Number: 303-765-5600
Fax Number: 303-765-0097
Market Orders: $15.00 per trade, and additional $0.015 per share for listed stocks.
Limit Orders: Same as market orders.
Option Trades: $15.00 per trade plus $2.50 per contract.
Telephone Trading: $55.00 per trade.
After-Hours Trading: None.
Products Available to Trade Online: Stocks and options.
Average Execution Time: Not divulged.
Minimum Deposit Required: $5,000 for cash or margin accounts.
Additional Fees: Special registration per issue: per cost. Funds wired out: $25.00. Legal item: per cost. Overnight courier: per cost. Regulation T extension: $10.00. Nonmandatory reorganization: $15.00. Returned check fee: $15.00. Rule 144 stock: $150.00. Extensions: $10.00. IRA fees: $40.00. IRA annual maintenance fee and $25.00 setup fee. Cancellations: $12.50. Postage: $3.50. Annual inactivity fee: $25.00.

Free Services and Financial Links: Mutual Fund Research, Lipper Reports, ASK Research Options Market Summary, Aantix Options Probability Calculator, Big Charts Options Chains, CBEO: All About Options, E-Analytics, Options Source.com, Options News Network, Options Club.

Real-Time Quotes: Free real-time quotes, although they are not streaming and must be refreshed.

States Registered In: CO, TX, WY, and NM.

Mutual Funds Offered: Several.

Payment for Order Flow: Yes.

Banking Services Offered: VISA card privileges offered through a Vision Account.

Company Background: Cales Investments, Inc., was founded in 1987 and is a full-service brokerage firm. Online trading was launched in 1999 to serve a range of individual and institutional investors. Cales Investments will work closely with its clients, providing them with portfolios that suite their individual investment goals. Clients' accounts are protected by SIPC up to $500,000, of which $100,000 is for cash protection. Additional protection of $2.5 million is provided by Emmett A. Larkin Company, Inc. Cales Investments offers its website in German as well as English.

Customer Service Rating: ★★★ Excellent

CASTLE SECURITIES CORP.

Brokerage Type: Direct-access brokerage

Mailing Address: 45 Church St.
Freeport, NY 11520

Web Address: www.castleonline.com

Email Address: paul@castleonline.com

Telephone Number: 800-661-5133, 800-891-1003

Fax Number: 516-868-5131, 516-868-0228

Market Orders: NYSE and Amex trades: $19.95 per trade plus $0.01 per share. Nasdaq NMS trades (SOES, SelectNet, and Island ECN trades): $19.95 up to 10,000 shares, $1.00 additional charge for partial execution. ECN orders other than ISLD: $19.95 per trade plus $0.015 per share.

Limit Orders: Same as market orders.

Option Trades: None.

Telephone Trading: If there is a problem with your computer or software, there is no commission fee to call and place your trade. Otherwise, the commission fees will be the same as online fees.

After-Hours Trading: 8:00 A.M. to 9:30 A.M. EST and 4:00 P.M. to 6:00 P.M. EST. $19.95 per trade, up to 10,000 shares.

Products Available to Trade Online: Stocks.

Average Execution Time: Market order: depends on market conditions when placing the trade.

Minimum Deposit Required: $5,000 for cash or margin account.

Additional Fees: Java Trader Level II quotes and the MyTrack Data Package: $150.00 per month (waived upon executing 100 or more trades per month, 50 round trips). Handling fee for all trades: $1.00. King Package: $300.00 per month (waived upon executing 150 or more trades per month, 75 round trips). Additional charge if using an ECN other than Island: $0.015 per share. Regulation T extensions: $25.00. Mailgrams: $15.00. Wiring of funds: $25.00. Overnight mail: $15.00. Involuntary reorganization items: $10.00. Voluntary reorganization items: $25.00. Account transfers, outgoing ACATs: $45.00. Transfer fee, per issue: $25.00. Legal transfer including rule 144s, per issue: $25.00. Returned checks: $25.00. Stop payment request on check: $25.00. Copies of back monthly statements: $10.00 per statement. Copies of any documentation that concerns correspondent customer activity that represents duplication of previously transmitted data: $25.00 per hour, 1 hour minimum. Option assignment fee: $20.00. Foreign security safekeeping (per issue/per quarter): $5.00. 144 stock registration: $25.00. Uncollected funds after settlement date (annualized rate, cash account): 18%.

Free Services and Financial Links: MyTrack Silver Data Package with intraday charts free to all Nasdaq Level II subscribers, professional stock analyst, Zeus-Holdings, DayTraders Stock Picks, technical analysis of Stocks and Commodities, Seidner's Market Wisdom, A Trader's Financial Resource Guide, Jack's Picks, Stocks plus, Buttonwood Financial Resources, Ltd., Day Trader Network, mawest.com, Tech Stock Investor, the Short Term Stock Selector, Teachdaq.

Real-Time Quotes: Free real-time quotes, although they are not streaming and must be refreshed. Clients with a Java Trader Account have access to Nasdaq Level II quotes.

States Registered In: AL, AR, CA, CO, CT, DC, DE, FL, GA, IL, LA, MA, MD, MI, MN, MT, NJ, NM, NV, NY, OH, OK, OR, PA, RI, SC, SD, TN, TX, UT, VA, WA, WI, WV, WY.

Mutual Funds Offered: None.

Payment for Order Flow: Primarily no.

Banking Services Offered: Free check writing through an Alliance money market account.

Company Background: Castle Online is operated by Castle Securities Corporation, which was founded in 1985 and launched online trading through Castle Online in April 1996. Castle Online has developed its own execution system, the Java Trader. This system was developed by day traders for day trading. Castle Online offers two trading packages to their clientele. The Castle King Package includes the Java Trader with AT Financial Major Attitude Package. The Castle Prince Package includes the Java Trader with Nasdaq Level II and the Mytrack Silver Data Package. Castle Online utilizes J. B. Oxford as its clearing firm.

Customer Service Rating: ★★★ Excellent

CHARLES SCHWAB

Brokerage Type: Full-service/discount brokerage

Mailing Address: NY Operations Center
P.O. Box 179
Newark, NJ 07101-9671

Web Address: www.schwab.com

Email Address: Available through website.

Telephone Number: 800-540-8120, 800-225-8570

Fax Number: 800-294-7565

Market Orders: $29.95 per trade, up to 1,000 shares, and additional $0.03 per share thereafter. High volume trading: $14.95 per trade. Stocks priced under $1.00 per share: 3% of principal amount for trades over 1,000 shares, subject to a $29.95 minimum.

Limit Orders: Same as market orders.

Option Trades: 20% discount off broker-assisted commission when trades are placed over the Internet.

Telephone Trading: Stock trades: $0–2,499, $30.00 plus 1.7% of principal; $2,500–6,249, $56.00 plus 0.66% of principal; $6,250–19,999, $76.00 plus 0.34% of principal; $20,000–49,999, $100.00 plus 0.22% of principal; $50,000–499,999, $155.00 plus 0.11% of principal; $500,000 or more, $255.00 plus 0.09% of principal. Minimum: $39.00. Option trades with premiums of $0.50 or under: 0–49 contracts, $1.80 per contract plus 1.5% of the principal; 50–149 contracts, $1.10 plus 1.8% of the principal; 150–499 contracts, $0.75 plus 2.0% of the principal; 500–1,499 contracts, $0.60 plus 2.0% of the principal, 1,500 or more contacts, $0.60 plus 1.5% of the principal. Overriding minimum: $39 per trade. Options with premiums greater than $0.50: $0–2,499 principal amount, $29.00 plus 1.6% of the principal; $2,500–9,999 principal amount, $49.00 plus 0.8% of the principal; $10,000 or more principal amount, $99 plus 0.3% of the principal. Overriding minimum: $37.25 plus $1.75 per contract. Maximum: $40.00 per contract on the first two contracts, plus $4.00 per contract thereafter.

After-Hours Trading: 4:15 P.M. to 8:00 P.M. EST, $29.95 per trade over the Internet.

Products Available to Trade Online: Stocks, options, mutual funds, treasuries, and corporate bonds.

Average Execution Time: Market order: Varies depending on market activity, liquidity in a particular stock, and other factors. Execution time can range from seconds to minutes.

Minimum Deposit Required: Schwab Account: $5,000. Schwab One Account: $10,000. Both accounts can be cash or margin accounts.

Additional Fees: Securities registered and shipped to individuals: $15.00. Voluntary and posteffective reorganization: $39.00. Account maintenance fees vary based on account balance.

Free Services and Financial Links: Priority service and enhanced research, the Analyst Center, Industry Closeup, Mutual Fund OneSource Online, upcoming events, watch lists, Stock Screener, Stock Analyzer, Equity Report Card, Schwab Portfolio Checkup, college planner, live investment forums, Estate Planning Calculator, Schwab Alerts, portfolio performance screen.

Real-Time Quotes: Free real-time quotes, although they are not streaming and must be refreshed. Schwab offers a Signature Service Platinum account that offers real-time streaming quotes to clients. Clients must have a $50,000 minimum in account and must place at least 49 commissionable trades a year, or they must have $1 million in assets in their account to qualify for this type of account.

States Registered In: All U.S. states.

Mutual Funds Offered: Over 1,600.

Payment for Order Flow: Yes.

Banking Services Offered: Schwab One Account: check writing and a VISA debit card. Schwab Access Account: online bill payment, unlimited ATM transactions with automatic fee reimbursements, Schwab Access Gold VISA debit card, and unlimited check writing.

Company Background: Charles Schwab & Co., Inc., was originally founded in 1971 and began offering online trading in 1995 with software and introduced trading through Schwab.com in May 1996. Charles Schwab currently has 3.7 million active online accounts, and a large portion of that is made up of individuals. Active traders at Schwab that have either $1 million or more in assets, or trade 48 times or more in one year, and have at least $50,000 in a Schwab account have access to Velocity trading software. Velocity is a desktop trading software offered exclusively to the active trader. Clients have access to equity trades as low as $14.95 per trade, and they can place multiple equity orders in multiple accounts, customize five real-time watch lists, monitor their portfolio, export files, and receive future enhancements. Charles Schwab protects clients' accounts up to $100 million. The SIPC provides up to $500,000 to protect clients' assets, with a limit of $100,000 for claims of cash. An additional $99.5 million of protection is provided only for securities, of which $500,000 is available for claims in cash through American International Group, Inc.

Customer Service Rating: ★★ Average
Gomez Rating: 7.99
Forrester PowerRankings: 59.95

CITICORP INVESTMENT SERVICES

Brokerage Type: Discount brokerage
Mailing Address: 111 Wall Street 3rd Fl.
New York, NY 10043
Web Address: www.citibank.com
Email Address: Available through website.
Telephone Number: 800-ASKCITI
Fax Number: 210-677-7370
Market Orders: $19.95 per trade, flat rate.
Limit Orders: Same as market orders.
Option Trades: None.
Telephone Trading: $29.95 per trade (0–100 shares). $20.00 per trade plus $0.18 per share (101–500 shares). $85.00 per trade plus $0.04 per share (501–1000 shares). $100 per trade plus $0.02 per share (1,001 or more shares). Stocks under $1.00: $29.95 or 3% of principal, whichever is greater.
After-Hours Trading: None.
Products Available to Trade Online: Stocks and mutual funds.

Average Execution Time: Market order: few seconds, depending on volume of security being traded.

Minimum Deposit Required: None for cash accounts. $2,000 for margin accounts.

Additional Fees: Postage and handling fee per online trade: $2.50. Postage and handling fee per Citicorp registered representative, per transaction: $5.00. Transfer of securities account: $50.00. Maintenance fee when no transactions occur in a 12 month period, with average monthly balances less than $10,000: $50.00 fee. Dividend reinvestment fee: $3.00. Domestic wire transfer: $15.00. Overnight check to client or third party: $15.00. Duplicate statements 6 months or older: $6.00. Re-register certificate from client name to another name: $25.00. Estate evaluation: $25.00. Failure to deliver cash or securities due by settlement date: $25.00. Copy of check: $6.00.

Free Services and Financial Links: Price and news alerts via email, portfolio tracking, market and company news, profile, charts. Reports: Market Guide's Quick Facts, Zacks II Earnings Estimates, Telescan Pro, Search Criteria Report, Insider Trading Report, symbol lookup, currency exchange rates.

Real-Time Quotes: Free real-time quotes, although they are not streaming and must be refreshed.

States Registered In: All U.S. states.

Mutual Funds Offered: Over 4,000.

Payment for Order Flow: No.

Banking Services Offered: Free Direct Access Service, which includes bill payment service.

Company Background: Citibank was originally founded in 1812 and launched its online trading in 1992 through Citicorp Investment Services, a member of NASD/SPIC. Clients' accounts are protected up to $500,000, of which $100,000 is for cash coverage, provided by SIPC.

Customer Service Rating: ★★★ Excellent

COMPUTEL SECURITIES

Brokerage Type: Discount brokerage
Mailing Address: 301 Mission St. 5th Floor
San Francisco, CA 94105
Web Address: www.computel.com

Email Address: support@computel.com

Telephone Number: 800-432-0327

Fax Number: 415-543-3714

Market Orders: $9.00 per trade (1,000 to 5,000 shares). $14.00 per trade, less than 1,000 shares. Flat rate for equity trades up to $5,000 shares. Orders over 5,000 shares: additional $0.01 per share. Stocks under $2.00 and Canadian shares are $19.75 plus 2% of the principal.

Limit Orders: $19.00 per trade.

Option Trades: $24.00 per trade plus $1.00 per contract, for any contract price.

Telephone Trading: Additional surcharge of $10.00 per trade.

After-Hours Trading: 9:00 A.M. to 9:30 A.M. EST and 4:00 P.M. to 6:30 P.M. EST. $29.00 per trade, with live broker only.

Products Available to Trade Online: Stocks, options, and mutual funds.

Average Execution Time: Market order: 2–3 seconds under normal market conditions, less than 10 seconds for listed for Nasdaq stocks.

Minimum Deposit Required: $2,000 for cash or margin account.

Additional Fees: Transaction service fee: $2.50. Money wires sent out: $15.00. Legal name change: $25.00 per certificate. Returned check: $15.00. Reorganizations: $35.00. 144 stock: $50.00.

Free Services and Financial Links: Annual account maintenance, money market fund with check privileges, IRA setup, Reuters Inc. link, personalized market snapshots, portfolio tracker, charting, option chains, Briefing.com, Zacks, Edgar Online.

Real-Time Quotes: 25 streaming real-time quotes per day and 100 free real-time quotes with each trade placed and free 20-minute delayed quotes are also available.

States Registered In: All U.S. states.

Mutual Funds Offered: Any available in the open market.

Payment for Order Flow: Not divulged.

Banking Services Offered: No-fee check writing privileges through Bank One.

Company Background: Computel Securities was founded in June 1995 and is a division of Thomas F. White and Co. Computel Securities deals with a great amount of high net worth clients. Computel is currently a considerably small firm that considers itself a "Boutique Shop" giving very personalized service to its clients. Customers' accounts are protected up to $50 million dollars. Computel offers a customer service guarantee that states that if customers are not satisfied with service while making a trade, they may write them within 15 days, and Computel will refund the commission for that trade.

Customer Service Rating: ★★ Average

CYBERCORP.COM INC.

Brokerage Type: Direct-access brokerage
Mailing Address: 115 Wild Basin Rd.
Austin, TX 78746
Web Address: www.cybercorp.com
Email Address: correspondence@cybercorp.com
Telephone Number: 888-76-CYBER, 512-320-5444
Fax Number: 512-320-1561
Market Orders: Cyber Trader: $17.95 per trade (1–249 trades), $14.95 per trade (250–499 trades), $9.95 per trade (500 or more trades). CyberX & CyberX2: $14.95 per trade (1–249 trades), $12.95 per trade (250–499 trades), $9.95 per trade (500 or more trades).
Limit Orders: Same as market orders.
Option Trades: Cyber Trader and CyberX2: $3.00 per contract or $19.95 per trade, whichever is greater.
Telephone Trading: Broker-assisted trading is only used in emergency situations and for closing positions.
After-Hours Trading: 8:00 A.M. to 9:30 A.M. EST and 4:00 P.M. to 8:00 P.M. EST Commission schedule is the same as that for online trading.
Products Available to Trade Online: Stocks and options.
Average Execution Time: Market order: instantaneous.
Minimum Deposit Required: $10,000 for all accounts.
Additional Fees: Cyber Trader and CyberX2 data fees: $99.00 per month (0–49 trades per month), free (50 or more trades per month). Options data fee: $60.00 per month. Exchange fees: REDI Direct, $0.002 per share; ARCA Direct, $0.005 per share; ATTN Direct, $1.00 per trade; INCA Direct, $0.015 per share; BTRD Direct, $0.005 per share; NYSE-Amex, $0.005. SelectNet Fees: SelectNet Direct, $1.00 per trade. SelectNet Broadcast, $2.50 per trade; NTRD-BRUT-INCA, $0.015 per share (through SelectNet, additional $1.00 per trade); ATTN-BTRD-ARCA, $0.005 per share (through SelectNet, additional $1.00 per trade); ISLD-REDI, $0.0025 per share; STRK, $0.01 per share (through SelectNet, additional $1.00 per trade). IRA open: $25.00. IRA annual fee: $40.00. IRA termination: $60.00. Roth open: $25.00. Roth annual fee: $45.00. Roth termination: $75.00. Returned check: $15.00.

Free Services and Financial Links: Not available.

Real-Time Quotes: Streaming real-time quotes with software package.

States Registered In: All U.S. states

Mutual Funds Offered: None.

Payment for Order Flow: No.

Banking Services Offered: Check writing with an online account.

Company Background: Cybercorp was founded in December 1995 and is a direct-access trading and technology brokerage group. Cybercorp is a wholly owned subsidiary of Charles Schwab Corporation. Cybercorp caters to the active professional trader. Cybercorp currently trades over 32,500 trades per day as of April 2000. More than 2,000 traders use Cybercorp's software both online and through live brokers, executing over 15 million shares a day. Clients must have an income of at least $35,000 a year and a net worth of at least $65,000 (exclusive of farm and home) and previous experience using a direct market access system or the completion of a training program in the use of SOES, Select-Net, and ECNs to open an account with Cybercorp.com using Cyber Trader. To open an account using CyberX, you only need previous experience in investing. All accounts at Cybercorp must maintain a minimum daily balance of $5,000, and the account will be restricted until it is restored with a balance of $7,500. Clients' accounts are protected up to $25 million. SIPC provides up to $500,000, of which $100,000 is for cash coverage, and Pension Financial Services provides the remaining $24.5 million. Cybercorp utilizes Pension Financial Services as their clearing firm.

Customer Service Rating: ★★ Average

DATEK

Brokerage Type: Discount brokerage

Mailing Address: P.O. Box 493
                 Iselin, NJ 08830-0493

Web Address: www.datek.com

Email Address: support@datek.com

Telephone Number: 888-463-2835, outside U.S. 732-635-8800

Fax Number: 732-635-8957

Market Orders: $9.99 per trade, up to 5,000 shares, and additional $9.99 per trade for each additional 5,000 shares.

Limit Orders: Same as market orders.

Option Trades: Expected to begin October 2000.

Telephone Trading: $25.00 per trade.

After-Hours Trading: 8:00 A.M. to 9:30 A.M. EST and 4:00 P.M. to 8:00 P.M. EST. $9.99 per trade over Internet (limit orders only).

Products Available to Trade Online: Stocks and mutual funds.

Average Execution Time: Market order: 60 seconds or less or the marketable trade is free.

Minimum Deposit Required: None, but funds must be deposited in account before placing a trade. $2,000 minimum deposit is required for a margin account.

Additional Fees: Stock certificate: $50.00. Wire transfer out: $9.99. Returned check fee: $9.99. Stop payment: $9.99 (single check). Stop payment: $25.00 (sequence book of checks).

Free Services and Financial Links: Charts, news, Bloomberg Online, Briefing.com, Big Charts, CBS Marketwatch, market summaries, weekly market commentaries, Zacks, Free fund withdrawals from your Datek Online account, free money transfers to and from your Datek Online account, free securities transfers.

Real-Time Quotes: "Streamer," which allows clients to watch up to 20 NYSE or Amex streaming ticker symbols in real-time, free of charge.

States Registered In: All U.S. states.

Mutual Funds Offered: Over 7,000.

Payment for Order Flow: Yes, in certain cases, and Datek will rebate any payment received back to the client.

Banking Services Offered: Check writing. The first check book is free, and additional check books are $9.99 each.

Company Background: Datek Online began offering online trading to its clientele in July 1996. Datek has opened approximately 570,000 active customer accounts with total assets exceeding $14 billion and currently executes more than 100,000 investment transactions each day. Datek Online customers may open a wide variety of accounts, including individual, IRA, joint, corporate, and custodial accounts. Datek Online is offering its clients the ability to trade Nasdaq stocks in pennies and nickels rather than in fractions. This transaction will take place through their alternative trading system, Island ECN. Datek Online provides customer account protection up to $10,500,000. Datek provides a guarantee that if a marketable order is not executed within 60 seconds, the trade will be commission free.

Customer Service Rating: ★★★ Excellent

Gomez Rating: 6.22
Forrester PowerRankings: 49.95

DIRECT ACCESS TRADER

Brokerage Type: Direct-access brokerage
Mailing Address: InvestIn Securities Corp.
Infomart, Suite 2016
1950 Stemmons Frwy.
Dallas, TX 75207
Web Address: www.directaccesstrader.com
Email Address: newaccounts@investin.com
Telephone Number: 800-327-1883, 214-939-0110
Fax Number: 214-939-0116
Market Orders: 1–100 trades per month: $13.95 per trade. 101–200 trades per month: $12.95 per trade. 201–250 trades per month: $11.95 per trade. 251–300 trades per month: $10.95 per trade. 301 or more trades per month: $9.95 per trade. Applies to all trades up to 1,000 shares. Bulletin Board and Penny Stock Orders: $20.00 per trade, flat fee.
Limit Orders: Same as market orders.
Option Trades: $25.00 per trade plus $1.75 per contract.
Telephone Trading: $10.00 additional surcharge.
After-Hours Trading: 8:00 A.M. to 9:30 A.M. EST and 4:00 P.M. to 6:30 P.M. EST. Trades are routed through Island and ARCA. Same commissions apply as online commission schedule.
Products Available to Trade Online: Stocks and options.
Average Execution Time: Market order: Immediate execution.
Minimum Deposit Required: $10,000 for a margin account. All direct-access accounts require signed margin agreements.
Additional Fees: Software fees for Direct Access Trader: $247.45 per month plus tax (includes fee for NYSE and Nasdaq Level II), fee will be waived upon exceeding 50 trades per month. Exchange/ECN fees: Island (Nasdaq) Direct Access Connection, $1.00 per trade; Island (NYSE listed) Direct Access Connection, $1.00 per trade; Archipelago (TNTO) Direct Access Connection plus ECN charges, $1.00 per trade, $0.0075 per share; SOES, $0.50 per trade; SelectNet (preference market maker), $1.00 per trade; SelectNet (Broadcast), $2.50 per trade; NYSE listed, $0.008 per share; SelectNet: Instinet (INCA), $1.00 per trade, $0.015 per share; SelectNet: Btrade (BTRD), $1.00 per trade, $0.015

per share; SelectNet: Archipelago (TNTO), $1.00 per trade, $0.0075 per share; SelectNet: Spear Leads (REDI), $1.00 per trade, $0.015 per share; SelectNet: Brass (BRUT), $6.50 per trade; SelectNet: Attain (ATTN), $1.00 per trade, $0.015 per share; SelectNet: Strike (STRK), $1.00 per trade, $0.0066 per share; SelectNet: Nextrade (NTRD), $1.00 per trade, $0.015 per share. SOES/SelectNet Cancels, $0.25 per trade. Wire fees: $15.00 per each outgoing wire. Rule 144 sales: $35.00 surcharge. ACAT: $5.00 per account transferred from Penson (outgoing). Safekeeping charge: clients with securities in account and with less than 2 trades during a calendar year will incur a $25.00 charge. Options exercise: $19.95. Additional exchange-permission fees: American Stock Exchange, $3.50; Options Price Reporting, $25.00; Chicago Board of Trade (Bond Futures), $5.00; Chicago Mercantile (S&P Futures), $5.00. Dow Jones news: $95.00.

Free Services and Financial Links: Sites that offer training, Traders Press book store, short list of over 4,500 stocks, customizable news, price alerts, real-time news, real-time options chain, AnalystGroup.com, Bay-Street.com, Big Play Stocks, DayTrading at About.com, Day Trading International, Day Traders USA, Doh! Stock Picks, Dowtrend.com, Economic NET, Emerging Economies Portfolio, Epic Investments, Fuller Markets, Fundbuster, global and domestic investment information, Green & Company, Inc., InvestorLinks, Investor's Compass, Jarrett Investment Research, OptionSmart.com, Orion Futures Group, Inc., Raw Data, Right Stock Right Time, StockSites on the Net, StockSniffer.com, Stockpickz.com, Technical Analysis of Stocks and Commodities, TradingData.com, Trading Ideas, WalkRich Value Line, Wall Street Courier—Tools for day trading.

Real-Time Quotes: Streaming live Level II quotes with their software package.

States Registered In: All U.S. states except NH and PR.

Mutual Funds Offered: None.

Payment for Order Flow: No.

Banking Services Offered: None.

Company Background: Direct Access Trader was founded in 1995 and is a division of InvestIn Securities Corp. The Direct Access Trader software is used daily by over 4,000 traders. With the Direct Access Trader software, clients can trade using a Nasdaq Level II screen and can directly route orders to market makers and ECNs. The software, along with many other features, offers an account management system that tells in real-time both when the order was executed and at what price and when a position is being held. It also tells subsequent market movements that affect the position by displaying this information instantly. Clients' accounts are protected up to $25 million per account. Direct Access Trader utilizes Penson Financial Services as its clearing firm. Direct Access caters to the very active investor and day traders who trade for a living.

Customer Service Rating: ★★ Average

1ST DISCOUNT BROKERAGE, INC.

Brokerage Type: Full-service/discount brokerage

Mailing Address: 5883 Lake Worth Road
Lake Worth, FL 33463

Web Address: www.1st-discount.com

Email Address: service@1db.com

Telephone Number: 888-642-2811, 561-642-2811

Fax Number: 561-439-8651

Market Orders: $14.75 per trade, up to 5,000 shares, and additional $0.02 per share thereafter.

Limit Orders: Same as market orders.

Option Trades: $25.00 plus $1.75 per contract, up to 5,000 shares, minimum $30.00.

Telephone Trading: $35.00 for 100 shares, $40.00 for 200 shares, increases $5.00 with every 100 shares thereafter.

After-Hours Trading: None.

Products Available to Trade Online: Stocks, options, and mutual funds.

Average Execution Time: Market order: 15–20 seconds for Nasdaq or exchange stock, pending market conditions. Bulletin Board of Pink Sheet stock may take a little longer.

Minimum Deposit Required: None for cash account.

Additional Fees: Postage and handling: $3.50 per trade. Further additional fees unavailable.

Free Services and Financial Links: Portfolio tracker, the Motley Fool, Quote.com, The Internet Stock Report, Stock Grade, Silicon Investor, Vcall, Big Charts, Stock Point, Multex Investor network, Bloomberg.com, TheStreet.com, Market Snapshot Report, market equity indices, currency rates, Hot Stocks research, company profiles, IPO information, Small-Cap OTC News.

Real-Time Quotes: Free real-time quotes, although they are not streaming and must be refreshed. Unlimited 20 minute delayed quotes are also available.

States Registered In: All U.S. states except HI.

Mutual Funds Offered: Over 2,500.

Payment for Order Flow: Not disclosed.

Banking Services Offered: Check writing.

Company Background: 1st Discount Brokerage, Inc., was founded in 1995 and is a wholly owned subsidiary of 1st Internet Financials Services, Inc. 1st Discount Brokerage's clientele consists of individuals and institutions. 1st Discount Brokerage offers its clients knowledge about investing along with experience and investment strategies. 1st Discount does not mind handholding and feels that its customer service is one of its strongest advantages. 1st Discount Brokerage utilizes Fleet Securities, Inc., as its clearing firm. Clients' accounts are protected up to $100 million per account. SIPC provides coverage up to $500,000, of which $100,000 is for cash coverage. The additional $99.5 million is provided by Asset Guaranty Insurance Company.

Customer Service Rating: ★★★ Excellent

DLJ DIRECT

Brokerage Type: Discount brokerage

Mailing Address: P.O. Box 2062
Jersey City, NJ 07303-9838

Web Address: www.dljdirect.com

Email Address: service@dljdirect.com

Telephone Number: 800-825-5723, 800-825-5873

Fax Number: 201-413-5268

Market Orders: $20.00 per trade, up to 1,000 shares, and additional $0.02 per share thereafter. Select Client commission: $20.00 per trade, up to 5,000 shares, and additional $0.02 per share thereafter. Stocks trading at less than $1.00 will incur an overriding minimum of $20.00 and a maximum of 5% of the principal.

Limit Orders: Same as market orders.

Option Trades: $35.00 per trade plus $1.75 per contract (no minimum charge). Select Client commission: $30.00 per trade plus $1.75 per contract.

Telephone Trading: $20.00 per trade.

After-Hours Trading: 8:00 A.M. to 9:15 A.M. EST and 4:15 P.M. to 7:00 P.M. EST. $20.00 per trade over the Internet or with live broker.

Products Available to Trade Online: Stocks, options, mutual funds, and treasuries.

Average Execution Time: Market order: generally less than 1 minute.

Minimum Deposit Required: None.

Additional Fees: Late payments for trades: $15.00. Certificate insurance: $15.00. Legal transfer: $15.00. Returned check: $20.00. Funds wired: $25.00. Voluntary reorganization: $25.00. Precious metal storage: 0.001875 of the total value of each position per quarter.

Free Services and Financial Links: Select client privileges, including a higher level of personal attention, more savings, expanded trading capabilities, and superior investment information, charts, reports, news and market commentary from S&P, Zacks, Lipper, Reuters, Business Wire, PR Newswire, First Call, Thomson's, Briefing.com, model portfolios, personal stock ticker, alerts, Stock Center, Fund Center.

Real-Time Quotes: 100 free streaming real-time quotes upon opening an account and an additional 100 free for each trade executed in your account.

States Registered In: All U.S. states.

Mutual Funds Offered: Over 7,000.

Payment for Order Flow: Yes.

Banking Services Offered: AssetMaster Account: free check writing and no annual fee Gold MasterCard debit card with worldwide ATM purchase privileges.

Company Background: DLJ Direct was established in 1988. DLJ Direct has executed over $50 billion in online transactions and serves over 600,000 online accounts. Currently, DLJ Direct is the only online brokerage that offers Donaldson, Lufkin & Jenrette Securities Corporation research and IPOs to the self-directed online investor. DLJ Direct can be found on all the major online services including America Online, Prodigy, CompuServe, and the Internet (www.DLJdirect.com). DLJ's businesses include securities underwriting, sales and trading, investment and merchant banking, financial advisory services, investment research, venture capital, correspondent brokerage services, online interactive brokerage services, and asset management. The company's common stock trades on the New York Stock Exchange under the ticker symbol DLJ. DLJ and its affiliates handle approximately 10% of the daily volume of the NYSE. DLJ allows investors to apply to open an account online and may approve trading up to $15,000 within seconds. Clients with at least $1 million of assets in their combined DLJ Direct accounts can qualify for Select Client status to receive a host of Select Client privileges.

Customer Service Rating: ★★ Average
Gomez Rating: 7.00
Forrester PowerRankings: 57.61

DREYFUS BROKERAGE SERVICES, INC.

Brokerage Type: Discount brokerage
Mailing Address: 401 N. Maple Drive
Beverly Hills, CA 90210
Web Address: www.edreyfus.com
Email Address: support@edryfus.com
Telephone Number: 800-416-7113
Fax Number: 310-276-2238
Market Orders: $15.00 per trade, unlimited shares.
Limit Orders: Same as market orders.
Option Trades: Options placed over the Internet: $15.00 minimum plus $1.75 per contract. Minimum commission: $25.00.
Telephone Trading: Stocks: $25.00 per order up to 5,000 shares, and additional $0.01 per share thereafter. Option trades below $1.00 per contract: $1.75 per contract. Options priced at or above $1.00 per contract: $2.25 per contract. Minimum: $25.00.
After-Hours Trading: 4:00 P.M. to 8:00 P.M. EST. $15.00 per trade over the Internet (limit order only).
Products Available to Trade Online: Stocks, options, and mutual funds.
Average Execution Time: Market order: time varies depending on market conditions.
Minimum Deposit Required: None, but you must have cash or securities in the account before placing a trade. $2,000 required for a margin account.
Additional Fees: E-Signal: $85.00, but with more than 5 trades a month your account will be credited back $75.00. Level II: $50.00 per month. Exchange fees: $50.00 per month. Marketline: $35.00 per month. Instant Adviser: $90.00 per month. Vickers Insider Trading Report: $30.00 per month. IPO Spotlight: $30.00 per month. Option exercise and assignment: $15.00.
Free Services and Financial Links: Zacks, Thompson, Big Charts,

News Alert, Wall Street on Demand, Future World News, CBS Market-watch, Dow Jones, Market Watch, investment data.

Real-Time Quotes: Free real-time quotes, although they are not streaming and must be refreshed.

States Registered In: All U.S. states.

Mutual Funds Offered: Many.

Payment for Order Flow: Yes.

Banking Services Offered: None.

Company Background: Established in 1976, Dreyfus Brokerage Services, Inc., formerly Pacific Brokerage Services, Inc., is a member firm of the NYSE and other principal U.S. securities exchanges. DBS is an affiliate of Mellon Bank, N.A., and its principal subsidiary the Dreyfus Corporation. Clients' accounts are protected by SIPC to a maximum of $500,000 (claims for cash are limited to a maximum of $100,000). DBS maintains other insurance coverage through private carriers of $24.5 million per account, which gives clients total coverage of $25 million per account. DBS is a member of all major national clearing organizations (Depository Trust Co., National Securities Clearing Corp., and the Options Clearing Corp). DBS has one of the most sophisticated order entry systems in the securities industry. Orders for the purchase or sale of securities or options are entered and executed on all major exchanges via a direct computer-to-computer link with the NYSE, the Nasdaq, and selected dealers as well as various options and other exchanges.

Customer Service Rating: ★★★ Excellent

Gomez Rating: 4.57

EMPIRE FINANCIAL

Brokerage Type: Full-service/discount brokerage

Mailing Address: 1385 West State Road 434
                Longwood, FL 32750

Web Address: www.empirenow.com

Email Address: clientsupport@empirenow.com

Telephone Number: 800-569-3337, 407-774-1300

Fax Number: 407-834-9995

Market Orders: Nasdaq stocks: $6.95 per trade, unlimited shares. Exchange listed: $6.95 per trade, up to 5,000 shares, and additional $0.01 per share on entire order thereafter. First 5 trades free, market orders only.

Limit Orders: Nasdaq stocks: $11.95 per trade, unlimited shares. Exchange listed: $11.95 per trade, up to 5,000 shares, and additional $0.01 per share thereafter.

Option Trades: $19.00 per trade plus $1.95 per contract.

Telephone Trading: Market orders: Nasdaq stocks, $19.00 per trade, unlimited shares; exchange listed, $19.00 per trade, up to 5,000 shares, and additional $0.01 per share on entire order thereafter. Limit orders: Nasdaq stocks, $19.00 per trade plus $0.01 per share on entire order on shares valued greater than $1.00; $19.00 per trade plus 3% of the total dollar amount of the transaction on shares valued at $1.00 per share or less.

After-Hours Trading: 4:05 P.M. to 6:30 P.M. EST, limit orders and round lots only. Minimum order: 100 shares. Internet or live broker trading available, $11.95 per trade.

Products Available to Trade Online: Stocks, options, bonds, and mutual funds.

Average Execution Time: Market order: depends on security being traded.

Minimum Deposit Required: $1,000 for cash account. $2,000 for margin account.

Additional Fees: Transfer and ship (per certificate physical delivery): $20.00. Domestic wires: $20.00. Foreign wires: $50.00. Overnight delivery: $20.00. Extensions: $20.00. IRA setup: $25.00, annually $50.00. IRA account termination fee: $75.00. Account transfer out fee: $50.00. Returned check: $49.00. Legal transfer: $25.00 per issue. Options exercise and assignment: $30.00. DTC transfer: $10.00 per issue. Tenders: $25.00 per position. Bond redemption: $25.00 per item. Foreign securities transfer fee: $100.00. Foreign securities safekeeping: $5.00 per position per quarter. Copies of back statements: $5.00 per item. Cash settlement: $20.00 plus interest to settlement date. 144 sales: $75.00. Accommodation transfer: $25.00. Service charge (applied to all except equity and option transactions): $4.95. SEC fee charged on equity sale transactions of $1/300$ of 1% of principal amount of trade.

Free Services and Financial Links: Stock alerts, personal portfolio, news search, personal news, news manager, market commentary, internet news, Market at a Glance, News by Industry, IPO calendar, market indexes, free safekeeping, News Search, IPO Commentary.

Real-Time Quotes: Real-time quotes available for a monthly fee of $14.95; clients quote bank will be credited on the first of each month with 250 free quotes, and 100 quotes will be credited for each online transaction. Quotes are not streaming and must be refreshed.

States Registered In: All U.S. states.

Mutual Funds Offered: Over 5,000 from 70 mutual fund families.

Payment for Order Flow: Yes.

Banking Services Offered: Unlimited check writing with a minimum account balance of $2,000. A VISA debit card is also available for a $60.00 annual fee.

Company Background: Empire Financial Group was established in 1990, and online trading was launched in 1996. Empire Financial Group introduced and upgraded empirenow.com in March of 2000 to enhance clients' investing experiences. Empirenow offers online trading services, portfolio management capabilities, and market data and research. Clients also have access to a personal representative with expertise in portfolio management, mutual funds, and financial planning to help the client achieve their investment objectives. Clients' accounts are protected by SIPC up to $500,000, of which $100,000 is for cash coverage; additional protection of $2 million is also provided.

Customer Service Rating: ★★★ Excellent

Gomez Rating: 5.65

EQUITY TRADING

Brokerage Type: Direct access

Mailing Address: Empire State Building
350 Fifth Avenue, Suite 630
New York, NY 10118

Web Address: www.equitytrading.com

Email Address: info@equitytrading.com

Telephone Number: 877-ET-TRADE, 877-388-7233, 212-279-7800

Fax Number: 212-279-7805

Market Orders: $22.50 per trade, 1–19 trades per month; $21.95 per trade, 20–40 trades per month; $19.95 per trade, 41–99 trades per month; $17.95 per trade, 100–199 trades per month; $17.95 per trade, 200–399; $14.95 per trade, 400 or more trades per month. All trades up to 2,000 shares: add $0.015 per share thereafter.

Limit Orders: Same as market orders.

Option Trades: $25.00 minimum or $2.50 per contract. Minimum charge $25.00 per trade.

Telephone Trading: Same commissions as online schedule.

After-Hours Trading: 8:00 A.M. to 9:30 A.M. EST and 4:00 P.M. to 8:00 P.M. EST. Same commission as online trading schedule.

Products Available to Trade Online: Stocks, options, and futures.

Average Execution Time: Market order: split second.

Minimum Deposit Required: $10,000 for all accounts.

Additional Fees: Exchange fees: Nasdaq stock exchange Level II (0–40 trades per month), $50.00 per month, free with 41 or more trades per month; Chicago Board of Trade (0–40 trades per month), $10.00 per month, free with 41 or more trades per month; Chicago Mercantile (0–40 trades per month), $55.00 per month, free with 41 or more trades per month; Options price reporting authorization: $5.00 per month. Data fees: Full Real Tick (0–40 trades per month), $250.00 per month, free with 41 or more trades per month; Fixed Real Tick (0–40 trades per month), $175.00 per month, free with 41 or more trades per month; Lite Real Tick (0–40 trades per month), $100.00 per month, free with 41 or more trades per month; Dow Jones (0–40 trades per month), $95.00 per month, free with 41 or more trades per month; News Watch (0–40 trades per month), call firm for price per month. Execution fees: ABN AMRO (ISI), $.005 per share; Insinet (INCA), $.015 per share. Wire transfer fee: $15.00. Transfer fee: $7.50. IRA transfer return: $25.00. Returned check fee: $15.00.

Free Services and Financial Links: Dow Jones Newswire, financial news retrieval, Newswatch, The FirstNews.com, JaqNotes, Business-Week, Forbes, Individual Investor, Online Investor, Wall Street Journal.

Real-Time Quotes: Free streaming real-time Level I quotes at no charge and Level II quotes $50.00 (0–40 trades per month); after 40 trades Equity Trading will rebate the $50.00 fee back to the client.

States Registered In: All U.S. states.

Mutual Funds Offered: None.

Payment for Order Flow: No.

Banking Services Offered: Check writing with a Vision Account.

Company Background: Equity Trading is a direct access firm founded in 1995 that caters to the active trader. Equity trader offers clients access to SOES, Archipelago (ARCA), Island (ISLD), Instinet (INCA), and REDI. Equity Trader offers $5.00 trades on all orders of 300 shares or less for the client's first 90 days of trading. This allows clients time to familiarize themselves with the Equity Trading software. The brokerage also offers one-week educational programs to help the trader have a better understanding of the market and online trading. The course fee is $2,900 with a $500.00 rebate for anyone who opens an account. Clients must have a minimum net worth of $50,000 and a minimum salary of $50,000 to open an account with Equity Trading. A minimum balance of $2,000 must remain in clients' account at all times.

Customer Service Rating: ★★★ Excellent

E*TRADE

Brokerage Type: Discount brokerage
Mailing Address: E*TRADE Securities, Inc.
2400 Geng Road
Palo Alto, CA 94303-3317
Web Address: www.e-trade.com
Email Address: accounts@etrade.com
Telephone Number: 800-ETRADE-1
Fax Number: 916-858-8989
Market Orders: Listed stocks: $14.95 per trade, up to 5,000 shares, additional $0.01 per share thereafter. Nasdaq stocks: $19.95 per trade. Commissions decline for active traders.
Limit Orders: $19.95 per trade. Commissions decline for active traders.
Option Trades: $20.00 per trade plus $1.75 per contract, $29.00 minimum per trade.
Telephone Trading: Additional surcharge of $15.00 per trade.
After-Hours Trading: 4:05 P.M. to 6:30 P.M. EST. $19.95 per trade over the Internet (limit order only).
Products Available to Trade Online: Stocks, options, mutual funds, bonds, and U.S. treasuries.
Average Execution Time: Market order: 2–3 seconds.
Minimum Deposit Required: $1,000 for cash account. $2,000 for margin account.
Additional Fees: Photocopies of checks: one check, $5.00; additional copies, $2.50. Account transfer out: $20.00. Issue stock certificate: $5.00. Overnight mail: $15.00. Returned check: $25.00. Wired funds out: $20.00. Stop payment request on E*TRADE check: $15.00. Restricted securities: $75.00. Voluntary reorganization: $10.00.
Free Services and Financial Links: Fully customizable portfolio manager, personalized market views, breaking news, live market commentary, First Call earnings estimates, posting privileges in discussion groups, United Airlines Mileage Plus miles, portfolio tracking, stock research and recommendations, Black Scholes option analysis, No-fee

IRAs, Bond trading and research, instant stock alerts, access to sub-
scribe to IPOs, Real-time up and down grades, Standard & Poor's news,
Clear Station, TheStreet.com, Zacks, Reuters, CNBC, Briefing.com, free
Nasdaq Level II quotes with 75 or more transactions per quarter.

Real-Time Quotes: Free streaming real-time quotes with 35 or more
trades per quarter. Clients can view 20 stocks at a time in one portfolio,
and they have access to numerous portfolios. If they do not exceed 35
trades per month, there is a $19.95 per trade fee per month.

States Registered In: All U.S. states.

Mutual Funds Offered: Over 5,000 from over 175 asset management
companies.

Payment for Order Flow: Yes.

Banking Services Offered: Check writing through a money market
fund. Clients can open an account through E*TRADE Bank online that
offers banking services such as check writing, ATM debit card, and online bill paying.

Company Background: In 1992, E*TRADE Securities Inc. was established and began offering online investing services through America
Online and CompuServe. In 1996, www.e-trade.com was launched and
E*TRADE went public. Its clientele currently exceeds 1.5 million, and
clients' accounts are protected up to $100 million. The company's stock
trades on the Nasdaq under the symbol EGRP.

Customer Service Rating: ★★★ Excellent

Gomez Rating: 7.84

Forrester PowerRankings: 49.83

FARSIGHT

Brokerage Type: Discount brokerage

Mailing Address: FarSight Financial Services, LLP
P.O. Box 1913
Boston, MA 02205-1913

Web Address: www.farsight.com

Email Address: service@ecapitalist.com

Telephone Number: 800-830-7483

Fax Number: 613-218-3835

Market Orders: $19.95 up to 5,000 shares, and additional $0.02 per
share thereafter.

Limit Orders: Same as market orders.

Option Trades: $19.95 plus $1.99 per contract. Minimum commission: $29.95.

Telephone Trading: $29.95 per trade, up to 5,000 shares, and additional $0.02 per share thereafter.

After-Hours Trading: None.

Products Available to Trade Online: Stocks, options, and mutual funds.

Average Execution Time: Market order: 5 seconds, dependent on market conditions.

Minimum Deposit Required: $2,500 for cash account. $10,000 for margin account.

Additional Fees: IRA annual maintenance fee: $25.00, waived for accounts over $25,000 equity. IRA setup: $25.00. Mailgrams: $20.00. Extensions: $20.00. Late payments: brokers discretion plus 2%. ACATS: $50.00. Legal transfer: $25.00. Tenders (voluntary or involuntary): $20.00. Restricted stock (144) processing fee: $150.00. Transfer and ship: $25.00. Outgoing wire transfer: $20.00. Overnight delivery of checks: $15.00. Overnight delivery of documents: $15.00. Return deposit check: $25.00. Duplicate noncurrent statement: $10.00. Inactive account fees: $50.00 per year. "Double ticket charge" for missing documents: $20.00 per transaction. Checking: stop payment, $15.00; check copy, $2.50; VISA Debit ATM card copy of sales draft, $2.50. Option exercise and assignment: $29.95.

Free Services and Financial Links: Company profile, charts, news, Zacks, free IRA termination.

Real-Time Quotes: Free real-time quotes, although they are not streaming and must be refreshed.

States Registered In: All U.S. states.

Mutual Funds Offered: All mutual fund families.

Payment for Order Flow: Yes.

Banking Services Offered: Check writing with an online account and check writing off of margin account and debit card privileges through an asset management account.

Company Background: Farsight.com was founded in 1995, and its parent company is Platinum Online International. The largest portion of Farsight's clientele is made up of individuals, with currently 10,000 active online accounts. Clients' accounts are protected up to $25 million each. Farsight launched a Chinese-language version of its website due to the growing number of requests from its clientele.

Customer Service Rating: ★★ Average

FBR.COM

Brokerage Type: Discount brokerage
Mailing Address: 1001 Nineteenth Street North
Arlington, VA 22209
Web Address: www.fbr.com
Email Address: webmaster@fbr.com
Telephone Number: 888-200-4350
Fax Number: 703-522-3397
Market Orders: $14.95 per trade, up to 5,000 shares, add $0.01 per share thereafter. Purchase orders will not be taken for OTC Bulletin Board stocks below $5.00.
Limit Orders: Same as market orders.
Option Trades: None.
Telephone Trading: $29.95 per trade, up to 5,000 shares, and additional $0.01 per share thereafter.
After-Hours Trading: None.
Products Available to Trade Online: Stocks and mutual funds.
Average Execution Time: Market order: within 5–10 seconds.
Minimum Deposit Required: $2,000 for cash or margin accounts.
Additional Fees: Handling fee of stock certificate: $3.00. Shipment of securities to third-party names: $25.00. Check reordering: $15.00 per box of 200. Stop payment: $25.00. Late payment: $25.00. Returned check fee: $25.00. Insufficient funds: $25.00. Account transfer: $25.00. Transfer of securities into name other than that on account (per issue): $25.00. Wire transfer: $25.00. Extension request: $25.00. IRA termination: $50.00. IRA transfer out: $50.00.
Free Services and Financial Links: Research reports provided by Friedman, Billings, Ramsey & Co., daily articles, industry profiles, Research Library, news, charts, events.
Real-Time Quotes: Real-time quotes through online account.
States Registered In: All U.S. states.
Mutual Funds Offered: Over 5,000 from over 160 fund families.
Payment for Order Flow: Yes.
Banking Services Offered: Free check writing for clients with online account. Checks must be written for $100.00 or more. Clients have access to a VISA check card for a $50.00 annual fee.
Company Background: Friedman, Billings, Ramsey Group, Inc. was founded in 1989 and launched online trading through FBR.com in April 1999. Clients must maintain a minimum of $2,000 equity at all times. Client accounts are protected up to $500,000, of which

$100,000 is for cash, provided by SIPC. Additional coverage is provided by a private insurer. FBR.com brokerage accounts are carried and cleared through Fiserv Securities, Inc. FBR Investment Services is a brokerage/dealer and a member of SEC and NASD/SIPC.

Customer Service Rating: ★★★ Excellent

Gomez Rating: 4.63

FIDELITY INVESTMENTS

Brokerage Type: Discount brokerage

Mailing Address: Fidelity Services, Inc.
Attn. Brokerage Operations
P.O. Box 770001
Cincinnati, OH 45277-0002

Web Address: www.fidelity.com

Email Address: info@fidelity.com

Telephone Number: 800-544-6666

Fax Number: None.

Market Orders: Gold Circle: (72 or more trades per year) $14.95 per trade, up to 1,000 shares, and additional $0.02 per share thereafter; (240 or more trades per month) $14.00 per trade, up to 1,000 shares, and additional $0.01 per share thereafter. Maximum: 5% of principal, subject to the minimum commission. Minimum: $14.95 (72 or more trades) and $14.00 (240 or more trades). Active Trader: $14.95 per trade up to 1,000 shares, and additional $0.02 per share thereafter. Maximum: 5% of principal, subject to minimum commission. Minimum: $14.95. Preferred: $14.95 per trade, up to 1,000 shares, and additional $0.02 per share thereafter. Maximum: 5% of principal, subject to minimum commission. Minimum: $14.95.

Limit Orders: Limit/stop orders: $5.00 surcharge per transaction.

Option Trades: Gold Circle: $25.00 per trade plus $1.75 per contract. Active Trader: $20.00 per trade plus $1.75 per contract. Standard discount: 25% discount off standard rate.

Telephone Trading: Stock trades, Gold Circle: $25.00 per trade, up to 1,000 shares, and additional $0.02 per share thereafter. Maximum: 5% of principal, subject to minimum commission. Minimum: $25.00. Active Trader: $45.00 per trade, plus $0.02 per share. Maximum: 5% of principal, subject to minimum commission. Minimum: $45.00. Limit/stop orders: $5.00 surcharge per transaction. Preferred: 25% discount off standard commission (the charge for limit/stop orders is applied after discount). Option trades, Gold Circle: $25.00 per trade plus $1.75 per contract. Active Trader: $35.00 per trade plus $1.75 per contract. Standard Discount: $0–2,500, $28.75 per trade plus 1.60% of principal; $2,501–10,000, $48.75 plus .80% of principal; over $10,000, $98.75 per trade plus .30% of principal.

After-Hours Trading: 7:30 A.M. to 9:15 A.M. EST and 4:00 P.M. to 8:00 P.M. EST. 100 share lots only. Online commission schedule applies. $5.00 limit surcharge applies.

Products Available to Trade Online: Stocks, bonds, options, and mutual funds.

Average Execution Time: Market order: Fidelity was unable to give this information.

Minimum Deposit Required: $2,500 for cash or margin account.

Additional Fees: Bank Wire redemption: $15.00 (waived for Gold Circle Accounts). Brokerage inactivity fee: subject to a $15.00 fee, four times per year. Late settlement: $15.00. Limited partnership: $75.00 transfer fee. Return check, stop payment: $15.00. Transferring and shipping certificate: $15.00 per certificate. Voluntary reorganization: $38.00 (waived for Gold Circle Accounts).

Free Services and Financial Links: My Fidelity, My Fidelity Weekend, Portfolio Selector, Mutual Fund Spotlight Fund Evaluator, Fund Screens, Lehman Brothers: Top 10 U.S. Stock Picks, CBS Marketwatch, Active Trader Newsletter, Option Resources, IPO calendar, Real-time research, reports, alerts, catalog, intraday stock screener, stock evaluator, fund evaluator.

Real-Time Quotes: Real-time quotes through Powerstreet Pro.

States Registered In: All U.S. states.

Mutual Funds Offered: Over 4,100.

Payment for Order Flow: Yes.

Banking Services Offered: Most money market and many bond funds offer check writing. Clients who have a nonretirement, individual, joint or estate or trust registration for Fidelity Brokerage Account have access to online bill payment. If the client has $30,000 or more in assets there is no monthly fee. If there is less than $30,000 in assets, clients will incur a $6.95 monthly fee. Eligible clients can receive a Fidelity Gold or Platinum Card.

Company Background: Fidelity was founded in 1946 and established Fidelity Brokerage Services Inc. in 1978. Online trading was first offered in 1996, and online trading through Powerstreet was launched in 1999. Powerstreet by Fidelity offers its active traders additional commission discounts. To receive the Gold Circle discount, clients must trade stocks, bonds, or options 72 times or more in a rolling 12-month period. Accounts that trade more than 240 trades in a rolling 12-month period will qualify for lower commissions. To receive the Active Trader discount, clients must trade stocks, bonds, or options 36 or more times in a rolling 12-month period. To receive the Preferred Trader discount one must make at least 12 trades in a rolling 12-month period or have $100,000 in mutual fund assets. Powerstreet Pro is offered to the active trader and is a Web-based trading workstation for the client who places at least 36 trades in a rolling 12-month period. This workstation offers the client extensive research and investment tools.

Customer Service Rating: ★★★ Excellent
Gomez Rating: 7.63
Forrester PowerRankings: 56.62

FIRSTRADE

Brokerage Type: Full-service brokerage
Mailing Address: First Securities, Inc.
136-21 Roosevelt Ave. 3rd Floor
Flushing, NY 11354
Web Address: www.firstrade.com
Email Address: service@firstrade.com
Telephone Number: 888-988-6168
Fax Number: 718-961-6202
Market Orders: $6.95 per trade, up to 5,000 shares, and additional $0.005 per share to entire order for stocks at or under $2.00. Market orders at or under $2.00 are charged a minimum of $9.95.
Limit Orders: $9.95 per trade, up to 5,000 shares and add $0.005 per share to entire order for stocks at or under $2.00.
Option Trades: $20.00 per trade plus $1.75 per contract. Minimum: $28.75.
Telephone Trading: $29.95 per trade for stocks at or under $2.00; trades over 5,000 shares add $0.005 to entire order.
After-Hours Trading: None.
Products Available to Trade Online: Stocks, options, and mutual funds.
Average Execution Time: Market order: 2–3 seconds under normal market conditions; 20 seconds or more in fast market conditions.

Minimum Deposit Required: None, but funds must be cleared prior to first trade.

Additional Fees: Communication mailgrams: $15.00. Sell out/buy in notices: $15.00. Returned checks: $25.00. Outgoing DTC transfer fee: $7.50. Wiring funds domestic: $25.00. Wiring funds foreign: $35.00. Legal transfer fee: $50.00. Issue stock certificate: $7.50. Option exercise assignment: $29.95.

Free Services and Financial Links: Zacks, Express Site, Briefing.com, interactive charts, Edgar Online, Marketguide, stock and fund screening tools, free IRAs funds without transaction fees, streaming real-time watch list.

Real-Time Quotes: Free streaming real-time quotes.

States Registered In: All U.S. states.

Mutual Funds Offered: Thousands.

Payment for Order Flow: Yes.

Banking Services Offered: None.

Company Background: Firstrade.com is the proprietary trading system of Firstrade Securities Inc., member of NASD and SIPC, founded in 1985. In 1997 Firstrade went online. Firstrade.com clears all securities transactions through U.S. Clearing Corp. Firstrade Securities Inc. has fully disclosed brokerage/dealer clearing agreements with U.S. Clearing Corp. Accounts at Firstrade.com are protected up to $100 million, limited to $100,000 in cash, through U.S. Clearing. SIPC provides coverage up to $500,000, of which $100,000 is for cash coverage.

Customer Service Rating: ★★★ Excellent

Gomez Rating: 6.30

FOLIOFN

Brokerage Type: Discount brokerage

Mailing Address: Customer Service Department
Foliofn Investments, Inc.
P.O. Box 3068
Merrifield, VA 22116-3068

Web Address: www.foliofn.com

Email Address: support@investments.foliofn.com

Telephone Number: 888-973-7890

Fax Number: 703-356-9591

Market Orders: Individual direct stock trade: $14.95 per trade. Up to three folios: $29.95 per month flat fee or $295.00 a year. (The flat fee covers all clients trading during the twice-daily trading windows. Each additional folio: $9.95 a month or $95.00 a year.)

Limit Orders: Same as market orders.

Option Trades: None.

Telephone Trading: $45.00 additional surcharge.

After-Hours Trading: None.

Products Available to Trade Online: Stocks.

Average Execution Time: Market order: depends on stock being traded.

Minimum Deposit Required: None.

Additional Fees: Express mail: $15.00. Wire transfer out: $30. Certificate delivery, same registration: $15.00. Physical corporate action: $35.00. Voluntary corporate action: $20.00. Transfer out: $50.00 per account. Returned check, ACH fee: $20.00. Late trade settlement: $15.00. Bounced check: $20.00. Noncollectible deposit: $5.00. Stop payment: $16.00. Check copy: $10.00. VISA receipt copy: $6.00. Paper copies of account statements, confirmations: $5.00 first statements, $2.50 subsequent statements. Restricted securities (Rule 144): $75.00.

Free Services and Financial Links: Financial calculators, cost calculators, the Motley Fool, social security administration, Investors Clearinghouse, the Bond Market Association, Investing Online Research Center, New York Stock Exchange, Nasdaq, Securities and Exchange Commission, the North American Securities Administrators Association, Financial Standards Accounting Board, American Savings Education Council, Internal Revenue Service.

Real-Time Quotes: No real-time quotes; free 20-minute delayed quotes.

States Registered In: All U.S. states.

Mutual Funds Offered: None.

Payment for Order Flow: Yes.

Banking Services Offered: Check writing; free debit card if clients own more than six folios at one time.

Company Background: Foliofn was founded in early May 2000 and combined the benefits of mutual funds investing with advantages of stock investing, while eliminating many disadvantages of both. A folio is a group of stocks that clients can purchase in a single transaction using the Foliofn system. Foliofn offers a diversified range of folios. There are "ready-to-go" folios, which usually consist of 20 to 30 stocks. Clients can also build their own from scratch, usually consisting of 1 to

50 stocks. Clients have the ability to trade entire folios at once or to re-balance and screen out any stocks or industries they choose as often as they wish. Foliofn does not give advice or recommend folios to clients. The client must figure out their own investment goals and preferences and then focus the characteristics on which folio best suits their needs. Foliofn will automatically cancel an order if it goes up or down more than 5%, unless the client requests otherwise. Clients can submit orders throughout the day, and Foliofn will hold the order until the time frame window closes. The two window frames are 10:15 A.M. and 2:45 P.M. After the window closes, Foliofn will match orders up against other clients, and the ones that do not match up will be sent to the market for execution. Foliofn offers its clients automatic dividend reinvestment. Clients' accounts are protected by SIPC up to $500,000, of which $100,000 is for cash coverage. Lloyd's of London provides a maximum of $2 million in coverage per account.

Customer Service Rating: ★★ Average

FRANKLIN ROSS, INC.

Brokerage Type: Direct-access brokerage
Mailing Address: 210 North University Dr.
Coral Springs, FL 33071
Web Address: www.franklinross.com
Email Address: service@franklinross.com
Telephone Number: 877-81-TRADE
Fax Number: 954-757-8999
Market Orders: Nasdaq: standard account, $17.95 flat rate. Rates negotiable for the more active trader.
Limit Orders: Nasdaq: standard account, $17.95 flat rate.
Option Trades: $25.00 per ticket, $2.00 per contract, on average.
Telephone Trading: Same commissions as online schedule.
After-Hours Trading: 8:00 A.M. to 8:00 P.M. EST. $25.00 per ticket, $2.00 per contract, on average. Same commission applies as online trading schedule.
Products Available to Trade Online: Stocks.
Average Execution Time: Market order: 3–5 seconds.
Minimum Deposit Required: $10,000 for standard account.
Additional Fees: Software data fee: Complete Real Tick III with order entry, Nasdaq Level II, charts, time and sales, web browser, NYSE, Nas-

daq/Amex Exchange, $299.95 per month. Data fees are prorated if account is open after the 15th of the month. If customer completes more than 50 trades per month, monthly fee is waived. Nasdaq quotes only: $250.00 per month. OPRA for option quotes: additional $2.50 a month. CME permissioning for futures: additional $10.00 a month. Dow Jones News Wire: $95.00 per month, waived dependent on amount of trades placed. Wire out: $15.00. International wire out: $25.00. ACATs out: $25.00. Returned check fee: $20.00. Rule 144: varies on a case-to-case basis.

Free Services and Financial Links: Funds wired in, checks mailed out, confirmations, name change, Regulation T extension, nonmandatory reorganization.

Real-Time Quotes: Streaming real-time quotes with software package.

States Registered In: All U.S. states except AL, AR, DC, DE, ME, MO, MS, MT, ND, NE, NH, RI, SD, WI, WV, and WY.

Mutual Funds Offered: None.

Payment for Order Flow: No.

Banking Services Offered: None.

Company Background: Franklin Ross is a full-service brokerage firm founded in 1997. Franklin Ross offers its clientele real-time online trading through the utilization of Real Tick III, which allows the client access to all market makers and stock exchanges. Franklin Ross accounts are a mix of individuals and corporations but lean toward the individual trader. Free training is provided to all clients. To open a standard account (for traders expecting to make fewer than 100 trades per month), the client must have at least one year equity/investment trading experience, a minimum annual income of $30,000, and a net worth of $100,000.

Customer Service Rating: ★★★ Excellent

FREEDOM INVESTMENTS, INC.

Brokerage Type: Discount brokerage
Mailing Address: 11422 Miracle Hills Dr. Suite 501
                    Omaha, Nebraska 68154
Web Address: www.freedominvestments.com
Email Address: support@freedominvestments.com
Telephone Number: 800-944-4033, 402-431-8500
Fax Number: None.

Market Orders: $15.00 per trade, unlimited shares. Stocks trading less than $2.00 per share for a maximum of 10,000 shares: $30.00 per trade. Stocks trading $2.00 per share or less for more than 10,000 shares: $30.00 per trade plus $0.005 per share.

Limit Orders: Same as market orders.

Option Trades: $40.00 per trade plus $2.00 per contract.

Telephone Trading: $45.00 per trade plus $0.03 per share. Options: $50.00 plus $3.50 per contract.

After-Hours Trading: None.

Products Available to Trade Online: Stocks, bonds, and options.

Average Execution Time: Market order: less than one minute under normal market conditions.

Minimum Deposit Required: $2,000 for cash or margin account.

Additional Fees: Wire transfer funds out: $15.00. Overnight deliveries: $20.00. Regulation T extensions: $20.00. Late payment fee: $15.00 plus all accrued interest charges. Mailing stock certificates: $50.00. Returned checks: $25.00. Legal transfers: $50.00. Back copies of statements or confirmations: $5.00 per item. Inactive account fee: $25.00 per quarter. Tenders (mandatory): $10.00. Tenders (nonmandatory): $25.00. Foreign securities: $75.00 plus agent fee. Foreign securities safekeeping fee: $5.00 per position per quarter. Restricted stock: $50.00 plus $0.02 per share. Account transfer fee: $50.00. IRA fees: $35.00. Exercise and assignments: $25.00.

Free Services and Financial Links: Zacks, Edgar Online, Investing Online Resource Center, Bloomberg News, Business Week Online, Douglas Gerlach's Invest-O-Rama, E-Line Financials, investor links, Investor Guide, Investors Business Daily, investor words, Morning Star Net, Prime Rate, Research Mag, the Web Investor, Securities and Exchange Commission, Daily Stocks, Stock Smart, Yahoo (U.S. Stock News, Reports, and Quotes), Active Traders Network, Trading Day, Audio and Video Links, Live Radio.

Real-Time Quotes: Free real-time quotes, although they are not streaming and must be refreshed.

States Registered In: All U.S. states.

Mutual Funds Offered: None.

Payment for Order Flow: Yes.

Banking Services Offered: None.

Company Background: Freedom Investments was founded in 1994 and is a member of NYSE, NASD, and SIPC. Freedom Investments is a wholly owned subsidiary of Fahnestock & Co., which is also its clearing firm. Clients' accounts are protected up to $500,000, of which $100,000 is for cash coverage, provided by SIPC.

Customer Service Rating: ★★★ Excellent

FREEMAN WELWOOD

Brokerage Type: Discount brokerage
Mailing Address: P.O. Box 21886
Seattle, WA 98111
Web Address: www.freemanwelwood.com
Email Address: service@freemanwelwood.com
Telephone Number: 800-729-7585, 206-382-5353
Fax Number: 206-382-5392
Market Orders: $14.95 per trade, up to 2,000 shares, and additional flat rate of $0.01 per share thereafter.
Limit Orders: $19.95 per trade, up to 2,000 shares, and additional flat rate of $0.01 per share thereafter.
Option Trades: 10% off of $34.00 plus $2.50 per contract.
Telephone Trading: $34.00 plus $0.05 per share up to 800 shares, and additional $0.025 per share thereafter. Maximum commission of $50.00 applies to first 1,000 shares priced between $1.00 and $5.00. $34.00 per trade plus 2.5% of principal applies to stocks priced under $1.00. Options: $34.00 per trade plus $2.50 per contract.
After-Hours Trading: 4:00 P.M. to 6:00 P.M. EST (live broker only). $34.00 per trade plus $0.05 per share.
Products Available to Trade Online: Stocks, options, and mutual funds.
Average Execution Time: Market order: within a few seconds.
Minimum Deposit Required: None for cash account, but cleared funds are required before placing first trade. $2,000 for a margin account.
Additional Fees: E-Signal real-time equity quotes: $59.00 per month. E-Signal real-time equity, futures, and options quotes: $130.00 per month. Certificate delivery: $15.00. Registration in another name: $25.00. Estate certificate deposit: $25.00. Restricted stock: $50.00. Voluntary reorganizations: $25.00. Mandatory reorganizations: $10.00. Withdrawals from offers: $25.00. Account research (including duplicate statements): within past 12 months, no charge; beyond past 12 months, $3.00 per month. Late payment or delivery: $15.00 plus inter-

est. Rebill trade to different account: $10.00. Returned check: $25.00 plus interest. Stop payment: $20.00. Wire transfer of funds: $20.00.

Free Services and Financial Links: Research, stock and mutual fund screening, charts, no-fee IRA, free dividend reinvestment, free earnings estimates, free safekeeping, Reuters News, intraday and historical charts, personal portfolio, commentary and analysis, portfolio tracking, StockWatch, financial calculators, SEC filings.

Real-Time Quotes: Streaming real-time quotes are offered to active traders. Unlimited delayed quotes are also available.

States Registered In: All U.S. states.

Mutual Funds Offered: Over 3,800.

Payment for Order Flow: Not divulged.

Banking Services Offered: Free check writing with Advantage Account.

Company Background: Freeman Welwood was founded in 1972 and went online in November 1997. Freeman Welwood is a privately held company with 10 offices nationwide. Clients' accounts are protected up to $500,000, of which $100,000 is for cash coverage, provided by SIPC. Additional protection of $95 million is provided through private underwriters. The clientele at Freeman Welwood is predominantly made up of individuals.

Customer Service Rating: ★★ Average

Gomez Rating: 5.73

FREETRADE

Brokerage Type: Discount brokerage

Mailing Address: None.

Web Address: www.freetrade.com

Email Address: customerservice@freetrade.com

Telephone Number: None.

Fax Number: None.

Market Orders: No commissions.

Limit Orders: $5.00 per trade. $5.00 per trade for stop and odd-lot orders also.

Option Trades: None.

Telephone Trading: None.

After-Hours Trading: None.

Products Available to Trade Online: Stocks.

Average Execution Time: Market order: 2–3 seconds under normal market conditions.

Minimum Deposit Required: $5,000 for all accounts.

Additional Fees: Certain fees will affect the customer depending on the situation.

Free Services: None.

Real-Time Quotes: Real-time quotes for a $20.00 per month fee, although they are not streaming and must be refreshed.

States Registered In: All U.S. states.

Mutual Funds Offered: None.

Payment for Order Flow: Yes.

Banking Services Offered: None.

Company Background: FreeTrade, founded in 2000, is a brokerage/dealer and a wholly owned subsidiary of Ameritrade Holding Corporation. FreeTrade is considered to be a new virtual broker catering to a specific niche market. All communication is done through the Internet. Email is used for all means of communication, including statements. There are no telephones and no employees to open mail; this is how the company keeps their commissions so minimal. This type of operation may not be for everyone, but if you are comfortable with no direct communication with a live person, it may work for you. All trades and customer service will go through the Internet. FreeTrade will only accept individual or joint accounts; no transfer accounts are accepted. To open an account, perspective clients must apply online after agreeing to the terms of an account with FreeTrade.

Customer Service Rating: ★★★ Excellent

FRONTIER FUTURES, INC.

Brokerage Type: Discount brokerage

Mailing Address: 4000 River Ridge Dr. NE
Cedar Rapids, IA 52402

Web Address: www.ffutures.com

Email Address: request@ffutures.com

Telephone Number: 800-278-6257

Fax Number: 319-393-6171

Market Orders: Listed and OTC stocks: $2.00 per share and higher. Up to 2,999 shares: $29.00 per trade. 3,000 shares and over: free. Listed stocks under $2.00 per share: $29.00 per share plus $0.01 per share. All orders subject to a $4.00 confirmation charge.

Limit Orders: Listed stocks under $2.00 per share: $29.00 plus $0.02 per share. All orders subject to a $4.00 confirmation charge.

Option Trades: $29.00 per trade plus $2.50 per contract.

Telephone Trading: Same commissions as online schedule.

After-Hours Trading: None.

Products Available to Trade Online: Futures, stocks, options, mutual funds, and bonds (futures).

Average Execution Time: Market order: less than 30 seconds under normal market conditions.

Minimum Deposit Required: $5,000 for cash or margin account.

Additional Fees: Reports from Wall Street by FAX, Standard & Poor's, First Call, Argus, Morningstar and more: approximately $1.50 each. Wire funds: $15.00. Returned checks: $25.00. Stop payment request: $15.00. Certificate delivered: $25.00. Trade extensions: $25.00. Mailgram: $15.00. Delinquent mandatory reorganization: $20.00. Legal return item: $25.00. Certificate requiring legal documents: $10.00. Full transfer of account: $30.00. Inactive account fee: $25.00. Research fee: $60.00 per hour. IRA annual fee: $30.00. IRA termination: $50.00.

Free Services and Financial Links: Investools, Market Guide, Pace Setters Stock Database, company annual reports, futures news & quotes.

Real-Time Quotes: Unlimited delayed quotes; real-time quotes for a fee.

States Registered In: All U.S. states.

Mutual Funds Offered: Funds Mart, a mutual funds supermarket.

Payment for Order Flow: Yes, on certain trades.

Banking Services Offered: Check writing and ATM debit card.

Company Background: Frontier Futures, Inc., a commodities trading company, was established in 1985. Frontier Futures launched its online trading through www.ffutures.com in the first quarter of 1999. Frontier appeals to customers who make their own trading decisions or employ a trading advisor and serves a national and international client base of individuals, institutional traders, and hedgers.

Customer Service Rating: ★★★ Excellent

GFN.COM (GAY FINANCIAL NETWORK)

Brokerage Type: Discount brokerage

Mailing Address: GFN Investments
C/o Brokerage Services Division, US Clearing
26 Broadway 12th Fl.
New York, NY 10004

Web Address: www.gfn.com
Email Address: bsd@usclearing.com
Telephone Number: 800-354-7429
Fax Number: 212-747-4850
Market Orders: $14.95 per trade, up to 1,000 shares, and additional $0.02 per share thereafter.
Limit Orders: Same as market orders.
Option Trades: Principal amount: $35.00 plus .009% of principal amount ($3,000 and under); $35.00 plus .008% of principal amount ($3,001 to $10,000); $35.00 plus .007% of principal amount ($10,001 and over). Maximum charge: $25.00 per contract (100 shares = 1 contract). Minimum: $3.00 per contract.
Telephone Trading: Stock trades: $35.00 plus .005% of principal amount ($15,000 and under); $35.00 plus .004% of principal amount ($15,000 to $50,000); $35.00 plus .002% of principal amount ($50,001 to $125,000); $35.00 plus .0015% of principal amount ($125,001 to $225,000); $35.00 plus .001% of principal amount ($225,001 to $500,000). Maximum charge: $45.00 per share for orders of 100 or more shares. Minimum charge: $0.06 per share on the first 1,000 shares plus $0.03 per share thereafter. Stocks priced less than $1.00: $35.00 plus .03% of principal per transaction. Option trades: $35.00 plus .009% of principal amount ($3,000 and under); $35.00 plus .008% of principal amount ($3,001 to $10,000); $35.00 plus .007% of principal amount ($10,001 and over). Maximum charge: $25.00 per contract. Minimum charge: $3.00 per contract. All options transactions are subject to a minimum commission of $35.00.
After-Hours Trading: None.
Products Available to Trade Online: Stocks, options, and mutual funds.
Average Execution Time: Market order: few seconds depending on market conditions and volatility of the market.
Minimum Deposit Required: None for cash account. $2,000 for margin account.
Additional Fees: Overnight checking: $15.00. Returned check fee: $15.00. Additional statements: $15.00 for each month pulled. Name change on stock certificate: $15.00. Wire out: $15.00.
Free Services and Financial Links: America-invest.com, BestCalls.com, CBS Marketwatch, Myvesta.org, EdgorOnline, Final Bell, IPO Info, ON24, TheStreet.com, Zacks.com, portfolio analysis, portfolio tracker (20 minute delayed).

Real-Time Quotes: Unlimited real-time quotes for $29.95 per month. The quotes are not streaming and must be refreshed. Free unlimited delayed quotes are also available to clients.

States Registered In: All U.S. states.

Mutual Funds Offered: Over 1,500.

Payment for Order Flow: No.

Banking Services Offered: E-Trade Bank Account through GFN.com provides check writing, ATM debit card, and online bill payment.

Company Background: GFN.com (Gay Financial Network) was founded in 1998. In July 1999 online trading began, and GFN states that they will not turn anyone away, but they do cater predominantly to the gay and lesbian community. Client accounts are protected up to $100 million. SIPC provides protection up to $500,000, of which $100,000 is for cash. The additional $99.5 million is provided by Asset Guaranty Insurance Co. Products and investments are purchased through U.S. Clearing.

Customer Service Rating: ★★ Average

GRO TRADER

Brokerage Type: Direct-access brokerage

Mailing Address: Gro Corporation
3000 Weslayan St. Suite 390
Houston, TX 77027

Web Address: www.grotrader.com

Email Address: info@grotrader.com

Telephone Number: 800-852-3862

Fax Number: 713-439-1799

Market Orders: 1–249 trades per month: $17.95 per trade, up to 5,000 shares, and additional $0.018 per share thereafter. 250–499 trades per month: $14.95 per trade, up to 5,000 shares, and additional $0.015 per share thereafter. 500 or more trades per month: $9.95 per trade, up to 5,000 shares, and additional $0.01 per share thereafter.

Limit Orders: Same as those for market orders.

Option Trades: None, but Gro Trader will work on a one-to-one basis with a client depending on the volume of the client's trading.

Telephone Trading: Guaranteed to pick up the phone within 2–3 rings. Commission schedule same as online trading.

After-Hours Trading: None.

Products Available to Trade Online: Stocks.

Average Execution Time: Market order: depends on market conditions and security being traded.

Minimum Deposit Required: $25,000 in cash or $50,000 in marginal securities.

Additional Fees: Software fees: Pro user fees, $327.50 per month (0–4 trades per month), $216.50 per month (5–99 trades per month). Fee waived for Pro clients who trade more than 100 trades per month. Pro exchange fee of $127.50 is included in software fee. Pro fees are for those who are licensed with Nasdaq, who work at a bank or insurance company, or who trade corporate funds. Non-Pro user fees: $200.00 per month (0–4 trades per month), $89.00 per month (5–39 trades per month). Fee waived for Non-Pro clients who trade 40 trades per month. Non-Pro fees include Nasdaq Level II quotes and NYSE and Amex exchange fees. Pass-through fees: (Direct Access) AMRO, $0.0125 per share; ATTN, $1.00 per trade; BTRD, $0.005 per share; REDI, $0.0025 per share; TNTO, $0.005 per share; SelectNet Preference, $1.00 per trade plus per share fee; ATTN, $0.015 per share; BTRD, $0.015 per share; INCA, $0.015; REDI, $0.0025 per share; TNTO, $0.005 per share. SelectNet Broadcast: $2.50 per trade; SOES, $1.00 per trade. Funds wired out: $15.00 (domestic), $50.00 (foreign). Overnight courier: $15.00, $23.50 (Saturday). Regulation T extension: $10.00 plus interest. Returned check: $20.00. Stop payment on check: $20.00. Transfer of accounts outbound: ACAT, $5.00; IRAs $60.00–100.00. Previous statement copies: $20.00 per hour. Rule 144 stock: $35.00 plus transfer agent fee. Name change on stock certificate: transfer agent fee. IRA acceptance: $25.00–100.00. IRA annual fee: $25.00–100.00. IRA termination: $60.00–100.00. Foreign securities safekeeping: Euroclear fees.

Free Services and Financial Links: Online Trading Academy, News Traders Live Wire, Zacks, View Island Book, Investment Bookstore, Financialchat.com, Rightline, Dynamic Traders, Millennium-Traders.com.

Real-Time Quotes: Streaming Level II quotes at a charge; fee is waived depending on the amount of trades placed per month.

States Registered In: All U.S. states.

Mutual Funds Offered: None.

Payment for Order Flow: No.

Banking Services Offered: Check writing privileges may be worked out between the client and Gro Trader.

Company Background: Gro Corporation was established in 1983, and online trading through Gro Trader was launched in 1981. Gro Trader is a brokerage/dealer offering direct-access order routing. Gro Trader is not web-based; clients can electronically route their orders through the appropriate market maker, ECN, specialist, or exchange. Gro Trader caters to individuals and money managers who are active traders. Clients' accounts are protected up to $25 million per account. SIPC provides up to $500,000, of which $100,000 is for cash coverage, and Pension Securities provides the remaining $24.5 million. To open a Gro Trader Platinum account, clients must have a yearly income of at least $35,000 and a net worth of $65,000 (exclusive of farm and home), at least 3 months of live trading on an electronic platform, or the completion of a training course covering the following topics: SOES, Select-Net, ECNs, order-handling rules, and Level II training. Clients must also maintain an equity balance of $15,000 in their Platinum accounts.

Customer Service Rating: ★★★ Excellent

HARRIS INVESTORLINE

Brokerage Type: Discount brokerage
Mailing Address: 303 West Madison St. Suite 400
Chicago, IL 60606
Web Address: www.harrisinvestorline.com
Email Address: maria@blcnet.com
Telephone Number: 800-621-0392, 312-346-8283
Fax Number: 312-346-3608
Market Orders: $13.00 per trade, up to 5,000 shares on NYSE, Amex, and Nasdaq stocks trading over $1.00. Over 5,000 shares: add $0.01 per share, retroactive to the first share.
Limit Orders: $18.00 per trade, up to 5,000 shares on NYSE, Amex, and Nasdaq stocks trading over $1.00. Over 5,000 shares: add $0.01 per share retroactive to the first share.
Option Trades: Option trades are discounted 10% from the standard commission schedule rate of $27.00 plus 0.35% of principal and $1.50 per contract. $34.00 minimum commission per transaction.
Telephone Trading: Equity trades: $0–3,000, $18.00 per trade plus .008 of principal; $3,001–7,000, $29.00 per trade plus .0048 of principal; $7,001–20,000, $49.00 per trade plus .0024 of principal; $20,001–40,000, $57.00 per trade plus .0022 of principal; $40,001–50,000, $72.00 per trade plus .0020 of principal; $50,001 and over, $133.00 per trade plus .00085 of principal. All transactions are subject

to a $34.00 minimum commission. Option trades: $27.00 plus $1.50 per contract plus .0035 of the transaction's principal. $34.00 minimum commission per transaction.

After-Hours Trading: 4:30 P.M. to 6:00 P.M. EST. Broker-assisted only; limit orders and round lots only. $34.00 per trade, up to 100 shares, based on quantity of shares and price per shares thereafter.

Products Available to Trade Online: Stocks and options.

Average Execution Time: Market order: less than one minute under normal market conditions.

Minimum Deposit Required: None for cash account, but funds or securities are required in account to place first trade. $2,000 for a margin account.

Additional Fees: Full or partial account transfer: $30.00. Returned check: $25.00. Restricted stock transaction: $25.00. Journal of individual security position to account at another firm: $15.00. Corporate reorganizations, tender offers, and exercising of warrants and rights: $15.00. Outgoing wire transfers: $15.00. Accommodation transfer: $10.00. Excessive (over 5) changes to order: $10.00. Duplicate statements or confirms: $5.00. HIL check writing returned check: $25.00. Stop payment: $10.00. Check copy: $2.50. Check reorders: 50 checks, $6.00; 100 checks, $10.00. Option exercise and assignment: $25.00 flat rate.

Free Services and Financial Links: Briefing.com, Mutual Fund and Equity Research Reports, Zacks, IPO News, company background information, calendar of future initial public offerings, TheStreet.com, Alert Me!, news manager, personal news, personal page, My Portfolio, News Search, News by Industry, Internet News, Merger News, Market Snapshot, Mutual Fund Quote, Company Digest, price chart.

Real-Time Quotes: 100 real-time quotes with new account plus an additional 100 with every trade placed, although they are not streaming and must be refreshed.

States Registered In: All U.S. states.

Mutual Funds Offered: Over 170 families.

Payment for Order Flow: Yes.

Banking Services Offered: Check writing.

Company Background: Harris InvestorLine began its operation on April 15, 2000, after Harris Bank and Harris Bancorp's brokerage unit Harris Investors Direct merged its operations. The firms combined have over 35 years of brokerage experience. Harris InvestorLine's clientele currently exceeds 40,000 and has over $2.9 billion in assets in client accounts. HIL is a self-clearing firm and is a member of the Depository Trust Company (DTC), The National Securities Clearing Corporation (NSCC), and the Options Clearing Corporation (OCC). HIL accounts are protected up to $500,000, of which $100,000 is for cash, by SIPC. An additional $2,000,000 of coverage is provided by a private insurance carrier.

Customer Service Rating: ★★★ Excellent
Gomez Rating: 4.48

INTERACTIVE BROKERS LLC

Brokerage Type: Direct access
Mailing Address: Two Pickwick Plaza
Greenwich, CT 06830
Web Address: www.interactivebrokers.com
Email Address: loconnor@interactivebrokers.com
Telephone Number: 877-442-2757, 203-618-5839
Fax Number: 203-618-5770
Market Orders: $0.01 per share with a $1.00 minimum.
Limit Orders: Same as market orders.
Option Trades: Equity options: $1.95 per contract. Index options: $1.95 per contract. Exercised options will be charged $1.00 per contract by the Options Clearing Corporation.
Telephone Trading: $30.00 additional surcharge.
After-Hours Trading: 8:00 A.M. to 9:30 A.M. EST and 4:00 P.M. to 8:00 P.M. EST. Internet trading only. $0.01 per share.
Products Available to Trade Online: Equities, options, and futures.
Average Execution Time: Market order: within seconds.
Minimum Deposit Required: $2,000 for cash account. $3,500 for margin account.
Additional Fees: None.
Free Services and Financial Links: S&P future price information, Zacks, the Commodity Futures Trading Commission (CFTC), NUMA (Numa Financial Systems), the Options Strategist, Waldemar's List, Futures Magazine, Futureweb, Current News from the SEC, the NASD, Barron's Online, the Futures Industry Association.
Real-Time Quotes: Free streaming real-time quotes.
States Registered In: All U.S. states.
Mutual Funds Offered: None.
Payment for Order Flow: No.

Banking Services Offered: None.

Company Background: Interactive Brokers was founded in 1993 and executes several thousand orders for clients each day. Interactive Brokers offers Timber Hill proprietary technology and execution network to its clientele. Interactive Brokers offers direct access to NYSE, Amex, Nasdaq, and ISE, and direct interfaces to major international exchanges. Clients' accounts are protected by SIPC up to a maximum of $500,000, of which $100,000 is for cash coverage.

Customer Service Rating: ★★★ Excellent

INTERNET TRADING.COM

Brokerage Type: Discount brokerage

Mailing Address: 100 Bush Street, Suite 1000
San Francisco, CA 94104

Web Address: www.internettrading.com

Email Address: webmaster@internettrading.com

Telephone Number: 800-696-2811

Fax Number: 415-362-0671

Market Orders: $19.95 per trade, up to 5,000 shares, and additional $0.0175 per share thereafter.

Limit Orders: Same as market orders.

Option Trades: $25.00 per trade plus $2.00 per contract.

Telephone Trading: $15.00 additional surcharge.

After-Hours Trading: 4:30 P.M. to 6:30 P.M. EST. $20.00 per trade. Broker-assisted trading only.

Products Available to Trade Online: Stocks and options.

Average Execution Time: Market order: 2–3 seconds.

Minimum Deposit Required: $10,000 for cash or margin account.

Additional Fees: Postage: $3.50. Wire out funds: $25.00. Order out securities: $25.00 per certificate. Voluntary reorganization and redemptions: $15.00 per issue. Transfer of account away from Internet Trading.com: $50.00. Accommodation transfer: $25.00 per issue. Rule 144 processing: $150.00 per certificate. Return check: $15.00. Annual inactivity fee: $25.00. IRA annual maintenance: $40.00. IRA setup: $25.00. Nonautomated trades: $6.00 additional fee. Foreign security transaction and safekeeping: at cost. Annual safekeeping fee (nonpublicly traded issues): $25.00 per issue.

Free Services and Financial Links: News links, charts, S&P First Call,

Vickers, Argus & Lipper, analyst upgrades and downgrades, option chains.

Real-Time Quotes: Real-time quotes for $0.02 a quote, although they are not streaming and must be refreshed. Free unlimited delayed quotes.

States Registered In: All U.S. states.

Mutual Funds Offered: Almost all major U.S. funds.

Payment for Order Flow: Yes.

Banking Services Offered: Online account: check writing. Map Account: unlimited check writing and a VISA debit card for a $60.00 annual fee.

Company Background: Emmett A. Larkin Company, Inc., was founded in 1959, and Internet accessibility through Internet Trading.com was introduced in 1997. Internet Trading.com executes on average 700 trades per day. Its clientele consists mainly of brokers and broker dealers (currently about 1000) but includes individual investors.

Customer Service Rating: ★★★ Excellent

INTLTRADER.COM

Brokerage Type: Discount brokerage

Mailing Address: 250 Park Avenue South Suite 201
Winter Park, FL 32789

Web Address: www.intltrader.com

Email Address: support@intltrader.com

Telephone Number: 888-345-INTL

Fax Number: 407-629-2378

Market Orders: U.S. listed and Nasdaq stocks: $14.99 per trade, up to 5,000 shares, and additional $0.01 per share to entire order thereafter. Nasdaq stocks under $1.00 per share: $25.00 per trade plus 2.75% of the principal amount. Foreign stocks, ordinary shares: $29.99 per trade, up to 5,000 shares, and additional $0.01 per share to entire order thereafter.

Limit Orders: $19.99 per trade, up to 5,000 shares, and additional $0.01 per share to entire order thereafter. Nasdaq stocks under $1.00 per share: $25.00 per trade plus 2.75% of the principal amount. Foreign stocks, ordinary shares: $29.99 per trade, up to 5,000 shares, and additional $0.01 per share to entire order thereafter.

Option Trades: Options less than $1.00 per contract: $1.75 per contract with a $27.50 minimum. Options $1.00 and greater per contract: $3.00 per contract with a $27.50 minimum.

Telephone Trading: $15.00 additional surcharge.

After-Hours Trading: 8:00 A.M. to 9:30 A.M. EST and 4:00 P.M. to 5:00 P.M. EST. $25.00 per trade surcharge. Foreign stocks: no additional fee.

Products Available to Trade Online: Stocks, options, and mutual funds.

Average Execution Time: Market order: U.S. securities: 5 seconds under normal market conditions. Foreign securities: common stock is quick; obscure stocks could take a few minutes.

Minimum Deposit Required: $2,000 for cash or margin account.

Additional Fees: IRA annual fee: $35.00. Voluntary reorganizations (conversions): $50.00; options exercise and assignments, $30.00; all other, $35.00. Stop payment fee: $20.00. Copy of cancelled check: $7.50. Duplicate statement: $5.00 minimum. Duplicate 1099: $15.00. Annual statement (duplicate copy): $25.00. Returned check fee: $25.00. Transfer certificate in customers name: $30.00. Regulation T extensions: $15.00. Mailgrams: $15.00. Outgoing funds wired: $25.00.

Free Services and Financial Links: Global Markets Spotlight, Global Market Risk–Return Robot, Global Industries Spotlight, Global Marriages, DJIA Global Comparable, Global News Headlines, Bank of New York ADR Profiles, glossary of financial terms, Email Bulletin, Stockfinder, Foreign Equity Research, personal portfolio tracker, full text global and U.S. news, Zacks, International Currency Updates, International Market Indices, Quick Charts, Market Guide Profiles, foreign equity profiles.

Real-Time Quotes: Real-time quotes on both U.S. and foreign stocks.

States Registered In: All U.S. states except ND.

Mutual Funds Offered: Approximately 75–100 families.

Payment for Order Flow: Yes.

Banking Services Offered: Free check writing through a federated money fund.

Company Background: INTLTRADER.com was founded in 1998 to give clients access to buy and sell securities around the world using the Internet. Through INTLTRADER.com clients can invest both in U.S. and international markets. INTLTRADER.com caters to self-directed investors and allows them access and resources to trade online in overseas securities as well as in U.S. markets. Clients' accounts are protected up to $500,000, of which $100,000 is for cash coverage, provided by SIPC. Additional protection covering the total amount of fully paid-for securities and cash balances without limit is provided by Wexford Clearing Services.

Customer Service Rating: ★★★ Excellent

INVEST EXPRESS ON-LINE

Brokerage Type: Discount brokerage

Mailing Address: Investex Securities Group, Inc. Accounts Dept.
50 Broad St.
New York, NY 10004

Web Address: www.investexpress.com

Email Address: investexpress@dellnet.com

Telephone Number: 800-392-7192

Fax Number: None.

Market Orders: $13.95 per trade, up to 4,999 shares, and additional $0.005 per share thereafter.

Limit Orders: $17.95 per trade, up to 4,999 shares, and additional $0.005 per share thereafter.

Option Trades: $20.00 per trade plus $1.75 per contract.

Telephone Trading: Stock trades: $30.00 per trade (1–500 shares); $33.00 per trade (501–1650 shares); $0.02 per share (over 1650 shares). Option trades: $25.00 per trade plus $2.50 per contract.

After-Hours Trading: None.

Products Available to Trade Online: Stocks, options, mutual funds, corporates, municipals and treasuries, CDs, precious metals, and foreign securities.

Average Execution Time: Market orders: immediate.

Minimum Deposit Required: $5,000 for a margin account; sufficient cash or securities to cover first purchase or sale for a cash account.

Additional Fees: Late payment: $15.00. Returned check: $35.00. Extensions: $5.00. Mailgrams: $5.00. Legal transfer fee: $15.00. Postage, handling, and insurance: $3.50 per transaction.

Free Services and Financial Links: Reuters, PR Newswire, Business Wire, UPI, Thomson Market Edge, Company reports, no charge for transfer and ship certificate, voluntary tenders, mandated tenders, inactive account fee, extensions, mailgrams, and bond redemptions.

Real-Time Quotes: Real-time quotes, although they are not streaming and must be refreshed.

States Registered In: All U.S. states except AK, AR, AZ, DE, HI, ID, IN, MS, MT, ND, NE, NM, OR, PR, RI, SD, VT, WV, WY.

Mutual Funds Offered: 300-400.

Payment for Order Flow: Yes.

Banking Services Offered: Free check writing and an ATM debit card.

Company Background: Investex Securities Group, Inc., was established in 1992. Invest Express On-line, a division of Investex Securities, was established in the beginning of 1997. Investex Express On-line protects clients' accounts up to $100,000 for cash and $400,000 for securities, and additional insurance is up to $99.5 million per account.

Customer Service Rating: ★ Poor

INVESTIN.COM

Brokerage Type: Discount brokerage

Mailing Address: InvestIN.com Corp. & InvestIN.com Securities Corp.
Infomart—Suite 2016
1950 Stemmons Frwy.
Dallas, TX 75207

Web Address: www.investin.com

Email Address: newaccounts@investin.com

Telephone Number: 800-327-1883, 214-939-0110

Fax Number: 214-939-0116

Market Orders: $9.95 per trade, up to 1,000 shares, and additional $0.01 per share thereafter.

Limit Orders: $9.95 per trade, up to 1,000 shares, and additional $0.01 per share thereafter. Bulletin Board and Penny stock trades are charged a flat rate of $20.00 per trade. In addition, Pension Financial charges a $20.00 clearing fee per trade.

Option Trades: $25.00 per trade plus $1.75 per contract.

Telephone Trading: $10.00 additional surcharge.

After-Hours Trading: None.

Products Available to Trade Online: Mutual funds, stocks, and options.

Average Execution Time: Market order: considerably fast.

Minimum Deposit Required: $1,000 for cash account. $2,000 for margin account.

Additional Fees: $19.95 per exercises. Wire fee out: $15.00. Rule 144 sales: $35.00 surcharge. ACAT: $5.00 per account transfer outgoing. Safekeeping charge for clients with securities in account and with less than 2 trades during a calendar year.

Free Services and Financial Links: InvestIN news, short list of over 3,000 stocks, Nasdaq provides research, NewsTrader.com, Briefing.com.

Real-Time Quotes: Unlimited real-time quotes for $50.00 per month (over 10 trades placed per month, fee is rebated). Clients will receive 100 free real-time quotes per month and 100 additional quotes credited with each executed trade. The quotes are not streaming and must be refreshed. Delayed quotes are also available at no charge to the client.

States Registered In: All U.S. states except MN, ND, NH, and PR.

Mutual Funds Offered: Approximately 1,000 from around 100 families.

Payment for Order Flow: No.

Banking Services Offered: Clients with balances exceeding $10,000: debit card.

Company Background: InvestIN.com was founded in 1996. It is a member of NASD, SIPC, SIA, the Bond Market Association, and MSRB. InvestIN.com appeals to the trader who prefers to be in charge of his or her own investments and does not need financial planning advice. InvestIN.com utilizes Pension Financial Services as its clearing firm. Clients' accounts are protected up to $25 million. SIPC provides coverage of $500,000, of which $100,000 is for cash, and the remaining $24.5 million is provided by Penson Financial Services.

Customer Service Rating: ★★ Average

INVESTRADE

Brokerage Type: Discount brokerage

Mailing Address: 950 North Milwaukee Ave, Suite 102
Glenview, IL 60025

Web Address: www.investrade.com

Email Address: support@investrade.com

Telephone Number: 800-498-7120

Fax Number: 847-298-6165

Market Orders: $7.95 per trade, unlimited number of shares. Listed and OTC stocks priced under $2.00 per share require broker assistance.

Limit Orders: $11.95 per trade, unlimited number of shares. Listed and OTC stocks priced under $2.00 per trade require broker assistance.

Option Trades: $14.95 per trade minimum plus $1.75 per contract.

Telephone Trading: $15.00 additional surcharge.

After-Hours Trading: None.

Products Available to Trade Online: Stocks, options, and mutual funds.

Average Execution Time: Market order: seconds to minutes.

Minimum Deposit Required: $2,000.

Additional Fees: IRA termination fee: $50.00. Option exercise and assignment: $14.95. Exercise rights and warrants: $13.95.

Free Services and Financial Links: Zacks, Investment Newsletters, Financial Web (Options Resources), Fination.com Newsletter, Investment Glossary, Option Analysis, Schaeffer's Investment Research, upon opening an account with InvesTrade clients receive 3 free trades, with each referral clients give InvesTrade they will receive 3 free trades, no-fee IRAs, InvesTrade has no charge for postage and handling, dividend reinvestment, IRA annual maintenance, and inactive account.

Real-Time Quotes: 100 free real-time quotes upon opening an account and 50 free with each execution placed in account, although these quotes are not streaming and must be refreshed. Unlimited delayed quotes are also available at no charge.

States Registered In: All U.S. states.

Mutual Funds Offered: Over 3,800.

Payment for Order Flow: No.

Banking Services Offered: None.

Company Background: InvesTrade was established in 1997 and is a division of Regal Discount Securities Inc. InvesTrade is a member of NASD and SIPC that has been working with long-term investors and active traders for more than 20 years. InvesTrade accounts are insured up to $100 million.

Customer Service Rating: ★★★ Excellent

Gomez Rating: 4.33

JB OXFORD & COMPANY

Brokerage Type: Discount brokerage

Mailing Address: 9665 Wilshire Blvd. 3rd Floor
Beverly Hills, CA 90212

Web Address: www.jboxford.com

Email Address: clientserv@jboc.com

Telephone Number: 800-782-1876, 800-799-8870

Fax Number: 310-777-8820

Market Orders: $14.50 per trade, up to 1,000 shares, additional $0.01 per share thereafter. Net-Trade account: $14.50 per trade, up to 3,000 shares, additional $0.01 per share thereafter. Listed and OTC equities priced less than $1.00 per share are charged the lesser of $0.03 per share or 5% of principal with a $25.00 minimum.

Limit Orders: $19.50 per trade, up to 1,000 shares, additional $0.01 per share thereafter. Net-Trade account: $19.50 per trade, up to 3,000 shares, additional $0.01 per share thereafter. Listed and OTC equities priced less than $1.00 per share are charged the lesser of $0.03 per share or 5% of principal with a $25.00 minimum.

Option Trades: $35.00 per trade plus $2.75 per contract.

Telephone Trading: Market order: $24.50 per trade. Limit order: $29.50 per trade.

After-Hours Trading: 8:30 A.M. to 9:30 A.M. and 4:30 P.M. to 5:30 P.M. EST. $60.00 per trade, broker-assisted trading only.

Products Available to Trade Online: Stocks, listed securities, options, index options, and certain foreign securities.

Average Execution Time: Market orders: immediately, depending on market conditions.

Minimum Deposit Required: $2,000 for cash or margin account.

Additional Fees: Option assignments: $20.00. Involuntary reorganizations: $10.00. Regulation T extension: $25.00. Mailgrams: $15.00. Wiring of funds: $25.00. Returned checks: $25.00. Legal transfer: $25.00. Voluntary reorganization: $25.00. Copies of monthly statements: $10.00. Copies of confirmation statements: $5.00 per month. Register and shipping fee: $15.00. Account transfer: $45.00. DTC deliveries: $15.00. Overnight mail: $15.00. Stop payment on check: $25.00. Inactive account fee: $25.00. 144 Stock regulation: $25.00. Uncollected funds after settlement date: 18% of cash account. Certificate registration and delivery: $25.00. Foreign securities transfer: $75.00. Foreign securities safekeeping: $5.00. Oxford Real-time Quotation Administrator: $75.00 to $300.00 per month (for personal real-time quotes, charts, and technical analysis). Over 10 checks per month: $0.25 per check. Return items (NFS): $30.00. Copies of checks: $3.00. Internet access provided by ISP Solutions: $15.95 per month if you maintain less than $2,000 cash in your account.

Free Services and Financial Links: Daily reports from Argus, Market Edge, Weekly Second Opinion, free postage and handling.

Real-Time Quotes: Real-time quotes, although they are not streaming and must be refreshed. Clients will receive 100 free real-time quotes upon opening an account and for each trade thereafter. Additional quotes are available for $5.00 per 200 quotes.

States Registered In: All U.S. states.

Mutual Funds Offered: Many.

Payment for Order Flow: No.

Banking Services Offered: Banking Center. Clients can sign up for the Banking Center's features through an N*Power account, free of charge with a minimum account balance of $2,000. Banking services are $4.95 a month for accounts with less than $2,000.

Company Background: JB Oxford & Company is a brokerage/dealer registered with the SEC and NASD. JB Oxford & Company was founded in 1994 and provides discount and online brokerage services and free internet access. JB Oxford offers clients free Internet access provided by ISP Solutions, Inc., with a $2,000 minimum balance in account. JB Oxford has experienced rapid growth and now boasts fully staffed branch offices in New York, Miami, and San Gabriel, CA. JB Oxford is a wholly owned subsidiary of Utah-based JB Oxford Holdings, Inc. JB Oxford Holdings is a publicly traded Nasdaq Small Cap issue, ticker symbol JBOH. Net-Trade accounts require a minimum of $250,000 in equity in account.

Customer Service Rating: ★★★ Excellent

Gomez Rating: 5.29

JPR CAPITAL

Brokerage Type: Direct-access brokerage

Mailing Address: 1800 Northern Blvd. Suite 111
                     Roslyn, NY 11576

Web Address: www.jprcapital.com

Email Address: arlene@jprcapital.com

Telephone Number: 800-JPR-2004, 516-621-8787

Fax Number: 516-621-7899

Market Orders: Nasdaq stocks: $10.00 per trade, up to 2,000 shares, and additional $0.015 per share thereafter. Trades placed using SOES: $0.50 per trade. Island: $1.00 per trade. SelectNet: $2.50 per trade. ARCA: $0.005 per share. Instinet: $0.015 per share. Listed stocks: CSS, $10.00 per trade up to 2,000 shares, and additional $0.015 per share thereafter; ISI, $10.00 per trade. Trades placed through NYSE: orders executed under 5 minutes, $0.004 per share; orders executed over 5 minutes: $0.012 per share. Trades placed through Amex: orders less than 2,099 shares, $0.004 per share; orders more than 2,099 shares, $0.012 per share; orders executed with competing market makers, $0.012 per share.

Limit Orders: Same as market orders.

Option Trades: None.

Telephone Trading: Same commissions as online schedule.

After-Hours Trading: 7:30 A.M. to 9:30 A.M. EST and 4:00 P.M. to 6:30 P.M. EST. Online trading or broker-assisted available. Same commissions as online schedule.

Products Available to Trade Online: Stocks.

Average Execution Time: Market order: 5 seconds or less depending on what the stock is doing at that time and current market conditions.

Minimum Deposit Required: $10,000 to open an account. All accounts opened are considered margin accounts.

Additional Fees: Real Audio: $50.00 per month (first two weeks free). Whisper: $100.00 per month. S&P Comstock data fee: $250.00 per month. Amex: $1.00. CME (S&P futures): $10.00. CBT (T Bond futures): $30.00. NYSE: $1.00. Nasdaq Level II: $50.00 (waived upon 200 or more round-trip trades per month).

Free Services and Financial Links: Morning Call, Pegasusri.com, Zdii.com, IPOlockup.com, TheStreet.com, TheStandard.com, Netstocks.com, ISLD.com, Murphymorris.com, Multexinvestor.com, JagNotes.com, Pristine.com, Freedgar.com, activetrading.com, Before market hours daily briefing at 8:45 A.M. EST and weekly trading meetings.

Real-Time Quotes: Streaming real-time quotes with software package.

States Registered In: All U.S. states except MS, MO (pending), ND, NE (pending), NM, PR, VT.

Mutual Funds Offered: None.

Payment for Order Flow: No.

Banking Services Offered: None.

Company Background: JPR Capital was founded in 1995 and launched online trading in 1998. This firm is run by day traders and caters to the active day trader. JPR is a member of Island, Instinet, and ARCA. JPR is a direct-access firm, using no middleman in order to give clients direct access to market makers and ECNs. JPR offers Whisper to its clientele, which is a trading software that automatically watches all charts by filtering each trade tick by tick, using screening formulas. Whisper automatically detects changes in price momentum, volume, and relative strength, all without having charts on the screen. JPR utilizes South-west Securities, Inc., as its clearing firm. Clients' accounts are protected by SIPC up to $500,000, of which $100,000 is for cash coverage. Additional coverage is provided by JPR Capital.

Customer Service Rating: ★★★ Excellent

LEIGHBALDWIN.COM

Brokerage Type: Discount brokerage
Mailing Address: Leigh Baldwin & Co., LLC
112 Albany St.
Cazenovia, NY 13035
Web Address: www.investtoday.com
Email Address: info@investtoday.com
Telephone Number: 800-659-8044, 315-655-2964
Fax Number: 315-655-9138
Market Orders: $19.95 per trade (0–10 trades per month). $14.95 per trade (11 or more trades per month). Exchange listed trades over 2,000 shares: additional $0.01 per share on entire order. Stop and GTC orders: additional $5.00 per trade.
Limit Orders: $24.95 per trade (0–10 trades per month). $19.95 per trade (11 or more trades per month). Exchange listed trades over 2,000 shares: additional $0.01 per share on entire order. Stop and GTC orders: additional $5.00 per trade.
Option Trades: Principal amount: $0–2,500, $29.00 plus $0.016 times principal; $2,501–10,000, $49.00 per trade plus $0.008 times principal; $10,001 or more, $99.00 per trade plus $0.003 times principal. Minimum commission: $2.00 per option contract. Minimum: $35.00.
Telephone Trading: Stock Trades: principal amount: $40.00–2,500, $19.00 per trade plus $0.038 times principal; $2,501–6,000, $35.00 per trade plus $0.0043 times principal; $6,001–22,000, $53.00 per trade plus $0.0024 times principal; $22,001–50,000, $70.00 per trade plus $0.0017 times principal; $50,001–500,000, $110.00 per trade plus $0.0008 times principal; $500,001 or more, $190.00 per trade plus $0.0005 times principal. Minimum fee for stock trade: $0.06 per share for the first 1,000 shares plus $0.03 per share thereafter. Minimum: $35.00. Option Trades: principal amount: $0–2,500, $29.00 per trade plus $0.016 times principal; $2,501–10,000, $49.00 per trade plus $0.008 times principal; $10,001 or more, $99.00 per trade plus $0.003 times principal. Minimum commission: $2.00 per contract.

After-Hours Trading: 8:00 A.M. to 9:30 A.M. EST and 4:00 P.M. to 5:30 P.M. EST. Commission schedule same as online trading.

Products Available to Trade Online: Stocks, options, and mutual funds.

Average Execution Time: Market order: within 30 seconds.

Minimum Deposit Required: $2,000.

Additional Fees: IRA annual fee: $30.00. Transfer and ship securities: $15.00. Wire transfer of funds: $20.00. Overnight delivery: $15.00. Stop payment: $15.00. TOA deliveries: $30.00. Extensions: $2.00. Returned check fee: $15.00. Legal transfer returns: $10.00. Voluntary tenders: $25.00 per position. Mandated tenders: $10.00 per position. Physical re-organizations: $20.00. Foreign securities transfer fee: $100.00.

Free Services and Financial Links: 90-day account history, portfolio tracking, charts, news, and company profiles, Morningstar Profile and Screener for Mutual Funds, balance sheet and income statements, research, market statistics, market summary, company search, No postage and handling fees.

Real-Time Quotes: 100 free real-time quotes with new account and 100 more with every trade executed. The quotes are not streaming and must be refreshed.

States Registered In: AL, AZ, CA, CO, CT, FL, GA, IL, ID, LA, MA, ME, MD, MI, NC, NH, NJ, NV, NY, OH, OR, PA, RI, SC, TN, TX, VA, WV.

Mutual Funds Offered: Over 5,000 from 325 fund families.

Payment for Order Flow: Yes, but not in all cases.

Banking Services Offered: Free check writing, debit cards, electronic funds transfer, and cash machine access through a Cash Management Account.

Company Background: Leigh Baldwin was founded in 1991 and began its online services in 1999. Leigh Baldwin caters primarily to the individual trader and utilizes National Financial Services as its clearing firm. Clients' accounts are protected up to $100 million per account. SIPC covers $500,000, of which $100,000 is for cash claims, and the remaining $99.5 million is provided by National Financial Services.

Customer Service Rating: ★★★ Excellent

LIVESTREET.COM

Brokerage Type: Direct-access brokerage

Mailing Address: The Franklin Avenue Plaza
1225 Franklin Avenue Suite 117
Garden City, NY 11530

Web Address: www.livestreet.com

Email Address: clientservice@livestreet.com

Telephone Number: 516-873-4200

Fax Number: 516-837-4229

Market Orders: $21.50 per trade (1–19 trades per month); $20.95 per trade (20–49 trades per month); $18.95 per trade (50–99 trades per month); $17.95 per trade (100–199 trades per month); $16.95 per trade (200–399 trades per month); $14.50 per trade (400 or more trades per month). (Based on orders less than 2,000 shares; anything over 2,000 shares: additional $0.015 cents per share.)

Limit Orders: Same as market orders.

Option Trades: $2.50 per contract; $25.00 minimum.

Telephone Trading: Same commissions as online schedule.

After-Hours Trading: 6:30 A.M. to 8:30 A.M. EST. Same commissions as online schedule.

Products Available to Trade Online: Stocks and options.

Average Execution Time: Market order: 10 seconds.

Minimum Deposit Required: $10,000 for cash account ($5,000 must be cash). $25,000 for margin account ($5,000 must be cash).

Additional Fees: Software fees: Super Livestreet.com (nonprofessional traders): $300 per month (1–19 trades per month); $150.00 per month (20–49 trades per month), fee waived upon 50 or more trades per month. Livestreet.com Plus (professional traders): $382.45 per month (1–24 trades per month); $100.00 per month (25–74 trades per month), fee waived upon 75 or more trades per month. Super Livestreet.com (professional traders): $457.45 per month (1–24 trades per month); $250.00 per month (25–74 trades per month), fee waived upon 75 or more trades per month. ECN fees: INCA, $0.015 per share. Optional fees: OPRA: nonpro, $2.50; pro, $26.00. Chicago Mercantile Exchange (CME): nonpro, $10.00; pro, $55.00. Chicago Board of Trade (CBOT): nonpro, $30.00; pro, $60.00. Returned check: $25.00. Stop payment within 10 days: $15.00. Overnight delivery: $12.00. Wire domestic: $20.00. Wire foreign: $40.00. Other account costs: as charged.

Free Services and Financial Links: Big Easy Investor.com, First Alert, free Realtime.com, JagNotes.com, Multex.com, Radio Wall St.com, SmartMoney, The Fly on the Wall.com, TheStreet.com, Worldly Investor.com, Zacks.

Real-Time Quotes: Streaming real-time quotes with software package.

States Registered In: All U.S. states.

Mutual Funds Offered: None.

Payment for Order Flow: No.

Banking Services Offered: Check writing and ATM debit card with Vision Account.

Company Background: Livestreet.com was established in November 1996 as an in-house day-trading firm and launched online trading in November 1998. Livestreet.com is a branch of Terra Nova Trading, LLC, and a member of NASD, PSE, and SIPC. Livestreet.com was created for clients who are interested in day trading their portfolio online. Livestreet.com is an order-entry firm only, giving its clients access to control their own portfolio trading decisions. Clients must maintain a minimum equity level of $5,000, of which $1,000 must be cash at all times. If the account falls below $5,000, the client has 5 business days to refund the account to at least $10,000, of which $1,000 must be cash. Clients' accounts are protected up to $25 million. The SIPC provides coverage up to $500,000, of which $100,000 is for cash coverage. Additional coverage of $24.5 million is provided by a private insurance company.

Customer Service Rating: ★★★ Excellent

MAIN STREET MARKET.COM

Brokerage Type: Discount brokerage

Mailing Address: U.S. Clearing/A Division of Fleet Securities
Attn. Brokerage Services
26 Broadway, 12th Floor
New York, NY 10004-1798

Web Address: www.mainstmarket.com

Email Address: bsd@usclearing.com

Telephone Number: 800-710-7160

Fax Number: 212-747-5339

Market Orders: $19.95 per trade, up to 1,000 shares, and additional $0.02 per share thereafter. Stocks less than $1.00: $35.00 per trade plus .03% of principal transaction.

Limit Orders: Same as market orders.

Option Trades: Principal amount: $3,000 and under, $35.00 per trade plus .009% of principal amount; $3,001–10,000, $35.00 per trade plus .008% of principal amount; $10,001 and over, $35.00 per trade plus

.007% of principal amount. Maximum charge: $25.00 per contract. Minimum charge: $3.00 per contract. All transactions subject to a $35.00 commission.

Telephone Trading: Same commissions as online schedule.

After-Hours Trading: None.

Products Available to Trade Online: Stocks, options, and mutual funds.

Average Execution Time: Market order: 1–2 minutes.

Minimum Deposit Required: None for cash account. $2,000 for margin account.

Additional Fees: Copies of statements: $10.00. Late fee settlement: $5.00. Returned check: $15.00. No activity in account for one year: $35.00. IRA termination fee: $50.00. Overnight courier: $15.00.

Free Services and Financial Links: Free dividend reinvestment and stock transfers, quote and symbol lookup, options quotes, options chains, price history, portfolio tracker, Market Snapshot.

Real-Time Quotes: Real-time quotes for a monthly fee of $29.95. The quotes are not streaming and must be refreshed. Clients are offered free 20-minute delayed quotes.

States Registered In: All U.S. states.

Mutual Funds Offered: Over 1,500.

Payment for Order Flow: Yes.

Banking Services Offered: Check writing with a money market account.

Company Background: Main Street Market, a discount trading firm founded in 1997, is a division of Fleet Securities, Inc. Main Street Brokerage services cater to the investor looking for little or no broker contact. Main Street Market utilizes U.S. Clearing as its clearing agent. Clients' accounts are protected up to $100 million per account. The SIPC provides up to $500,000, of which $100,000 is for cash coverage. The remaining $99.5 million is provided by Asset Guaranty Insurance Company.

Customer Service Rating: ★★★ Excellent

MB TRADING

Brokerage Type: Direct access

Mailing Address: MB Trading
214 Main Street, PMB 241
El Segundo, CA 90245

Web Address: www.mbtrading.com

Email Address: newaccounts@mbtrading.com

Telephone Number: 310-414-4535, 888-790-4800

Fax Number: 310-414-0899

Market Orders: Commissions are based on a sliding scale. Trades per month: 1–19, $22.95 per trade; 20-49, $21.95 per trade; 50–99, $19.95 per trade; 100–199, $17.95 per trade; 200–399, $16.95 per trade; 400 or more, $14.95 per trade. Each trade is defined as 10,000 shares or less for Nasdaq trades and 2,000 shares or less for listed equities.

Limit Orders: Same as market orders.

Option Trades: 1–5 contracts: $7.00 each. 6–20 contracts: $4.00 each. 21 or more contracts: $3.00 each. Minimum ticket charge: $20.00.

Telephone Trading: Same commissions as online schedule.

After-Hours Trading: 877-414-9299. Island and Arca: 8:00 A.M. to 9:30 A.M. EST and 4:00 P.M. to 8:00 P.M. EST. SelectNet: 9:00 A.M. to 9:30 A.M. EST and 4:00 P.M. to 6:30 P.M. EST. Instinet: 8:00 A.M. to 9:30 A.M. EST and 4:00 P.M. to 6:45 P.M. EST. Broker-assisted trading only.

Products Available to Trade Online: Stocks and options.

Average Execution Time: Market order: 1 to 2 seconds, under normal market conditions and dependent on trade being placed.

Minimum Deposit Required: $5,000 for cash account. $10,000 for margin account.

Additional Fees: MB Lite (real-time Level I quotes, interest list, and full order entry module): 1–19 trades per month, $115.00 per month, free after 19 trades per month, $165.00 per month if Nasdaq Level II data feed is requested. MB Custom (real-time Level II quotes, interest list, charting with limited stochastics, ticker, major indices indicators): 1–19 trades per month, $200.00 per month, free after 20 trades per month, refundable when account is closed. MB Trader (Complete Realtick III professional trading platform with real-time Level II quotes, interest list, charting, time sales, T/A, stochastics, major indices indicators): 1–19 trades per month, $300.00 per month; 20–49 trades per month, $100.00 per month; free after 50 trades per month, refundable when account is closed. ECN fees: Instinet (INCA), $0.015 per share. Optional fees: NewsWatch, $75.00 per month (additional $15.00 for Zacks); Dow Jones News Wire, $95.00 per month; SortWizard, $30.00 per month; StockWatch tiered pricing per month, Storm Tracker $100.00–125.00 per month (fee waived after 30 trades per month); Fly on the Wall, $40.00 per month (fee waived after 50 trades per month). Returned check fee: $15.00. Stop payment within 10 days: $10.00. IRA termination fee: $25.00. Registry and delivery of certificate: $15.00. Overnight delivery: $16.55. Transfer fees: $7.50 per transaction. Exercising employee stock options: $35.00. Exercising warrants or rights subscriptions: $25.00. Courtesy transfer: $25.00. Inactive account: $15.00. Customer transfer out: $50.00. Wire transfer fee: $15.00. Equity redemption or tender: $0.04 per share with $4.00 minimum and $80.00 maximum. SEC fee: $0.01 per $300.00 value on the sell side of all listed securities, including options. Customer name safekeeping: $15.00 per issue.

Free Services and Financial Links: Zacks, no-charge cancellations, no-charge partial fills, TI Online Chatrooms, newsletter links, regulatory and announcement sites, stock research sites, online tutorials, suggested reading lists.

Real-Time Quotes: Level II quotes.

States Registered In: All U.S. states.

Mutual Funds Offered: None.

Payment for Order Flow: No.

Banking Services Offered: Free check writing with Vision Checking Account.

Company Background: MB Trading is a privately held online brokerage firm that was founded in 1997. MB Trading caters to the professional trader or the very active individual trader. To open an MB Trading account, clients must have a minimum net worth of $50,000 and a minimum annual income of $50,000. MB Trading offers direct access trading through all ECNs (Redi, Island, ARCA, SelectNet, SOES, and Instinet). This allows clients flexibility to route their own orders, so their exposure is not limited. Clients have more control when placing their trades, which can allow for much faster execution and confirmation. Customer service is valued very highly and is a top priority service to MB Trading's clients. SIPC protects clients' accounts up to $500,000, limited to $100,000 on claims for cash. A second level of coverage is provided up to an additional $25.5 million by a private insurer.

Customer Service Rating: ★★★ Excellent

MERRILL LYNCH DIRECT

Brokerage Type: Discount brokerage
Mailing Address: P.O. Box 173807
Denver, CO 80217-3807

Web Address: www.mldirect.com

Email Address: askmld@ml.com

Telephone Number: 877-653-4732

Fax Number: None.

Market Orders: Commission-based account: $29.95 per trade, up to 1,000 shares, plus $0.03 per share thereafter. Unlimited Advantage Account through Merrill Lynch: minimum annual fee of $1,500, and a percentage fee based on eligible assets. Customized pricing offered.

Limit Orders: Same as market orders.

Option Trades: None.

Telephone Trading: $50.00 to $150.00 per trade plus $0.03 per share per trade.

After-Hours Trading: None.

Products Available to Trade Online: Stocks, mutual funds, fixed income products, CDs, and bonds.

Average Execution Time: Market order: within 90 seconds, depending on volume of security being traded and current market conditions.

Minimum Deposit Required: $2,000 for cash or margin account.

Additional Fees: Cancelled check fee: $3.00. Returned check fee: $20.00. Stop payment fee: $20.00. ATM transaction fee: $1.00 per transaction. Bill payment: $7.50 per month. Return deposits: $20.00. Cash advance fee (non-ATM): 0.3% of the principal ($5.00 minimum). Wire transfer fee (domestic): $25.00. Wire transfer fee (international): $40.00. Legal transfer fee: $50.00. Register and ship: $15.00. Overnight mail request: $25.00. Municipal bond coupon processing: $5.00. Government security transfer fee: $125.00. FTS return: $10.00. Past due exchanges: $50.00. Past due redemptions: $50.00. Optional exchange fee: $20.00. Mandatory exchange fee: $50.00.

Free Services and Financial Links: Additional check printing; Merrill Lynch research; real-time quotes; Dow Jones news service; Standard & Poor's stock reports; dividend reports; stock, bond, and earnings guides; stock, fixed-income, and mutual fund scanners; market data; News.

Real-Time Quotes: Free unlimited real-time quotes, although they are not streaming and must be refreshed.

States Registered In: All U.S. states.

Mutual Funds Offered: Over 2,400.

Payment for Order Flow: Not divulged; Merrill Lynch Direct relayed that this was proprietary information.

Banking Services Offered: Check writing, VISA Signature debit card, and online bill payment service through a Cash Management Account.

Company Background: Merrill Lynch Direct was launched on December 1, 1999, and is made up of individual investors. Merrill Lynch Direct is an online brokerage firm that supplies the tools and benefits for clients to trade on their own but does not give investment advice. Clients' accounts at Merrill Lynch Direct are protected up to $500,000 for securities and $100,000 for cash by SIPC. Merrill Lynch offers its clients an Ultimate Advantage Account, which is a nondiscretionary brokerage service designed to give investors access to a broad range of resources for one annual fee. Clients have access to unlimited trading in eligible securities and professional advice and guidance through an Ultimate Advantage Account. Clients pay an asset-based fee on the value of their eligible assets instead of paying separate commission fees.

Customer Service Rating: ★★★ Excellent

Gomez Rating: 6.89

Forrester PowerRankings: 58.54

================ **MORGAN STANLEY DEAN WITTER ONLINE** ================

Brokerage Type: Discount brokerage

Mailing Address: 333 Market St. 25th Floor
                  San Francisco, CA 94105-2812

Web Address: www.msdw.com

Email Address: clientsupport@onlinemsdw.com

Telephone Number: 800-584-6837, 800-688-6896

Fax Number: 801-902-6770

Market Orders: Commission based through Morgan Stanley Dean Witter Online: $29.95 per trade, 1,000 shares or less, and additional $0.03 per share on entire order thereafter; stocks under $1.00 per share, $25.00 per trade plus 2.75% of principal amount. Choice Account offered through Morgan Stanley Dean Witter: minimum annual fee, $1,000. A quarterly fee applies depending on the amount of assets held with Morgan Stanley Dean Witter.

Limit Orders: Same as market orders.

Option Trades: 20% discount off standard broker-assisted commission for Internet trades.

Telephone Trading: Stocks: $39.95 per trade, 1,000 shares or less, and additional $0.04 per share on entire order thereafter; stocks under $1.00 per share, $25.00 per trade plus 2.75% of principal amount. Options selling at $0.50 or less: 0–49 contracts, $1.80 per contract plus 1.5% of principal, 50–149 contracts, $1.10 per contract plus 1.8% of principal; 150–499 contracts, $0.75 per contract plus 2.0% of principal; 500–1,499 contracts, $0.60 per contract plus 2.0% of principal; 1,500 or more contracts, $0.60 per contract plus 1.5% of principal; overriding minimum, $35.00. Options selling greater than $0.50: $0–2,499 principal amount, $29.00 plus 1.5% of principal; $2,500–9,999 principal amount, $49.00 plus 0.8% of principal; $10,000 or more principal amount, $99.00 plus 0.3% of principal; overriding minimum, $37.25 plus $1.75 per trade.

After-Hours Trading: 4:30 P.M. to 8:00 P.M. EST, Monday through Thursday. $29.95 per trade. Internet trading available.

Products Available to Trade Online: Stocks, options, mutual funds, municipal bonds, and U.S. treasuries.

Average Execution Time: Market order: 15–30 seconds.

Minimum Deposit Required: $2,000 for cash or margin account.

Additional Fees: IRA termination fee: $50.00. Returned check fee: $25.00. Buy in/sell out notices: $15.00. Outgoing money wires: domestic, $30.00; foreign, $50.00. Outgoing DTC transfers: $7.50. Voluntary reorganizations: $35.00. Called bonds: $30.00. Name change on request of stock certificate: $25.00. Legal transfer fee: $50.00. Extra statement copies: $7.50 per statement. Option assignment and exercise (broker-assisted trades): up to 4,999 shares, $34.00; 5,000–19,999 shares, $50.00; 20,000 or more shares, $100.00.

Free Services and Financial Links: Unlimited real-time graphs, Morgan Stanley Dean Witter research reports, Zacks, Thomson Financial Proprietary Research, Reuters, download into Quicken and Money, Dividend Reinvestment Program, company news, e-commerce news, Global Economic Forum, Global Strategy Bulletin, U.S. Strategic Commentary.

Real-Time Quotes: Free unlimited real-time quotes for options, market indices, and stocks. Amex stock quotes are 20-minute delayed. The quotes are not streaming and must be refreshed.

States Registered In: All U.S. states.

Mutual Funds Offered: Over 5,300 from 190 families.

Payment for Order Flow: Yes.

Banking Services Offered: Unlimited check writing privileges with the first 50 checks free; reorders are $12.95 per 200 checks.

Company Background: Morgan Stanley Dean Witter (MSDW) Online was formed as a result of the 1997 merger of Dean Witter, Discover & Co., and Morgan Stanley Group, Inc. MSDW Online has been offering Web-based investing to its clientele since 1995. Morgan Stanley Dean Witter & Co. is the parent company of MSDW On-line, and it services over 4 million clients. MSDW Online protects clients' accounts up to $500,000, of which $100,000 is for cash coverage, provided by SIPC. MSDW offers a Choice Account exclusively to suitable investors who have a MSDW account or a retirement account. This account is an alternative way to pay for securities transactions. Clients will pay one quarterly fee, based on the amount of assets they have with MSDW. There are no single commission charges per trade, and clients have access to guidance and service with a financial advisor at any time.

Customer Service Rating: ★★★ Excellent

Gomez Rating: 6.48

MOST ACTIVES

Brokerage Type: Full-service discount brokerage

Mailing Address: 8723 4th Avenue
Brooklyn, NY 11209

Web Address: www.mostactives.com

Email Address: info@mostactives.com

Telephone Number: 718-491-6650, 888-409-4773

Fax Number: 718-491-6653

Market Orders: $9.99 per trade (all Nasdaq, NYSE, and Amex orders).

Limit Orders: $14.95 per trade.

Option Trades: $25.00 plus $2.50 per contract.

Telephone Trading: Nasdaq, NYSE, Amex, and market orders: $19.99 per trade. Limit orders: $24.99 per trade.

After-Hours Trading: 4:00 P.M. to 6:30 P.M. EST; broker-assisted trades only, and broker-assisted commissions apply.

Products Available to Trade Online: Stocks, options, and mutual funds.

Average Execution Time: Market order: 3 seconds, depending on volatility of stock.

Minimum Deposit Required: $100.00 for cash account. $2,500.00 for margin account.

Additional Fees: Postage and handling per trade: $3.00. Option assignment and exercise: $20.00. Regulation T extension: $10.00. Mailgrams: $15.00. Wiring of funds: $25.00. Returned checks: $25.00. Legal transfer: $25.00. Reorganization: $10.00. Copies of monthly statements: $10.00 per month. Copies of confirmation statements: $5.00. Copies of checks over 6 months old: $20.00. Register and ship per issue: $15.00.

Account transfer (out-ACAT, plus draft charges if any): $45.00. Partial DTC delivery (per issue): $10.00. Overnight mail upon request: $15.00. Stop payment request on checks: $25.00. Foreign securities transfer: $75.00 plus additional transfer agent fee. Foreign securities safekeeping: $5.00.

Free Services and Financial Links: CBS Marketwatch, market updates, Super Star Funds, Mutual Understanding, IPO News Stock Alerts sent to your cell phone, research, charts, graphs.

Real-Time Quotes: Real-time quotes, although they are not streaming and must be refreshed.

States Registered In: All U.S. states except PR.

Mutual Funds Offered: Hundreds of families and access to almost every mutual fund.

Payment for Order Flow: No.

Banking Services Offered: None.

Company Background: Benson York Group, Inc., was founded in September 1995 and launched online trading through Most Actives in 1999. As a full-service brokerage, Most Actives helps investors achieve their goals by giving proper guidance and rapid access to the markets. All trades are executed through the Benson York Group. Most Actives utilizes JB Oxford as its clearing firm. A special feature offered by Most Actives is a computerized human voice that will call the client back on the phone and state that a trade has been completed. This feature was created to save the customer any unnecessary frustration while trading. All accounts at Most Actives are protected by SIPC up to $500,000, of which $100,000 is for cash coverage.

Customer Service Rating: ★★★ Excellent

MR. STOCK, INC.

Brokerage Type: Discount brokerage

Mailing Address: 505 14th St., Suite 500
Oakland, CA 94612

Web Address: www.mrstock.com

Email Address: info@mrstock.com

Telephone Number: 800-470-1896, 510-587-5500

Fax Number: 510-587-5518

Market Orders: $14.95 per trade, up to 5,000 shares, and additional $0.0125 per share thereafter.

Limit Orders: $0.0125 per share, $16.00 minimum.

Option Trades: Contracts $10.00 and under: $16.00 plus $1.75 per contract. Contracts over $10.00: $16.00 plus $2.25 per contract.

Telephone Trading: $7.00 additional surcharge; if trade commission exceeds $100.00, phone trading fee does not apply.

After-Hours Trading: None.

Products Available to Trade Online: Stocks and options.

Average Execution Time: Market order: 2-3 seconds depending on market conditions.

Minimum Deposit Required: $2,000.

Additional Fees: Returned checks: $20.00. Legal transfer: $15.00. Physical DVP: $15.00. Regulation T extensions: $25.00. Document reprinting: $3.00. Printing duplicate statements: $2.00. Outgoing wires ($2,000 or more): $5.00. IRA annual fee: $40.00. IRA closing fee: $40.00. Ordering out physical security: $45.00. SEC fee (sell trades only): $0.01 per $300.00. Options assignment and exercise: $0.25 per contract, $20.00 minimum.

Free Services and Financial Links: Economic indicators, charts, research and company news, Zacks, market commentary, balance sheets, income statements, global market commentary, free trial to ZWSS Network, EDGAR online database, 2nd Opinion, Reuters, Inc. Link Co. News, stock charting, option chains, volatility charting, News Alert.

Real-Time Quotes: 100 real-time quotes per trade, although they are not streaming and must be refreshed. Access to free unlimited delayed quotes.

States Registered In: All U.S. states.

Mutual Funds Offered: None.

Payment for Order Flow: No.

Banking Services Offered: Free check-writing.

Company Background: Mr. Stock, Inc. was founded in 1993, and in 1997 Mr. Stock launched online trading due to the tremendous growth of the Internet. Mr. Stock is privately owned and executes more than 1.5 million shares of stock and 45,000 option contracts each trading day. All orders are executed through Mr. Stock. Mr. Stock protects its clients' accounts up to $500,000.

Customer Service Rating: ★★★ Excellent

Gomez Rating: 5.02

■ SIEBERTNET ■

Brokerage Type: Discount brokerage

Mailing Address: 885 Third Ave., 17th Floor
New York, NY 10022

Web Address: www.msiebert.com
Email Address: service@seibertnet.com
Telephone Number: 800-USA-0711, 212-644-2400
Fax Number: 212-486-2784
Market Orders: $14.95 per trade, up to 1,000 shares, and additional $0.015 per share thereafter.
Limit Orders: Same as market orders.
Option Trades: Options priced below $1.00: $2.00 per contract, minimum $34.00 per order. Commissions vary as the price per option and the number of options vary. SiebertNet offers 10% discount for online option trading.
Telephone Trading: Stock trades: $37.50–45.00 per trade (100 shares or fewer), depending on price of stock; $75.00 to buy or sell up to 2,500 shares of an exchange listed stock; $60.00 to buy or sell up to 3,000 shares of an OTC or Nasdaq stock. SiebertNet will negotiate rates depending on the size of account. Option trades: options priced below $1.00 are $2.00 per contract; minimum $34.00 per order. Commissions vary as the price per option and the number of options vary.
After-Hours Trading: 7:30 A.M. to 9:30 A.M. EST: Instinet, broker-assisted (Internet commission applies). 4:30 P.M. to 6:00 P.M. EST: Instinet, broker-assisted (Internet commission applies). 4:00 P.M. to 8:00 P.M. EST: trades routed through computer, $50.00 up to 1,000 shares, additional $0.05 a share thereafter. 100-share lots and limit orders only.
Products Available to Trade Online: Stocks, bonds, and mutual funds.
Average Execution Time: Market order: seconds to minutes.
Minimum Deposit Required: None for cash account. $2,000 for margin account.
Additional Fees: Standard & Poor's Reports: $1.50. First Call Earnings Reports: $1.50. Argus Reports: $1.50. Vickers Reports: $4.50. Business Wire press releases: $1.50. Five-year historical price charts: $1.50. Lipper Mutual Fund Reports: $1.50.
Free Services and Financial Links: Performance fax, research by fax (guaranteed delivery in five minutes), Zacks, custom charting capabilities, CBS Marketwatch, free tender offers, Nelsons Publications, gain and loss tracking, postage and handling, transfer and shipping, free dividend reinvestment, free legal transfers.
Real-Time Quotes: Free real-time quotes during market hours, although they are not streaming and must be refreshed. Streaming quotes available for a fee.
States Registered In: All U.S. states except NE and NM.
Mutual Funds Offered: More than 7,065 from more than 325 families.

Payment for Order Flow: No.

Banking Services Offered: Unlimited check writing, VISA debit card, and access to ATMs worldwide.

Company Background: Muriel Siebert & Co., Inc., has been in business and an NYSE member since 1967. Muriel Siebert, chairwoman and president, was the first woman ever to become a member of the exchange. In 1975, the first day NYSE member firms were permitted to negotiate commissions, Siebert became one of the very first to announce that it would become a discount brokerage house. SiebertNet is a Nasdaq-traded company under the symbol SIEB. SiebertNet has headquarters in Manhattan and branches in Beverly Hills, CA, and in Boca Raton, Naples, Palm Beach, and Surfside, FL. Assets in customer accounts are protected up to $100 million; SIPC provides up to $500,000, of which $100,000 is for cash coverage, and Asset Guaranty Insurance Co. provides the remaining $99.5 million. If a client is unsatisfied with a trade for any reason, that trade will be commission-free.

Customer Service Rating: ★★★ Excellent

MYDISCOUNTBROKER.COM

Brokerage Type: Discount brokerage

Mailing Address: 1201 Elm Street, Suite 121
Dallas, TX 75270

Web Address: www.mydiscountbroker.com

Email Address: service@mydiscountbroker.com

Telephone Number: 888-882-5600, 214-859-6400

Fax Number: 214-859-6440

Market Orders: $12.00 per trade, up to 5,000 shares, and additional $0.01 per share if stock is priced at $1.00 or more, and additional $0.005 if stock is priced less than $1.00 thereafter.

Limit Orders: Same as market orders.

Option Trades: $12.00 per trade plus maximum $2.00 per contract, contract price of $1.00 or more.

Telephone Trading: $25.00 (0–1,000 shares); $35.00 (1,001–2,500 shares); $45.00 (2,501–5,000 shares); $45.00 plus $0.02 per share (5,000 or more shares). Options: $25.00 plus $2.00 per contract (up to 5,000 shares); $45.00 per trade plus $0.02 per share (over 5,000 shares).

After-Hours Trading: 4:30 P.M. to 8:00 P.M. EST. $12.00 plus $0.01 per share with a minimum of $1.50 and a maximum of $5.00. Broker-assisted trading and limit orders only.

Products Available to Trade Online: Stocks, options, and mutual funds.

Average Execution Time: Market order: 75.7% of orders are routed to a market maker between 0–1 seconds.

Minimum Deposit Required: None, but sufficient cash or securities are needed to place a trade. $2,000 for margin account.

Additional Fees: Shipping fee: $12.00 (excluded if registered for DRIP program). Ship certificates: $25.00. Issued certificates: $12.00.

Free Services and Financial Links: No-fee IRA, SEP, and 401k accounts; monthly newsletter; Quote.com; free IRA transfers; charts and graphs; full-text company news; Zacks; Market Guide; portfolio tracker; quote chain for options; ticker symbol searches; the Wall Street Journal "Guide to Understanding Money and Investing"; interactive calculators; bimonthly newsletter.

Real-Time Quotes: Free unlimited real-time quotes, although they are not streaming and must be refreshed. Clients can receive unlimited streaming real-time quotes for a fee of $10.00 a month.

States Registered In: All U.S. states.

Mutual Funds Offered: Over 6,400.

Payment for Order Flow: Yes.

Banking Services Offered: Vision Cash Management Account: free unlimited check writing privileges. Clients also have access to a full array of banking services through MyBankUSA.com.

Company Background: Sovereign Securities, Inc., a traditional discount brokerage, was founded in 1996. In 1998 Sovereign began offering internet investing services through its web site www.mydiscountbroker.com, and in 1999 Sovereign changed its name completely to Mydiscountbroker.com. Mydiscountbroker protects clients' accounts up to $25 million per account. It offers clients a broad spectrum of investment vehicles and provides research to help clients make their own investment decisions without the need of a broker. Telephone and email technical support is always available to clients 24 hours a day, 7 days a week. The largest portion of online accounts is made up of individuals.

Customer Service Rating: ★★★ Excellent

Gomez Rating: 6.41

NATIONAL DISCOUNT BROKERS (NDB.COM)

Brokerage Type: Discount brokerage
Mailing Address: 7 Hanover Square, 4th Floor
New York, NY 10004
Web Address: www.ndb.com
Email Address: info@ndb.com
Telephone Number: 800-888-3999
Fax Number: 212-863-4400
Market Orders: $14.75 per trade, up to 5,000 shares, and additional $0.01 per share thereafter. Foreign Securities: ordinary shares, $0.02 per share plus $125.00; Canadian shares, $0.02 per share plus $30.00.
Limit Orders: $19.75 per trade, up to 5,000 shares, and additional $0.01 per share thereafter. Foreign Securities: ordinary shares, $0.02 per share plus $125.00; Canadian shares, $0.02 per share plus $30.00.
Option Trades: $20.00 per trade plus $1.75 per contract. $29.00 minimum.
Telephone Trading: Stock trades: $24.95 per trade (market order), $27.95 per trade (limit order). Option trades: $35.00 per trade plus $2.50 per contract.
After-Hours Trading: 7:30 A.M. to 9:30 A.M. EST and 4:00 P.M. to 5:30 P.M. EST. $19.75 per trade, up to 5,000 shares, and additional $0.01 per share thereafter. Limit orders only.
Products Available to Trade Online: Stocks, options, and mutual funds.
Average Execution Time: Market order: under 10 seconds.
Minimum Deposit Required: None for cash account. $2,000 for margin account.
Additional Fees: Transfer and shipping: $15.00 per certificate. Wires: $20.00. Overnight delivery: $15.00. IRA: $35.00, annually waved for accounts over $10,000. IRA termination: $50.00 plus annual fee. Restricted security processing fee: $50.00. Returned check: $25.00. Legal transfers: $25.00. Voluntary tenders: $25.00. Mandatory tenders: $10.00. Bond redemptions: $5.00. Rapid research line (increments): $1.50 each. Copies of back statements: $5.00 per month.
Free Services and Financial Links: Thomson Report Service, EasyPay, free assets management account, Market Guide fundamental analysis reports, technical analysis charting, option chains, Insider Trading reports, SEC filings, analysts recommendations, earnings forecast, Dow Jones Business Newswire, Reuters, Briefing.com, TheStreet.com, The Wall Street transcript, First USA, AST, Stock Plan Inc., Time Inc. New Media, eLogic Communications, Stock Point, Vickers, Best Calls.com,

Wall Street on Demand, Zacks, Amazon.com, Research on Demand (includes a database of over $500,000 detailed financial reports).

Real-Time Quotes: Free real-time quotes: 100 per trade execution. The quotes are not streaming and must be refreshed.

States Registered In: All U.S. states.

Mutual Funds Offered: Over 9,000.

Payment for Order Flow: Yes.

Banking Services Offered: Unlimited check writing privileges with free Resource Checking Account. Clients can receive check writing, direct deposit, and online bill payment and can apply for a Platinum VISA credit card with a Procash Plus Account. The minimum deposit for this type of account is between $10,000 and $20,000.

Company Background: National Discount Brokers was originally founded in 1968, and online trading was launched through NDB.com in 1994. National Discount Brokers specializes in brokerage and financial services for individuals and institutions. NDB has over 178,000 accounts, with more than $8.9 billion in assets. SIPC provides $500,000 of insurance per account: $100,000 for cash and $400,000 for securities. NDB will return your commission fee within 7 days of purchase if you are not fully satisfied with the service.

Customer Service Rating: ★★★ Excellent

Gomez Rating: 6.69

NETBANK

Brokerage Type: Discount brokerage

Mailing Address: P.O. Box 2368
Alpharetta, GA 30023

Web Address: www.netbank.com

Email Address: customerservice@uvest.com

Telephone Number: 770-343-6006, 888-256-6932

Fax Number: 770-343-6464

Market Orders: $25.00 per trade, up to 2,000 shares, and additional $0.015 per share thereafter.

Limit Orders: Same as market orders.

Option Trades: $35.00 plus $2.50 per contract.

Telephone Trading: $39.00 per trade, up to 2,000 shares, and additional $0.015 per share thereafter.

After-Hours Trading: None.

Products Available to Trade Online: Stocks, options, mutual funds, bonds, and unit investment trusts.

Average Execution Time: Market order: usually within seconds.

Minimum Deposit Required: $500.00 for money market. $2,000 for margin.

Additional Fees: Accommodation transfers: $25.00. Bond redemption: $20.00. Exchange fee: $10.00. Foreign securities surcharge: $100.00. IRA maintenance (annual): $35.00. Legal transfer: $25.00. Margin or cash extension (late fee): $10.00. Reorganization (tender) charges: $40.00. Safekeeping fee (if annual commission level does not reach $45.00): $35.00. Securities delivery charge: $15.00. Wire fee: $15.00.

Free Services and Financial Links: NetBank offers "Tips & Tools," a financial education resource designed to help with financial decisions.

Real-Time Quotes: 50 real-time quotes with new account plus 50 free real-time quotes with each trade placed and 50 real-time quotes every month. Clients have access to unlimited delayed quotes.

States Registered In: All U.S. states.

Mutual Funds Offered: Over 9,000.

Payment for Order Flow: No.

Banking Services Offered: Banking services and trading with NetBank NetWorth Investment Account, which includes unlimited check writing, worldwide ATM access, a NetBank VISA check card (if approved), online funds transfer capabilities, and online bill payment.

Company Background: NetBank was founded in 1996 as a federal savings bank operating exclusively through the Internet and offering a full line of financial services. NetBank does not charge its customers a fee for brokerage services. Clients' accounts are protected up to $75 million. The SIPC provides up to $500,000, of which $100,000 is for cash coverage. The remaining $74.5 million is provided through a commercial insurer.

Customer Service Rating: ★★★ Excellent

NETFOLIO

Brokerage Type: Registered Investment Advisor, using broker Bear, Stearns

Mailing Address: Netfolio, Inc.
P.O. Box 4570
New York, NY 10163

Web Address: www.netfolio.com
Email Address: suggestions@netfolio.com
Telephone Number: None.
Fax Number: None.
Market Orders: $19.95 per trade if trade is placed after purchasing portfolio. Netfolio ebasket portfolio: $19.95 per month or $199.95 per year, unlimited trading.
Limit Orders: Same as market orders.
Option Trades: None.
Telephone Trading: Same commissions as online schedule.
After-Hours Trading: None.
Products Available to Trade Online: Stocks.
Average Execution Time: Not divulged.
Minimum Deposit Required: $5,000 for ebasket portfolio.
Additional Fees: None.
Free Services and Financial Links: Netfolio Insights, My Netfolio, tax-sensitive portfolio advice, Strategy Watch.
Real-Time Quotes: Real-time quotes with software package. The quotes are not streaming and must be refreshed.
States Registered In: All U.S. states.
Mutual Funds Offered: None.
Payment for Order Flow: No.
Banking Services Offered: None.
Company Background: In January 2000, O'Shaughnessy Capital Management was renamed Netfolio, Inc. In June 2000, Netfolio began developing online investment services. Netfolio is an investment-advisory firm that allows clients to buy a portfolio of stocks without a per trade commission fee. Netfolio has new clients fill out a short online questionnaire called Net Profiler. This allows Netfolio to evaluate each clients individual investment goals and needs. Netfolio then recommends a portfolio of stocks, made up of 5 to 40 stocks, called an ebasket portfolio. The client can either pay a monthly fee of $19.95 or a yearly flat fee of $199.95 to invest with Netfolio. This type of investing strategy allows the client to invest in a whole portfolio of stocks rather than on a stock-by-stock basis. Clients will incur no sales commission fees, no transaction fees, and no management costs. Trades placed through Netfolio are handled by Bear Stearns.
Customer Service Rating: ★★★ Excellent

NETSTOCK INVESTMENT CORPORATION

Brokerage Type: Discount brokerage
Mailing Address: P.O. Box 1728
Bellevue, WA 98009-1728
Web Address: www.netstock.com
Email Address: customercare@netstock.com
Telephone Number: 888-638-7865
Fax Number: 888-NET-STOK
Market Orders: Dollar-based investing.
Limit Orders: Dollar-based investing.
Option Trades: None.
Telephone Trading: None.
After-Hours Trading: None.
Products Available to Trade Online: Stocks.
Average Execution Time: Not applicable.
Minimum Deposit Required: None.
Additional Fees: ShareBuilder individual and joint account purchases: $2.00 (recurring). ShareBuilder custodial account purchases: $1.00 (recurring). ShareBuilder purchase: $5.00 (one-time). Funds wired in: $10.00. Funds wired out: $25.00. Stock certificate insurance and delivery: $25.00. Legal transfer: $30.00. Returned checks: $25.00. Stop payment: $25.00. Overnight courier: $25.00. Inactivity fee of $11.95 waived for first year and will continue to be waived as long as there are at least four transactions per year in account.
Free Services and Financial Links: Check with Netstock on services offered.
Real-Time Quotes: Real-time quotes to clients only; 20-minute delayed quotes always available.
States Registered In: All U.S. states.
Mutual Funds Offered: None.
Payment for Order Flow: No.
Banking Services Offered: None.
Company Background: Netstock Direct Corporation was founded in 1996 and is a privately held Internet company. Netstock offers "ShareBuilder" to clients. ShareBuilder is a long-term investing service that allows individual investors to buy stocks in dollar-based amounts for a flat $2.00 fee, or $1.00 in a custodial account. Investors buy stock in dollar amounts rather than share amounts. The idea is to accumulate a position in a company over a long period of time. This product emphasizes accumulating stock, rather than trading stock. Individuals can

make periodic investments, with a $2.00 transaction fee per trade, which helps the individual build up a portfolio of stocks. ShareBuilder covers more than 3,000 of the largest market cap securities on the NYSE/Nasdaq and more than 60 index products like the Nasdaq 100 QQQ. Netstock offers unlimited account protection on client accounts. The SIPC covers the first $500,000 and Netstock provides the remaining coverage.

Customer Service Rating: ★★★ Excellent

NETVEST

Company Name: NetVest
Brokerage Type: Discount brokerage
Mailing Address: 823 Third Ave., Suite 206
Seattle, WA 98104-9910
Web Address: www.netvest.com
Email Address: info@investorservices.net
Telephone Number: 800-961-1500
Fax Number: 713-350-3777
Market Orders: $14.00 per trade.
Limit Orders: $19.00 per trade.
Option Trades: $20.00 per trade plus $1.50 per contract.
Telephone Trading: Stock trades: market order, $24.00 per trade; limit order, $29.00 per trade. Option trades: $30.00 per trade plus $1.50 per contract.
After-Hours Trading: 4:30 P.M. to 6:30 P.M. EST. Same commission schedule as online trading or telephone trading.
Products Available to Trade Online: Stocks, options, mutual funds, bonds, T bills, and government securities.
Average Execution Time: Market order: Depends on market conditions and size of order.
Minimum Deposit Required: $2,000 for cash or margin.
Additional Fees: Options exercised and assignment: $24.00. Reorganization fees: Exchange offers: elective, $25.00. Tender offers: elective, $25.00. Rights subscription: $25.00. Optional dividend elections: $25.00. Replacement statements (per month): $5.00. Re-register and/or deliver certificate (per issue): $25.00. Wire transfer of funds (per item): $20.00. Late payment (past settlement): $15.00. Returned checks: $20.00. ACAT transfer (outgoing): $25.00. Foreign securities transfer: varies. IRA termination: $30.00. Overnight express delivery: $15.00. Restricted stock processing (per issue): $250.00.

Free Services and Financial Links: Postage, mailing, handling. No inactive account fee. IRA setup, charts, delayed ticker, quote-symbol lookup, investor calendar, stock screening, NYSE and Nasdaq gainers and losers, NYSE and Nasdaq most active lists.

Real-Time Quotes: 100 real-time quotes with new account and 100 more with each trade placed; not streaming, must be refreshed.

States Registered In: All U.S. states.

Mutual Funds Offered: More than 7,000.

Payment for Order Flow: No.

Banking Services Offered: None.

Company Background: TradeStar was founded in 1984 and launched TradeStar Express Investments in 1997. NetVest, a division of TradeStar, began in February 2000 and has an online client base of approximately 15,000 clients. The majority of its clients are individual traders. All NetVest accounts (except retirement and fiduciary accounts) require a margin account. Client accounts are protected by SIPC up to $500,000, including $100,000 in cash and an additional $99.5 million provided by Travelers Casualty and Surety Co. of America.

Customer Service Rating: ★★★ Excellent

Gomez Rating: 5.08

ONEINVEST

Brokerage Type: Discount brokerage

Mailing Address: Banc One Securities Corp. OneInvest
300 S. Riverside Plaza
MS IL 0745
Chicago, IL 60606-0745

Web Address: www.oneinvest.com

Email Address: None.

Telephone Number: 888-843-6382

Fax Number: None.

Market Orders: $19.95 per trade, up to 1,000 shares, and additional $0.02 per share thereafter. $3.00 confirmation fee for all orders.

Limit Orders: $19.95 per trade, up to 1,000 shares, and additional $0.02 per share thereafter. $3.00 confirmation fee for all orders.

Option Trades: $0–3,000: $35.00 per trade plus 1.5%. $3,000–10,000: $50.00 per trade plus 0.85%. $10,000 or more: $60.00 per trade plus 0.70%. Minimum $38.00 per trade, $3.00 per contract; maximum $25.00 per contract.

Telephone Trading: 25% off client service center fees.
After-Hours Trading: None.
Products Available to Trade Online: Stocks, options, and mutual funds.
Average Execution Time: Market order: under one minute.
Minimum Deposit Required: None for cash account.
Additional Fees: Postage and handling: $3.00. Dividend reinvestment: $1.00 per transaction. Registration and shipping: $15.00 per security. Other fees may apply.
Free Services and Financial Links: Morning Market Comment, Market Wrap-Up, credit and interest report, economic and market indicators, week in review, individual stock reports, Wall Street on Demand (Standard & Poor's, Argus, Lipper, First Call, Renaissance, Business Wire, Micropal), online annual reports.
Real-Time Quotes: With online account; quotes are not streaming and must be refreshed.
States Registered In: All U.S. states except AL and PR.
Mutual Funds Offered: More than 7,000.
Payment for Order Flow: No.
Banking Services Offered: Bank One online banking services.
Company Background: OneInvest was founded in January 1997 and is a service of Banc One Securities Corp. OneInvest was launched to provide online investment services and securities trading via the Internet while allowing clients to make their own investment decisions. OneInvest is a registered broker/dealer and a member NASD/SIPC.
Customer Service Rating: ★★★ Excellent

ONLINETRADING.COM

Brokerage Type: Direct access
Mailing Address: 2700 North Military Trail, Suite 200
Boca Raton, FL 33431
Web Address: www.onlinetrading.com
Email Address: info@onlinetrading.com
Telephone Number: 800-995-1076
Fax Number: 561-995-0606
Market Orders: $24.95 per trade, up to 1,000 shares, and additional $0.02 per share thereafter. Commissions exceeding $1,000 a month earn client a 10% discount on commission charges; those exceeding $2,000 a month earn a 15% discount.
Limit Orders: Same as market orders.

Option Trades: $30.00 per trade plus $2.00 per contract. Commissions exceeding $1,000 a month earn client a 10% discount on commission charges; those exceeding $2,000 a month earn a 15% discount.

Telephone Trading: $39.95 per trade up to and including 1,000 shares, and additional $0.02 per share thereafter. Bulletin-board stock trades under $1.00 are $23.95 per trade plus 2.75% of principal. Stock trades over $1.00 are $23.95 per trade plus $0.02 per share.

After-Hours Trading: 7:00 A.M. to 9:30 A.M. EST and 4:00 P.M. to 6:00 P.M. EST. Broker-assisted trades only. $39.95 per trade, up to and including 1,000 shares, and additional $0.02 per share thereafter.

Products Available to Trade Online: Stocks and options.

Average Execution Time: Market order: 15 seconds.

Minimum Deposit Required: $10,000 for all accounts.

Additional Fees: Overnight delivery: $14.00. IRA annual fee: $35.00. IRA termination: $50.00. Returned checks: $20.00. Options exercise and assignment: $25.00 per position. Foreign securities transfer: varies based on nation. Foreign accounts: based on nation; additional fees may apply. Orders software: $249.00 a month with volume discounts (50–99 trades per month, $125.00 monthly credit; 100 or more trades per month, $249.00 monthly credit).

Free Services and Financial Links: Transfer and ship, wires, extensions, mailgrams, restricted securities processing fee, fixed income transfer, legal transfer, voluntary tenders, mandated tenders, inactive account custody fee, copies of back statements, CBS Market Watch.

Real-Time Quotes: Real-time quotes, streaming.

States Registered In: All U.S. states.

Mutual Funds Offered: None.

Payment for Order Flow: No.

Banking Services Offered: Banking services.

Company Background: Onlinetrading.com is a privately owned direct-access firm founded in 1995. Clients at Onlinetrading.com are primarily hedge funds and institutional clients. Bear Stearns Securities Corp. is the clearing firm that is utilized and Onlinetrading.com is a member of SIPC. Clients' accounts are protected by SIPC up to $500,000, of which $100,000 is for cash coverage; additional unlimited coverage is provided by Bear Stearns. To open an account clients must have a minimum net worth of $300,000 and at least two years' trading and investing experience (this firm caters mainly to the experienced investor). The direct-access system allows orders to be directed to a number of electronic locations while the option to trade directly with a live broker is still maintained. Orders software is a point-and-click order handling system that allows clients to enter their orders directly to the market makers through a variety of execution routes, including Instinet, Island, Archipelago, SelectNet, NYSE via SuperDOT, and others.

Customer Service Rating: ★★ Average

ON-SITE TRADING, INC.

Brokerage Type: Direct access
Mailing Address: 98 Cutter Mill Road Suite 100
Great Neck, NY 11021
Web Address: www.onsitetrading.com
Email Address: sales@onsitetrading.com
Telephone Number: 888-402-0533 or 516-482-9292 (ext. 190)
Fax Number: 516-482-9388
Market Orders: Nasdaq trades: 1–200 trades per month, $19.95 per trade; 201–400 trades per month, $18.95 per trade; 401–600 trades per month, $17.95 per trade; 601–1,000 trades per month, $16.95 per trade; 1,001 or more trades per month, $15.95 per trade. NYSE/Amex trades: 1–200 trades per month, $14.95 per trade plus $0.01 per share; 201–400 trades per month, $13.95 per trade plus $0.01 per share; 401–600 trades per month, $12.95 per trade plus $0.01 per share; 601–1,000 trades per month, $11.95 per trade plus $0.01 per share; 1,001 or more trades per month, $10.95 per trade plus $0.01 per share. Bulletin securities are not available for trading.
Limit Orders: Same as market orders.
Option Trades: None.
Telephone Trading: Same commissions as online schedule.
After-Hours Trading: 7:30 A.M. to 9:30 A.M. and 4:00 P.M. to 10:00 P.M. EST. Same commission applies as for online schedule.
Products Available to Trade Online: Stocks.
Average Execution Time: Market order: fastest market will allow, depending on trade being placed.
Minimum Deposit Required: $25,000.
Additional Fees: ECN fees: Island, add $1.00 per trade; Instinet, add $0.015 per share; Archipelago, add $0.005 per share; Attain, add $0.005 per share; Bloomberg Book, add $0.005 per share with $1.50 per trade minimum; Brass Utility, add $0.015 per share; Nextrade, add $0.015 per share; Strike, add $0.015 per share. Industry rates at cost, determined by clearing firm.

Free Services and Financial Links: Dow Jones News Service, First
Call, Reuters, Bloomberg, Jag Notes, software training manual, Market
Guide, news, market analysis.

Real-Time Quotes: Streaming real-time quotes with online account.

States Registered In: All U.S. states.

Mutual Funds Offered: None.

Payment for Order Flow: No.

Banking Services Offered: None.

Company Background: On-Site Trading, Inc., is a direct-access brokerage firm, founded in 1994, that allows clients access to electronic stock
trading. On-Site Trading caters to the professional, active trader and offers a virtual-trading desktop that allows the client to choose from
many of the most popular quote and charting applications. The software offered to clients is called On-Site Trader and is a fully integrated,
dynamic, real-time U.S. equities remote trading system. Clients may either route their own orders or use S.M.A.R.T. Trading Technology, an
order-routing and execution technology that sends the order to
whomever is offering to buy or sell the requested shares at the best possible price. To open an account clients must have an annual income of
at least $50,000 and a net worth of at least $150,000. Client accounts
are protected up to $500,000, of which $100,000 is for cash coverage
provided by SIPC. Additional coverage is provided by Aetna up to $100
million.

Customer Service Rating: ★★★ Excellent

PACIFIC ON-LINE TRADING AND SECURITIES, INC.

Brokerage Type: Direct access

Mailing Address: 1030 The Alameda
San Jose, CA 95126

Web Address: www.day-trade.com

Email Address: customer_service@day-trade.com

Telephone Number: 408-297-8000, 800-STOCKS-9

Fax Number: 408-297-8020

Market Orders: $19.95 per trade. Listed issues (NYSE, Amex) $19.95
per trade up to 2,000 shares, and additional $0.01 per share thereafter.

Limit Orders: Same as market orders.

Option Trades: None.

Telephone Trading: Same commission as for online schedule.

After-Hours Trading: 5:00 A.M. to 9:30 A.M. EST and 4:00 P.M. to 5:00 P.M. EST. Same commission as for online schedule.

Products Available to Trade Online: Stocks.

Average Execution Time: Market order: depends on market volatility and access.

Minimum Deposit Required: $5,000.

Additional Fees: Software and data feed: POTS Lite, $100.00 per month (1–199 trades per month), fee waived upon placing 200 or more trades per month; POTS Custom, $175.00 per month (1–199 trades per month), fee waived upon placing 200 or more trades per month; POTS Trader, $250.00 per month (1–99 trades per month), $100.00 per month, (100–199 trades per month), fee waived upon placing 200 or more trades per month. ECN fees: ISI for NYSE, $0.0129 per share; Instinet (INCA), $0.0129 per share ($12.90 per 1,000 shares); Island (ISLD), $0.0025 per share; SelectNet (SNET), $2.50 per fill; Small Order Execution System (SOES), $0.50 per fill; BTRD, ATTN, etc., $0.015 per share; ARCA, $0.50 per fill; cancels, $0.25 per cancel. Exchange fees: NYSE (non-pro), $5.25 per month; Amex (non-pro), $3.25 per month; NASD Level II (non-pro), $50.00 per month; NASD Level I (non-pro), $4.00 per month; Options, $5.00 per month; CME, $55.00 per month; CBOT, $60.00 per month. Returned checks: $15.00. Stop payment (within 10 days): $10.00. Overnight delivery: $7.50. Foreign transfer: ACAT, $25.00–50.00. Wire: domestic, $15.00; foreign, $35.00.

Free Services and Financial Links: News Watch, CNBC, *The Wall Street Journal,* Bloomberg.com, Nasdaq, CNNfn, Chicago Board of Options Exchange, *Inter@ctive* Investor, TheStreet.com, Yahoo Finance, NYSE, StockTax98, Storecoupon.com, TradersPressBookstore.com, free seminars.

Real-Time Quotes: Streaming real-time quotes with software package.

States Registered In: AK, CA, CO, FL, HI, MO, NV, OK, TN, TX, UT, VA, WA.

Mutual Funds Offered: None.

Payment for Order Flow: No.

Banking Services Offered: Free check writing with online account.

Company Background: Pacific On-Line Trading and Securities, Inc., founded in 1996, is a brokerage/dealer and a member of the NASD and SIPC. Pacific On-Line Trading and Securities offers clients direct-access order execution and tools to help in electronic trading. Townsend Analytics' Real-Tick III is the professional software offered to clientele; Southwest Securities, Inc., is the clearing agent.

Customer Service Rating: ★★★ Excellent

PAINE WEBBER

Brokerage Type: Full-service brokerage
Mailing Address: The PaineWebber Building
1285 Avenue of Americas, 17th Floor
New York, NY 10019-6096
Web Address: www.painewebber.com
Email Address: edgeservice@painewebber.com
Telephone Number: 212-713-7800
Fax Number: None.
Market Orders: $1,250 minimum annual fee for Insight One Account up to 500% turnover of asset value.
Limit Orders: Same as market orders.
Option Trades: Broker-assisted only. Part of the Insight One Account annual fee.
Telephone Trading: No additional fee.
After-Hours Trading: Monday–Friday, 8:00 A.M. to 9:00 A.M. EST; Monday–Thursday, 4:30 P.M. to 6:30 P.M. Broker-assisted trades only. Commission charge is part of the Insight One Account annual fee.
Products Available to Trade Online: Stocks.
Average Execution Time: Market order: within 20 seconds, depending on market volatility, conditions, and volume traded.
Minimum Deposit Required: $50,000.
Additional Fees: May apply in certain cases.
Free Services and Financial Links: CBSMarketWatch.com, most active stocks, statistics, global brief, economic reports, IPO information, company news, company overview, key ratios, historic charts, intraday graphs, highlights, company research, portfolio tracker, E-lert Message Summary, Market Snapshot, Watch List, PaineWebber Spotlight, market summary.
Real-Time Quotes: Unlimited real-time quotes, although they are not streaming and must be refreshed.
States Registered In: All U.S. states.
Mutual Funds Offered: 90% of all mutual funds.
Payment for Order Flow: No.
Banking Services Offered: Free online bill payment through a Resource Management Account. Clients can also receive twenty free bill payments per month through a Business Service Account and will incur a $50.00 charge per bill payment thereafter.
Company Background: PaineWebber was originally founded in 1879 and is a full-service securities firm. Clients can trade online, via the

PaineWebber Edge, through a nondiscretionary, fee-based account called PaineWebber Insight One. PaineWebber Insight One is different from the average brokerage account; it combines personal service and advice with the access to trade for a single asset-based fee. Clients pay one flat fee instead of separate commission charges. PaineWebber is a member of the SIPC and protects clients' accounts up to $500,000, of which $100,000 is for cash coverage.
Customer Service Rating: ★★★ Excellent

PATAGON.COM

Brokerage Type: Discount brokerage
Mailing Address: Patagon.com Securities Corp.
At the Long Island Tech Center
3500 Sunrise Highway, Suite T200
Great River, NY 11739
Web Address: www.patagon.com
Email Address: info@Keytradeonline.com
Telephone Number: 888-539-8723
Fax Number: 631-501-0456
Market Orders: $12.00 per trade, exchange listed stocks, orders over 5,000 shares, and additional $0.01 per share on entire order.
Limit Orders: Same as market orders.
Option Trades: $20.00 per trade plus $1.50 per contract.
Telephone Trading: Stock trades: $25.00 per trade, exchange listed stocks over 5,000 shares, and additional $0.01 per share on entire order. Option trades: $25.00 per trade plus $1.50 per contract.
After-Hours Trading: None.
Products Available to Trade Online: Stocks, options, and mutual funds.
Average Execution Time: Market order: 5 seconds.
Minimum Deposit Required: None for cash account. $2,000 for margin account.
Additional Fees: Money wire outgoing: $10.00. Overnight check request: $10.00. Buy in/sell out: $10.00. Yearly inactivity fee: $50.00. Options exercise and assignment: $25.00. ACAT transfer out: $50.00. Returned checks: $10.00. Stop payment request on check: $10.00. Fees not listed here are negotiated as they occur.
Free Services and Financial Links: CBS MarketWatch, Market Snapshot, Thom Calandra's Stock Watch, Silicon Stocks and Tech Report,

Movers and Shakers, Analyst Opinion, Baseline, Lipper, News Alert, Standard & Poor's, Zacks, Stock Charts.com, Patagon.com, University, financial community page containing chat room and discussion boards.

Real-Time Quotes: Choice of streaming real-time quote packages. Clients receive 100 free quotes with each trade executed.

States Registered In: All U.S. states except ME (pending).

Mutual Funds Offered: Over 4,500.

Payment for Order Flow: Yes.

Banking Services Offered: None.

Company Background: Patagon.com has recently merged with the discount brokerage Keytrade Online, which was founded in 1997. Online trading at Keytrade began in 1999. Patagon has created a full-featured financial site that allows clients to buy and sell stocks, options, and mutual funds and also offers financial data suites. Clients' securities are held by Herzog, Heine, and Geduld Inc., and accounts are protected up to $500,000, of which $100,000 is for cash coverage, by SIPC. Additional coverage up to $24.5 million is provided by Herzog, Heine, and Geduld Inc. through a private insurer.

Customer Service Rating: ★★★ Excellent

Gomez Rating: 5.00

PEREMEL ONLINE

Brokerage Type: Discount brokerage

Mailing Address: Peremel & Company, Inc.
Woodholme Business Center
1829 Reisterstown Rd., Suite 120
Baltimore, MD 21208

Web Address: www.peremel.com

Email Address: info@peremel.com

Telephone Number: 877-PEREMEL, 410-486-4700

Fax Number: 410-486-4728

Market Orders: Peremel Direct Account: $18.00 per trade, up to 2,000 shares, and additional $0.01 per share on entire order thereafter. Peremel Personal Accounts: $38.00 per trade (up to 100 shares); $40.00 per trade (101–200 shares); $42.00 per trade (201–300 shares); $35.00 plus $0.03 per share (over 300 shares). Stocks under $1.00 per share: $35.00 plus 3% of principal.

Limit Orders: Same as market orders.

Option Trades: Peremel Direct Account: $25.00 plus $1.50 per contract (options trading under $4.00); $25.00 plus $2.00 per contract (options trading $4.00 and over). Peremel Personal Account: options trading under $1.00, $3.75 for any number of contracts; options trading over $1.00, $6.50 per option (1–10 contracts), $6.00 per option (11–20 contracts), $5.50 per option (21–49 contracts), $4.75 per option (50 and over contracts).

Telephone Trading: Stock trades: $38.00, up to 2,000 shares, and additional $0.02 per share on entire order thereafter. Option trades: options trading under $4.00, $35.00 plus $2.00 per contract; options trading $4.00 and over, $35.00 plus $2.50 per contract. Overriding minimum: $35.00.

After-Hours Trading: None.

Products Available to Trade Online: Stocks, options, and mutual funds.

Average Execution Time: Market order: within seconds, depending on stock.

Minimum Deposit Required: $2,000 for Peremel Account. $15,000 for VIP Account.

Additional Fees: Certificate: $15.00. Reorganization: $20.00. Legal transfer: $25.00. Redemption or call: $15.00. Outgoing wire payment: $20.00. Overnight delivery: $20.00. Returned check: $25.00. Stop payment: $25.00. Extension: $10.00. Mailgram: $15.00. Copy of confirmation or statement: $5.00. Postage and handling per trade: $2.75.

Free Services and Financial Links: Quotes on stocks, funds, and options; company and economic news; track personalized quote lists; customized stock charts; company profiles; market roundup; bond focus; market features; The Coming Week; Standard & Poor's Stock Reports; Morningstar Mutual Fund Reports; ValueLine Stock Reports; Personal Portfolio Analysis.

Real-Time Quotes: Real-time quotes.

States Registered In: All U.S. states.

Mutual Funds Offered: Over 7,000.

Payment for Order Flow: Yes, but not in all cases.

Banking Services Offered: Free check writing with a Money Market Account; free unlimited check writing and a VISA Gold debit card to access funds from over 240,000 ATM machines with a Peremel VIP Asset Management Account.

Company Background: Peremel & Company, Inc. was founded in 1974. It launched Peremel Online in 1998, offering clients discount savings, personal guidance and research, and 24-hours-a-day electronic access. Peremel Online utilizes Secure Socket Layer technology for a secure connection every time clients log in. Clients' accounts are protected by SIPC up to $500,000, of which $100,000 is for cash. Further coverage up to $100 million is provided by a private insurer.

Customer Service Rating: ★★★ Excellent

Gomez Rating: 5.72

POLAR TRADING

Brokerage Type: Direct-access brokerage

Mailing Address: 49 Macomb Place, Suite 200
Mt. Clemens, MI 48403

Web Address: www.polartrading.com

Email Address: customersupport@polartrading.com

Telephone Number: 877-771-POLR, 810-463-0140

Fax Number: 810-463-3151

Market Orders: $22.95 per trade (1–19 trades per month), $21.95 per trade (20–49 trades per month), $19.95 per trade (50–99 trades per month), $17.95 per trade (100–199 trades per month), $15.95 (200–399 trades per month), $14.95 per trade (400 or more trades per month). All trades are up to 2,000 shares; additional $0.01 per share thereafter.

Limit Orders: Same as market orders.

Option Trades: Broker-assisted only: lot size 1–5, $7.00 per option; lot size 6–20, $4.00 per option; lot size 21 or more, $3.00 per option. Minimum: $20.00 per trade.

Telephone Trading: Same commissions as online schedule.

After-Hours Trading: ARCA and Island: 8:00 A.M. to 9:30 A.M. EST and 4:00 P.M. to 8:00 P.M. EST. Instinet: 8:00 A.M. to 9:30 A.M. EST and 4:00 P.M. to 6:30 P.M. EST. $22.95 per trade plus 1½ cents per share.

Products Available to Trade Online: Stocks.

Average Execution Time: Market order: a few seconds, depending on market conditions, type of order being placed, order size, and methods of execution.

Minimum Deposit Required: $10,000. All accounts are established as margin accounts.

Additional Fees: Software and exchange fees: the "Full" Polar Trader including Turbo Options, $300.00 (1–19 trades per month), $100.00 (20–49 trades per month), free (50 or more trades per month); the "Fixed Page" Polar Trader, $225.00 (1–19 trades per month), free (20 or more trades per month); the Polar Trader Jr., $125.00 (1–19 trades per month), free (20 or more trades per month). Polar Turbo Options is included in the "Full" Polar Trader at no additional costs but requires either CBOT or OPRA exchange-data fees. Optional exchange fees: CEM futures, $10.00 (fee waived upon placing 50 trades per month); CBOT, $30.00; OPRA, $2.50. ECN fees: Instinet (INCA), $0.0150 per share. Returned check: $15.00. Stop payment within 10 days: $10.00. IRA termination fee: $25.00. Registry and delivery of certificate: $15.00. Overnight delivery: $16.55. Foreign transfer (ACAT), $25.00–50.00. Wire domestic: $15.00. Wire foreign: $35.00.

Free Services and Financial Links: TheStreet.com, Baseline, NewsAlert, Businesswire, Futures World News, M2 Newswire, Newsbytes, PR Newswire, Reuters, UPI, U.S. Newswire, AM Best, Edgar Online, Electronic Traders Association, Equity Analytics, Internal Revenue Service, Internet Traffic Report, Nasdaq, Nasdaq SEC Investor Education, VIWesInvest Info—short positions, ZDNet, Chicago Board Options Exchange, Chicago Board of Trade, Chicago Mercantile Exchange.

Real-Time Quotes: Streaming real-time quotes with software package.

States Registered In: All U.S. states.

Mutual Funds Offered: None.

Payment for Order Flow: No.

Banking Services Offered: Banking services through a separate account.

Company Background: Polar Trading.com, a privately owned electronic stock trading company, was founded in August 1997. Polar Trading is a branch of Terra Nova Trading, which offers all securities. Polar Trading utilizes Southwest Securities as its clearing firm. The electronic trading software offered to clients allows access to trade through SOES, other ECNs, and Super Dot linked to Nasdaq, NYSE, and Amex. Polar Trading offers Polar Ice, an internet continuing education program that consists of self-paced modules, structured courses, and special seminars to give a trader the skills, strategies, and experience to become a successful trader. Some modules are free of charge, but others incur a fee. Polar Trader also offers a special "Novice Trader" commission, which is available upon request for 60 days from the date an account is opened and includes Polar Ice, free bimonthly on-site seminars, free monthly online classes, free weekly chat, and free education modules. This offer does not include any software or third-party rebates. Clients' accounts are protected up to $25 million per account.

SIPC provides up to $500,000, of which $100,000 is for cash coverage, and National Union Fire Insurance Company provides the remaining $24.5 million.

Customer Service Rating: ★★★ Excellent

PREFERRED TRADE

Brokerage Type: Direct access
Mailing Address: 220 Montgomery St. Suite 777
         San Francisco, CA 94104
Web Address: www.deltatrader.com
Email Address: preferredtrade@preftech.com
Telephone Number: 888-781-0233, 415-73-3000
Fax Number: 415-398-5428
Market Orders: Nasdaq OTC: $7.75 flat rate per trade on eligible Nasdaq orders. Auto trade: $0.02 per share, up to 2,000 shares, and additional $0.01 per share thereafter; $15.00 minimum. New York listed: $0.02 per share, up to 2,000 shares, and additional $0.01 per share thereafter; $15.00 minimum. All listed orders subject to a minimum of $15.00 per trade.
Limit Orders: Nasdaq OTC: $7.75 flat rate per trade on eligible Nasdaq orders. Auto trade: $0.02 per share, up to 2,000 shares, and additional $0.01 per share thereafter; $15.00 minimum. New York listed: $0.03 per share, up to 2,000 shares, and additional $0.01 per share thereafter; $15.00 minimum. All orders subject to a minimum of $15.00 per trade.
Option Trades: Options trading up to $10.00: $2.00 per contract. Options trading at $10.00 and above: $3.00 per contract. Minimum: $19.95 per option order.
Telephone Trading: Same commissions as online schedule.
After-Hours Trading: 9:00 A.M. to 9:30 A.M. EST and 4:00 P.M. to 5:00 P.M. EST. $0.03 per share with a minimum of $35.00 per order. Broker-assisted (limit orders only).
Products Available to Trade Online: Stocks and options.
Average Execution Time: Market order: 0.5 seconds to 1 minute, depending on security traded time ranges.
Minimum Deposit Required: $5,000 for cash account, and funds must be available in the account before trading. $5,000 for margin account.
Additional Fees: Sending securities in certificate form: $15.00 per item. Returned check fee: $20.00. Inactive fee (if less than 3 trades per year): $35.00. Outward money wire or express mail transfers: $20.00. IRA set

up: $25.00. IRA termination: $100.00. IRA annual maintenance: $45.00.

Free Services and Financial Links: Options quotes, news, charts, equity reviews, trade listing of orders, trading tutorial, Yahoo Finance, TheStreet.com, the Motley Fool, interactive investor, Bloomberg, Hoovers Online, Multex, Zacks, Standard & Poor's, Options Clearing Corp., Options Industry Council, the Options Strategist, OptionInvestor.com.

Real-Time Quotes: Access to many leading quote system providers, and clients can subscribe to those services.

States Registered In: All U.S. states.

Mutual Funds Offered: Several.

Payment for Order Flow: No; payment is not received when placing trade through Auto Trade System. Yes; payment is received for directing $7.75 orders to a third-party dealer.

Banking Services Offered: None.

Company Background: Preferred Capital Markets, Inc., was founded in 1982. Preferred Trade online trading software was launched in May 1997. Preferred Trade currently has over 11,000 online accounts, with a majority being individual users. Preferred Trade utilizes Preferred Capital as its clearing firm. Clients' accounts are protected by SIPC up to $500,000, of which $100,000 is for cash coverage, and additional coverage is provided by an independent firm. Preferred Trade caters to the active investor. Clients can use the Auto Trade System, which automatically routes the order in various ways to search for the best liquidity depending on the pricing for the order; or, depending on if it is a listed stock, an OTC stock, or an option, users can choose to override the automated option routing and route orders to a specific exchange for execution.

Customer Service Rating: ★★★ Excellent

PRUDENTIAL SECURITIES

Brokerage Type: Full-service brokerage
Mailing Address: 1 Seaport Plaza
New York, NY 10292
Web Address: www.prudentialsecurities.com
Email Address: prumaster@prusec.com
Telephone Number: 800-PRUSEC2, 800-778-7322
Fax Number: None.

Market Orders: Prudential Advisor: Asset-based annual fee is based on the total assets in the portfolio. $50,000–249,999 in assets: Asset Group A, 1.500%; Asset Group B, 0.750%. $250,000–499,999 in assets: Asset Group A, 1.250%; Asset Group B, 0.625%. $500,000–999,999 in assets: Asset Group A, 1.000%; Asset Group B, 0.500%. $1,000,000–1,999,999 in assets: Asset Group A, 0.900%; Asset Group B, 0.450%. $2,000,000–4,999,999 in assets: Asset Group A, 0.750%; Asset Group B, 0.375%. $5,000,000–24,999,999 in assets: Asset Group A, 0.600%; Asset Group B, 0.300%. $25,000,000–74,999,999 in assets: Asset Group A, 0.500%; Asset Group B, 0.250%. $75,000,000–124,999,999 in assets: Asset Group A, 0.400%; Asset Group B, 0.200%. $125,000,000–174,999,999 in assets: Asset Group A, 0.300%; Asset Group B, 0.150%. $175,000,000 or more in assets: Asset Group A, 0.250%; Asset Group B, 0.125%. Group A includes common stock, mutual funds, cash-covered options, and all others not included in Group B. Group B includes corporate bonds, government bonds, municipal bonds, preferred securities, and mortgage-backed securities. $24.95 per trade transaction fee applies to each trade.

Limit Orders: Same as market orders. $24.95 per trade, up to 2,000 shares, and additional $0.01 per share thereafter.

Option Trades: Same as Prudential Advisor schedule.

Telephone Trading: Same as Prudential Advisor schedule.

After-Hours Trading: 4:00 P.M. to 6:30 P.M. EST. Same commissions as online schedule.

Products Available to Trade Online: Stocks, options, and mutual funds.

Average Execution Time: Market order: very high speed.

Minimum Deposit Required: Prudential Advisor: $50,000. Prudential Advisor II: $100,000.

Additional Fees: Contact Prudential Securities.

Free Services and Financial Links: Research reports, analyst notes, Dow Jones News Retrieval Service, daily market commentaries, Standard & Poor's, Zacks Equity Research, Lipper Mutual Fund Portfolio Analysis, new issue listing, portfolio reviews, access to PSIs select list.

Real-Time Quotes: Free real-time quotes, although they are not streaming and need to be refreshed.

States Registered In: All U.S. states.

Mutual Funds Offered: Over 7,000.

Payment for Order Flow: No.

Banking Services Offered: Banking services through a Command Account, which will consolidate both the clients' investment portfolios and their banking needs in one account. Account features are a state of the art statement, online account access, bill payment, check writing, and a VISA card.

Company Background: Prudential Securities Incorporated is a fully diversified global securities firm serving clients in the United States and overseas. Prudential Securities offers online trading through Prutrade, an Internet-based trading system. Clients can trade online while still fully utilizing a financial advisor for expert guidance. In May 1999 Prudential Securities began offering Prudential Advisor, an innovative investment advisory program. This program charges clients an asset-based fee, and the program enables enrolled investors to execute most trades for $24.95 per trade. The program separates the cost of advice and execution, enabling clients to understand clearly what the firm charges for each of its services. The firms financial advisors will be compensated for advice, not clients' trading activities. Prudential Securities also offers Prudential Advisor II, a discretionary wrap fee program with an asset-based advisory fee that is negotiable between the financial advisor and the client, and no fee for transactions.

Customer Service Rating: ★★★ Excellent

QUICK & REILLY ONLINE

Brokerage Type: Discount brokerage
Mailing Address: 26 Broadway
                      New York, NY 10004-1899
Web Address: www.qronline.com
Email Address: info@quick-reilly.com
Telephone Number: 800-539-0409, 212-753-1289
Fax Number: 212-753-9203
Market Orders: $14.95 per trade, up to 5,000 shares, and additional $0.02 per share thereafter.
Limit Orders: $19.95 per trade, up to 5,000 shares, and additional $0.02 per share thereafter.
Option Trades: 10% discount off broker-assisted commission for Internet trades.
Telephone Trading: Stock trades: $0–2,500 principal amount, $22.00 plus .014 times principal; $2,501–6,000 principal amount, $38.00 plus .0045 times principal; $6,001–22,000 principal amount, $59.00 plus .0025 times principal; $22,001–50,000 principal amount, $77.00

plus .0017 times principal; $50,001–500,000 principal amount, $120.00 plus .00085 times principal; $500,001 or more principal amount, $205.00 plus .00068 times principal. $37.50 per trade minimum overriding commission. Option trades: $0–2,500 principal amount, $29.00 plus .016 times principal; $2,501–10,000 principal amount, $49.00 plus .008 times principal; $10,001 or more principal amount, $99.00 plus .003 times principal. Overriding minimum $37.50 plus $1.75 per contract.

After-Hours Trading: None.

Products Available to Trade Online: Stocks, options, mutual funds, and U.S. Treasury bills.

Average Execution Time: Market order: 2–3 seconds; often less than 1 second.

Minimum Deposit Required: None for online account, but an acceptable deposit may be required prior to the acceptance of any order.

Additional Fees: Communication mailgrams: $5.00. Returned checks: $10.00. Registration of stock certificates: $15.00. Duplicate copies of monthly statements: $5.00 first page, $2.00 each additional page. Stopped check: $7.50. Wiring of funds: $15.00. IRA transfer: $50.00. Galaxy Money Reserve checks returned: $12.00. Duplicate copies of checks over six months ago: $10.00.

Free Services and Financial Links: Reuters, Big Charts, Zacks, Baseline, MarketEdge, Briefing.com, portfolio tracker, Investools, Market updates, no-fee check writing, economic indicators, hot stocks, international market summary, no-fee for life IRAs, free dividend reinvestment, Lipper.

Real-Time Quotes: Free real-time quotes, although they are not streaming and need to be refreshed.

States Registered In: All U.S. states.

Mutual Funds Offered: Over 3,000.

Payment for Order Flow: No.

Banking Services Offered: Free check writing through a Quick Assets Management Service. Clients also can set up a joint account with Fleet Bank to utilize a fully integrated Internet Banking & Internet Brokerage combined account.

Company Background: Quick & Reilly was founded in 1974. Quick & Reilly went online in 1984 and launched online trading in 1996. Clients' accounts are protected up to $100 million. Quick & Reilly utilizes U.S. Clearing as its clearing firm. Quick & Reilly's clientele consists mainly of individuals and has 1.3 million accounts in the firm overall, approximately 150,000 of which are active Internet trading accounts.

Customer Service Rating: ★★★ Excellent
Gomez Rating: 6.09

RJT.COM

Brokerage Type: Discount brokerage
Mailing Address: R. J. Thompson Securities, Inc.
13305 Birch Ave. Suite 200
Omaha, NE 68164
Web Address: www.rjt.com
Email Address: newaccounts@rjy.com
Telephone Number: 800-273-3212, 402-951-2600
Fax Number: 800-273-3025
Market Orders: $5.00 per trade, flat rate.
Limit Orders: Same as market orders.
Option Trades: $20.00 per trade plus $2.00 per contract.
Telephone Trading: Stock trades: $15.00 per trade. Option trades: $20.00 per trade plus $5.00 per contract.
After-Hours Trading: None.
Products Available to Trade Online: Stocks, options, and mutual funds.
Average Execution Time: Market order: 2.8–5.1 seconds. Rjt.com provides its clients with a detailed chart of their current execution speeds.
Minimum Deposit Required: $2,000 for cash or margin account.
Additional Fees: Returned checks: $20.00. Stop payment: $15.00. Transfer out: $50.00. Partial DTC transfer fee in: $6.00 per position. Partial DTC transfer fee out: $25.00 per position. Annual IRA fee: $35.00. Wire fee: $15.00. Mailgrams: $15.00. Voluntary reorganization: $20.00. Duplicate copies of monthly statements: $5.00 per item. Duplicate copies of confirmations: $5.00 per item. Certificate registration and delivery: $50.00. Overnight mail: $20.00. Foreign securities transfer fee: $75.00 plus any additional transfer agent fee. Foreign ordinary shares registration fee: $70.00 per position. Copies of checks: $5.00.
Free Services and Financial Links: Free postage and handling, involuntary reorganization, links to exchanges, government documents, investor education, links to IPOs. Market data: Bigcharts.com, Bloomberg.com. Mutual Funds: Morningstar.net, Findafund.com. News: Abcnews.com, Cbs.marketwatch.com, Cnnfn.com, Ft.com, Foxmarketwire.com, Msnbc.com, Thestreet.com. Options: Cboe.com,

Optionscentral.com, Optionsource.com. Research tools: Bestcalls.com, Companiesonline.com, Companysleuth.com, Contingencyanalysis. com, Earningswhispers.com, Multex.com, Rapidsearch.com, zacks.com. Technical analysis: Clearstation.com.

Real-Time Quotes: Free unlimited streaming real-time quotes.

States Registered In: All U.S. states.

Mutual Funds Offered: Thousands.

Payment for Order Flow: Yes, Nasdaq.

Banking Services Offered: None.

Company Background: R. J. Thompson, Inc., a brokerage/dealer registered with the NASD and SEC, was founded in 1999, launched rjt.com online services in April 2000, and currently executes over 4,000 trades per day. Clients' accounts are protected up to $2.5 million per account. The SPIC provides coverage up to $500,000, of which $100,000 is for cash coverage. Additional coverage up to $2 million is provided by clearing agent Kirkpatrick Pettis.

Customer Service Rating: ★★★ Excellent

Gomez Rating: 3.83

RML TRADING, INC.

Brokerage Type: Discount brokerage

Mailing Address: 12503 Bel Red Road, Suite 101
Bellevue, WA 98005

Web Address: www.rmltrading.com

Email Address: info@rmltrading.com

Telephone Number: 888-765-4403, 425-456-0186

Fax Number: 425-452-0312

Market Orders: OTC stocks: $14.95 per trade. Listed stocks: $14.95 per trade plus $0.01 per share.

Limit Orders: Same as market orders.

Option Trades: $19.95 per trade plus $2.00 per contract. Broker-assisted trades only.

Telephone Trading: RML will accommodate clients placing trades under certain circumstances over the phone. $19.95 per trade.

After-Hours Trading: 8:00 A.M. to 9:30 A.M. EST and 4:00 P.M. to 8:00 P.M. EST. $14.95 per trade.

Products Available to Trade Online: Stocks and mutual funds.

Average Execution Time: Market order: approximately 10 seconds, subject to volatility of the market.

Minimum Deposit Required: $10,000 for all accounts.

Additional Fees: Additional news: $75.00 per month. Funds wired out: within the U.S., $15.00; International, $50.00. Overnight delivery: $13.50. Nonmandatory reorganization: $10.00. Regulation T extension: $10.00. Returned check: $20.00. Stop payment on check: $20.00. Transfer of accounts outbound: ACAT fee, $5.00. Extensions: $10.00. IRA fees: mailgrams, $25.00 to open and $40.00 per year. Option assignment fee: $19.00 per trade plus $2.00 per contract. Foreign security safekeeping: $25.00 per account with less than 2 trades per year.

Free Services and Financial Links: All active trading accounts receive live audio-video support from the Stockcam; training manuals, charts, news, CBS Marketwatch.

Real-Time Quotes: Real-time quotes for a fee. Package one offers streaming Level I quotes for $100.00 per month; RML will rebate the fee to $25.00 with 25–49 trades per month or waive the entire fee with 50 or more trades per month. Package two offers streaming Level I quotes for $125.00 per month; RML will rebate the fee to $50.00 with 25–49 trades per month or waive the entire fee with 50 or more trades per month. Package three offers streaming Level II quotes for $225.00 per month; RML will rebate the fee to $150.00 with 25–49 trades per month or to $75.00 with 50–99 trades per month or waive the entire fee with 100 or more trades per month. Package four offers streaming Level II quotes for $300.00 per month; RML will rebate the fee to $225.00 with 25–49 trades, to $150.00 with 50–99 trades, or to $75.00 with 100–199 trades per month or waive the entire fee with 200 or more trades per month. Packages include other research and data services.

States Registered In: All U.S. states except HI, ME, MN, MO, and PR.

Mutual Funds Offered: Many.

Payment for Order Flow: RML was unable to answer this question.

Banking Services Offered: Check writing.

Company Background: RML Trading was founded in July 1998 and launched online trading in October 1998. Clients at RML consist mainly of individuals, but include several corporations as well as a few partnerships and a few IRAs, although RML does not recommend day trading an IRA. RML caters to active day/swing traders, so the majority of its business is in securities trading. The Realtick III software platform that RML uses allows clients to have full control of how and when they trade. The client is directly connected to the market via the ECN routes. RML uses ARCA, ISLD, ISI, and SOES. Clients' accounts are protected by SIPC up to $100,000 in cash coverage and up to $24 million in securities.

Customer Service Rating: ★★★ Excellent

RT TRADER

Brokerage Type: Direct-access brokerage
Mailing Address: InvestIN Securities Corp.
Infomart, Suite 2016
1950 Stemmons Frwy.
Dallas, TX 75207
Web Address: www.rttrading.com
Email Address: investin@investin.com
Telephone Number: 800-327-1883, 214-939-0110
Fax Number: 214-939-0116
Market Orders: $13.95 per trade (1–100 trades per month), $12.95 per trade (101–200 trades per month), $11.95 per trade (201–250 trades per month), $10.95 per trade (251–300 trades per month), $9.95 per trade (301 or more trades per month).
Limit Orders: Same as market orders.
Option Trades: $25.00 per trade plus $1.75 per contract.
Telephone Trading: $10.00 additional surcharge.
After-Hours Trading: 8:00 A.M. to 9:30 A.M. EST and 4:00 P.M. to 6:30 P.M. EST. Same commissions as online schedule.
Products Available to Trade Online: Stocks and options (through InvestINOptions.com).
Average Execution Time: Market order: instantaneous, depending on security being traded.
Minimum Deposit Required: $10,000.
Additional Fees: RT Trader software fee: $50.00 per month, waived upon placing 10 or more trades per month. ECN fees: Island (Nasdaq), $1.00 per trade; Island (NYSE listed), $1.00 per trade; Archipelego (direct-access connection plus ECN charges), $1.00 per trade and $0.0075 per share; SOES, $0.50 per trade; SelectNet (preference), $1.00 per trade; SelectNet (broadcast), $2.50 per trade; NYSE listed, $0.008 per share; SelectNet (Instinet), $1.00 per trade and $0.015 per share; SelectNet (Btrade), $1.00 per trade and $0.015 per share; SelectNet (Archipelego), $1.00 per trade and $0.0075 per share; SelectNet (Spear Leads), $1.00 per trade and $0.015 per share; SelectNet (Brass), $6.50 per trade; SelectNet (Attain), $1.00 per trade and $0.015 per share; SelectNet (Strike), $1.00 per trade and $0.0066 per

share; SelectNet (Nextrade), $1.00 per trade and $0.015 per share; SOES-SelectNet cancels, $0.25 per trade. Wire fees: $15.00. Rule 144 sales: $35.00 surcharge. ACAT: $5.00 per account, outgoing. Safekeeping charge (customer accounts with securities in the account, and less than 2 trades during a calendar year): $25.00.

Free Services and Financial Links: InvestIN News, Nasdaq, NewsTraders.com, Briefing.com.

Real-Time Quotes: Direct line to Nasdaq that accesses streaming real-time quotes called the Nasdaq Quotation Dissemination Service.

States Registered In: All U.S. states.

Mutual Funds Offered: All.

Payment for Order Flow: No.

Banking Services Offered: None.

Company Background: InvestIn Securities Corp. is a fully disclosed brokerage/dealer that provides direct-access trading to investors. InvestIn offers clients software through RT Trader to trade directly to the financial markets. Smart Order Routing, which immediately dispatches the order to any market maker or ECN offering to buy or sell at the best possible price, is also available to clients. The RT Smart software package includes Trade Manager, Account Manager, Top List, Charts, Ticker, Trading Window, ECN Book, and Time and Sales. The RT Trader software package includes Trade Manager, Account Manager, Market Minder, Top List, Charts, Trading Window, Ticker, Position Minder, Time of Sales, and ECN Book. Clients' accounts are protected up to $500,000, of which $100,000 is for cash coverage, provided by SIPC. Additional coverage up to $24.5 million is provided by Penson Financial Services.

Customer Service Rating: ★★★ Excellent

SALOMON SMITH BARNEY, INC.

Brokerage Type: Full-service brokerage

Mailing Address: 388 Greenwich Street
New York, NY 10013

Web Address: www.smithbarney.com

Email Address: None.

Telephone Number: 212-615-9544

Fax Number: None.

Market Orders: Asset One Account: annual fee ranging from 0.5% to 1.5%, based on eligible account value.

Limit Orders: Same as market orders.

Option Trades: Check with local branch.

Telephone Trading: Check with local branch.

After-Hours Trading: 4:30 P.M. to 8:00 P.M. EST.

Products Available to Trade Online: Stocks, bonds, options, closed-end funds, ADRs, foreign equities, select mutual funds, and UITs.

Average Execution Time: Not divulged.

Minimum Deposit Required: $100,000 for Asset One Account.

Additional Fees: Not divulged.

Free Services and Financial Links: Free dividend reinvestment, quarterly performance reporting, financial management account, waived IRA annual fee, watch list, Bill Pay, investment ideas, financial planning, research, market commentaries, Young Investors Network, Dow Jones News, free 24-hour access to your portfolio.

Real-Time Quotes: Real-time quotes with online account.

States Registered In: All U.S. states.

Mutual Funds Offered: Thousands.

Payment for Order Flow: Not divulged.

Banking Services Offered: Asset One Account: complimentary Financial Management Account, which offers clients direct online access and bill payment services through Quicken and Microsoft Money. The services offered are balancing checkbooks, paying bills, organizing financial statements, and tracking expenses. Clients with an Asset One Select Account have access to an FMA Card, unlimited check writing, and electronic funds transfers and direct deposits.

Company Background: Salomon Smith Barney was founded in 1873, and online Trading was first offered in Fall 1999. Salomon Smith Barney offers its online clientele the Asset One Account, which allows the client to pay one annual fee based on the value of the client's eligible program assets. The fee is billed quarterly and allows the client to buy and sell a large range of securities and eligible mutual funds without individual commission costs. Online clients who have a less active trading profile and a minimum account size of $1 million can open the Asset One Select Account. This account is tailored to meet the needs of the high–net worth investor.

Customer Service Rating: ★★ Average

SCOTTRADE

Brokerage Type: Discount brokerage

Mailing Address: 2780 Middle Country Rd. #211
Lake Grove, NY 11755-2121

Web Address: www.scottrade.com
Email Address: support@scottrade.com
Telephone Number: 800-619-SAVE
Fax Number: 314-909-9227
Market Orders: $7.00 per trade (stocks priced above $1.00). All stocks priced under $1.00: $22.00 plus 2% of principal, must be placed with a broker. All bulletin board and foreign stocks over $1.00: $22.00 plus $0.02 per share, must be placed with a broker.
Limit Orders: $12.00 per trade (stocks priced above $1.00). All stocks priced under $1.00: $22.00 plus 2% of principal, must be placed with a broker. All bulletin board and foreign stocks over $1.00: $22.00 plus $0.02 per share, must be placed with a broker.
Option Trades: $20.00 plus $1.60 per contract.
Telephone Trading: Market order: $17.00 per trade. Limit order: $22.00 per trade.
After-Hours Trading: 4:15 P.M. to 6:30 P.M. EST. Commission free.
Products Available to Trade Online: Stocks, options, mutual funds, and CDs.
Average Execution Time: Market order: within a few seconds.
Minimum Deposit Required: $500.00 for cash account. $2,000 for margin account.
Additional Fees: Wired funds: $20.00. Returned check: $15.00. Legal item: $25.00. Certificate delivered out: $25.00. Accommodation transfer: $25.00. Nonmandatory reorganization: $25.00. Termination of IRA account: $60.00. Sell-out notice: $15.00. Overnight fees: $15.00. Outgoing account transfer: $25.00. Stock reregistration: $25.00. Duplicate statement: $3.00. Roth IRA deconversion fee: $50.00. Regular mail confirmation: $1.00. Fed Ex overnight delivery: $15.00. Option assignment and exercise: $17.00. IRA closing fee: $60.00. Sell out notice: $15.00.
Free Services and Financial Links: Charts, Zacks, news, Briefing.com, Edgar, Vickers, Reuters, market commentary, portfolio.
Real-Time Quotes: 100 free real-time quotes with new account and 100 free real-time quotes for each trade placed. The free quotes are not streaming and must be refreshed. Scottrade has arrangements through North American Quotations to offer unlimited streaming real-time quotes for $30.00 per month plus exchange fees. Unlimited 20-minute delayed quotes are also available to clients.
States Registered In: All U.S. states.
Mutual Funds Offered: Over 200 families.

Payment for Order Flow: Information not available according to Scottrade.

Banking Services Offered: Free check writing.

Company Background: Scottsdale Securities, Inc., was established in 1980 and changed its name to Scottrade in fall 1997. The company currently has 105 branch offices nationwide. Scottrade protects clients' accounts up to $5 million, provided by SIPC. Additional coverage of $4.5 million is provided by a supplemental insurance company.

Customer Service Rating: ★★★ Excellent

SMARTVEST

Brokerage Type: Discount brokerage

Mailing Address: H & R Block Financial Corporation, Inc.
751 Griswold, Suite 200
Detroit, MI 48226-3274

Web Address: www.smartvest.com

Email Address: customerservice@smartvest.com

Telephone Number: 800-249-5500

Fax Number: 313-961-2211

Market Orders: $19.95 per trade, up to 2,500 shares, and additional $0.01 per share thereafter.

Limit Orders: $24.95 per trade, up to 2,500 shares, and additional $0.01 per share thereafter.

Option Trades: $19.95 per trade plus $2.50 per contract.

Telephone Trading: Stock trades: $45.00 per trade, up to 2,500 shares, and additional $0.01 per share thereafter. Option trades: $35.00 per trade plus $2.50 per contract.

After-Hours Trading: None.

Products Available to Trade Online: Stocks, options, and mutual funds.

Average Execution Time: Market order: within seconds, depending on stock being traded.

Minimum Deposit Required: $2,500 for standard brokerage account.

Additional Fees: Certificate delivery: $25.00 per certificate. Certificate special registration: $15.00 per certificate. Checks: photocopy, $2.00; returned check, $25.00; stop payment, $25.00 (no charge if check is cashed within 10 days). Duplicate confirm statement: $2.00. Foreign securities: $50.00. IRA closing fee: $50.00 (no transfer out fee if closing fee is charged). Legal item (death, estate stock, same-name affidavit); $15.00 minimum. Overnight courier: $15.00 weekdays, $20.00 Saturday (foreign address at cost). Mandatory reorganization: $20.00. Non-mandatory reorganization: $40.00. Account transfer out: $50.00 (no charge if transferred to OLDE). Wired funds out: $25.00.

Free Services and Financial Links: No Canadian stock fee, free dividend reinvestment, no-fee account transfer in or wire in, Standard & Poor's research, Quote.com, Zacks, stock screening, technical analysis, historical quotes, portfolio monitor, account activity filters, investor education, prepopulated stock order screen, mutual fund selector, investment glossary.

Real-Time Quotes: 200 real-time quotes with new account and 100 more with each security purchase or sale. If quote bank is depleted, clients can purchase real-time quotes for a fee of $5.00 per 100 quotes. Quotes are not streaming and must be refreshed. Unlimited delayed quotes are also available to clients.

States Registered In: All U.S. states except FL.

Mutual Funds Offered: Thousands.

Payment for Order Flow: Yes.

Banking Services Offered: None.

Company Background: Through a recent acquisition of Olde Financial Corporation, H & R Block now provides financial planning and investment services to millions of clients. H & R Block launched online trading through SmartVest.com in January 2000. The clientele base at SmartVest consists mainly of individuals. SmartVest utilizes OLDE Discount Corporation as its clearing firm. Clients' accounts are protected up to $25 million, with SIPC protection up to $500,000, of which $100,000 is for cash, and the remaining $24.5 million is provided by National Union.

Customer Service Rating: ★★★ Excellent

Gomez Rating: 5.32

STOCKWALK.COM

Brokerage Type: Discount brokerage

Mailing Address: Stockwalk.com Inc.
5500 Wayzata Blvd., 6th fl., Suite 620
Minneapolis, MN 55416

Web Address: www.stockwalk.com

Email Address: custservice@stockwalk.com

Telephone Number: 800-259-2800

Fax Number: 800-259-9250

Market Orders: $18.95 per trade, 5,000 shares or less, and additional $0.01 per share on entire order thereafter. Stocks under $1.00 per share: $25.00 plus 1% of principal amount.

Limit Orders: Same as market orders.

Option Trades: Options trading: less than $1.00 per contract, $27.50 plus $1.75 per contract; $1.00–3.78 per contract, $27.50 plus $3.00 per contract; $4.00 and up per contract, $30.00 plus $3.00 per contract.

Telephone Trading: Stock trades: $34.00 per trade plus $0.02 per share. Stocks under $1.00 per share: $25.00 plus 1% of the principal amount. Option trades: less than $1.00 per contract, $27.50 plus $1.75 per contract; $1.00–3.875 per contract, $27.50 plus $3.00 per contract; $4.00 and up per contract, $30.00 plus $3.00 per contract.

After-Hours Trading: 7:30 A.M. to 8:30 A.M. CST and 3:00 P.M. to 5:30 P.M. CST. Broker-assisted trading and limit orders only.

Products Available to Trade Online: Stocks, options, and mutual funds.

Average Execution Time: Market order: 15 seconds, depending on stock and volatility.

Minimum Deposit Required: $1,000 for cash account. $2,000 for margin account.

Additional Fees: Options exercise and assignments: 1–4,999 shares, $34.00; 5,000–19,999 shares, $50.00; 20,000 or more shares, $100.00. Debit card: $50.00 per year with an account balance under $10,000. IRA termination fee: $50.00. Returned check fee: $25.00. Buy in/sell out notices: $15.00. Outgoing money wires: domestic, $30.00; foreign, $50.00. Outgoing DTC transfer: $750.00. Voluntary reorganizations: $35.00. Called bonds: $30.00. Name change request on stock certificate: $20.00. Legal transfer fee: $20.00. Extra statement copies: $7.50 per statement. Copy of check: $5.00. Stop payment of individual check: $15.00. Stop payment of block range of checks: $25.00 per block. Regulation T late payment: $10.00 per trade.

Free Services and Financial Links: Charts, company news, company info, analysts reports, insider trading, message board, industry groups, options reports, fund screening, mutual fund techniques, Market Snap Shot, portfolio performance, tools and alerts, financial updates.

Real-Time Quotes: Real-time quotes, although they are not streaming and must be refreshed.

States Registered In: All U.S. states except ME.

Mutual Funds Offered: Over 3,000 funds from 200–250 families.

Payment for Order Flow: No.

Banking Services Offered: Free check writing and a debit card through a money market account. There is no minimum deposit required, but the client will be charged an annual fee if the account has less than $10,000.

Company Background: Stockwalk.com Group, Inc., is a publicly traded company that was founded in 1981. It launched its online trading in 1999 with Nasdaq under the symbol STOK. Stockwalk.com protects clients' accounts up to $20 million. SIPC provides protection up to $500,000, of which $100,000 is for cash, and the remaining $19.5 million is provided by Lloyd's of London.

Customer Service Rating: ★★★ Excellent

Gomez Rating: 5.24

STOXNOW

Brokerage Type: Direct-access brokerage

Mailing Address: 7464 E. Tierra Buena Ln. #203
Scottsdale, AZ 85260

Web Address: www.stoxnow.com

Email Address: info@stoxnow.com

Telephone Number: 877-872-3372, 480-991-7979

Fax Number: 480-991-3705

Market Orders: $16.95 per trade (1–100 trades per month); $15.95 per trade (101–200 trades per month); $14.95 per trade (201–300 trades per month); $13.95 per trade (301–500 trades per month); $9.95 per trade (501 or more trades per month). Up to 1,000 shares, and additional $0.01 per share thereafter.

Limit Orders: Same as market orders.

Option Trades: $25.00 per trade plus $1.75 per contract minimum.

Telephone Trading: $4.00 additional surcharge.

After-Hours Trading: 8:00 A.M. to 9:30 A.M. EST and 4:00 P.M. to 6:00 P.M. EST. Same commissions as online schedule.

Products Available to Trade Online: Stocks and options.

Average Execution Time: Market order: depends on market conditions.

Minimum Deposit Required: $10,000 for all accounts.

Additional Fees: Software fees: Traderunner, $115.00 per month;

TraderPro, $250.00 per month (21 or more trades per month, $100.00 rebate: 51 or more trades per month, $250.00 rebate). ECN fees: NYSE listed, $0.008 per share; SOES, $0.50; Island, $1.00. SelectNet (preference): $1.00. SelectNet (broadcast): $2.50. Instinet-Bloomberg-REDI-Attain-NTRD: $1.00 plus $0.015 per share. Archipelago (ARCA): $1.00 plus $0.0075 per share. Strike (STRK): $1.00 plus $0.0066 per share. Brass Utility (BRUT): $6.50. Options exercise and assignments: $19.95. Overnight mail: $15.00. Wire transfer: $15.00. Wiring funds: $20.00. Outgoing account transfer: $25.00. Stop payment: $15.00. Returned check fee: $40.00. Legal transfer: $25.00. Regulation T extension: $5.00. Copies of back statements: $5.00.

Free Services and Financial Links: Easy Runner software package.

Real-Time Quotes: Streaming real-time Level II quotes with software package.

States Registered In: All U.S. states except NH and PR.

Mutual Funds Offered: None.

Payment for Order Flow: No.

Banking Services Offered: None.

Company Background: Stoxnow is a branch office of InvestIN.com and was founded in 1998. Stoxnow provides its predominantly individual trader clientele with real-time execution and trading systems. The direct-access trading system provided is TraderPro, which includes the following features: Level II quotes, Trade Scout predefined order routing system, direct access to ISLD and ARCA, access to ECNs and Instinet, complete charting and analytic packages, and detailed trade blotters and position managers. Stoxnow also offers its clientele a free software package, Easy Runner, which includes Level I products such as best bid and ask and real-time data. Clients' accounts are protected up to $25 million per account.

Customer Service Rating: ★★★ Excellent

SUNLOGIC SECURITIES

Brokerage Type: Discount brokerage

Mailing Address: Sunlogic Securities, Inc.
5333 Thornton Ave.
Newark, CA 94560

Web Address: www.sunlogic.com

Email Address: newaccount@sunlogic.com

Telephone Number: 800-556-4600

Fax Number: 510-793-0436

Market Orders: Nasdaq: $15.99 per trade, flat fee, round-lot only, security at $1.00 or more. Listed: $0.02 per share, $15.99 minimum.

Limit Orders: Nasdaq: $0.01 per share, $32.00 minimum, round-lot only, security at $1.00 or more. Listed stock: $0.02 per share, $32.00 minimum, round-lot only, security value at $1.00 or more.

Option Trades: Principal amount $0–2,000: $18.00 per trade plus 1.6% of principal. Principal amount $2,001–10,000: $39.00 per trade plus 0.7% of principal. Principal amount $10,001 and more: $76.00 per trade plus 0.3% of principal. Minimum option commission: $6.00 first five contracts, $2.50 per contract thereafter. Minimum: $34.00 per trade.

Telephone Trading: Nasdaq: $0.01 per share, $32.00 minimum (round-lot security at $1.00 or more). Listed stock: $0.02 per share, $32.00 minimum (round-lot security at $1.00 or more).

After-Hours Trading: 9:15 A.M. to 9:30 A.M. EST and 4:00 P.M. to 6:00 P.M. EST (round-lots, multiples of 100, and limit orders only). Internet or broker-assisted trades: Market order, $35.00 per trade plus $0.02 per share ECN fees; limit order, $32.00 unlimited shares. GTC orders incur a $5.00 surcharge.

Products Available to Trade Online: Stocks and options.

Average Execution Time: Market order: within 1.5 minutes.

Minimum Deposit Required: $2,000 for cash or margin account.

Additional Fees: Shipping and handling: $3.00, subject to all trades. Accounts transferred out: $45.00. Issue stock certificate: $20.00 per issue. Overnight mail (upon request): $15.00. Returned check fee: $25.00. Wire funds out: $25.00. Stop payment request on Sunlogic-issued check: $10.00. Restricted securities: $75.00. Fed call extensions: $10.00. Voluntary reorganization: $20.00. Copy of account statement: $20.00. Check deposit holding before withdraw: 10 business days, SEC fee, and ODD lot differential charges at $0.125 per share may apply to certain trades. GTC order: additional $5.00.

Free Services and Financial Links: Sunlogic Daily Newsletter.

Real-Time Quotes: Free real-time quotes, although they are not streaming and must be refreshed.

States Registered In: AZ, CA, GA, MI, NV, NY, VA, WA.

Mutual Funds Offered: None.

Payment for Order Flow: Sunlogic was unable to answer.

Banking Services Offered: Free check writing ($100.00 minimum). Clients holding a margin account can write checks against margin credit.

Company Background: Sunlogic Securities, Inc., was founded in 1995. It has a client base of approximately 1,000 individual traders, 99% of whom are Chinese. Its website is in Chinese as well as English. Sunlogic clients are protected up to $10,500,000 per account: $500,000 is protected by SIPC, of which $100,000 is for cash protection.
Customer Service Rating: ★★ Average

SUNTRUST

Brokerage Type: Full-service/discount brokerage
Mailing Address: SunTrust Securities
1349 West Peachtree St. Suite 1180
Atlanta, GA 30309
Web Address: www.suntrust.com
Email Address: Available through website.
Telephone Number: 800-874-4770
Fax Number: 404-588-8359
Market Orders: $29.95 per trade, up to 1,000 shares, and additional $0.03 per share thereafter.
Limit Orders: Same as market orders.
Option Trades: 10% discount for Internet trades. Up to $2,500: $30.00 plus 1.6% of principal. $2,501–10,000: $50.00 plus 0.08% of principal. $10,001 or more: $100.00 plus .03% of principal. Minimum: $38.25 plus $1.75 per contract. Maximum: $40.00 per contract for first 2 contracts plus $5.00 per contract thereafter.
Telephone Trading: $38.00 plus 0.5% of total dollar.
After-Hours Trading: None.
Products Available to Trade Online: Stocks, options, and mutual funds.
Average Execution Time: Market order: instantly routed for trading with immediate execution.
Minimum Deposit Required: None for cash account. $2,000 for margin account.
Additional Fees: Wire funds out: $15.00. Returned check fee: $25.00. Transfer IRA out: $50.00. Annual maintenance fee for IRA: $24.00. Overnight delivery: $12.00. Postage and handling: $2.95.
Free Services and Financial Links: Standard & Poor's Stock Reports, Morningstar, stock screener, Lehman Brothers Morning Meeting Flash Report, online calculators.
Real-Time Quotes: Real-time quotes, although they are not streaming and must be refreshed.

States Registered In: All U.S. states.

Mutual Funds Offered: Over 30 STI Classic mutual funds.

Payment for Order Flow: No.

Banking Services Offered: Active Investor Account: This is an asset management account that combines a checking account, including check card use, with investment flexibility of a brokerage account. All Active Investor customers can utilize Internet Investing.

Company Background: SunTrust Securities, an indirect subsidiary of SunTrust Banks, Inc., was founded in 1986 when SunTrust Bank and Crestar Securities merged. In May 2000 SunTrust Internet Investing began its online trading. Crestar Securities offered online trading for many years before the merger with SunTrust Bank; thus, although the SunTrust site is new, the online trading experience of Crestar is still a part of the organization. It currently has over 200,000 accounts, all of which can be accessed online. SunTrust is a brokerage/dealer registered with the SEC. SunTrust utilizes NFSC as its clearing firm. SIPC provides clients with up to $500,000 in protection, of which $100,000 is for cash.

Customer Service Rating: ★★★ Excellent

SURETRADE

Brokerage Type: Discount brokerage

Mailing Address: Suretrade, Inc.
P.O. Box 862
Lincoln, RI 02865-9807

Web Address: www.suretrade.com

Email Address: service@suretrade.com

Telephone Number: 401-642-6900

Fax Number: 401-642-5262

Market Orders: $7.95 per trade, stocks over $2.00, and up to 5,000 shares. Stocks priced below $2.00: additional $5.00 for first 5,000 shares, and additional $0.01 per share on entire order for all trades over 5,000 shares.

Limit Orders: $9.95 per trade, stocks over $2.00, and up to 5,000 shares. Stocks priced below $2.00: additional $5.00 for first 5,000 shares, and additional $0.01 per share on entire order for all trades over 5,000 shares.

Option Trades: $20.00 per trade plus $1.70 per contract. $28.95 minimum.

Telephone Trading: $25.00 additional surcharge.

After-Hours Trading: None.

Products Available to Trade Online: Stocks, options, mutual funds, and bonds.

Average Execution Time: Market order: 5 seconds.

Minimum Deposit Required: None, but clients must have cleared funds in their accounts prior to placing first trade for a cash account. $2,000 for margin account.

Additional Fees: Communication mailgrams: $5.00. Wiring funds: $20.00. Returned checks: $20.00. Duplicate copies of checks issued over 6 months ago: $10.00. Stock certificates sent: $20.00. Overnight delivery fee: $15.00. Option assignments and exercise: $34.95. Duplicate copies of monthly statement, 1099 forms, and trade confirmations: $5.00 first page, $2.00 each additional page.

Free Services and Financial Links: Baseline, Big Charts, Briefing.com, Investools research, Market Edge, Fund Finder, news, Zacks, Stockpoint, Wall Street Source.

Real-Time Quotes: 100 real-time quotes per day on stocks, mutual funds, and indices.

States Registered In: All U.S. states.

Mutual Funds Offered: Approximately 100.

Payment for Order Flow: Yes.

Banking Services Offered: Account balance of $150,000: check writing. This service is available by request only.

Company Background: Suretrade was launched in November 1997 and has grown to over 360,000 customer accounts and $2 billion in customer assets. Suretrade is a member of the SIPC. Suretrade customer accounts are carried by U.S. Clearing, a division of Fleet Securities, Inc. SIPC protection is $500,000 in assets per account, of which up to $100,000 may be cash. Total account protection for our customers is $100,000,000 in assets per account, of which $100,000 may be cash.

Customer Service Rating: ★★★ Excellent

Gomez Rating: 6.32

Forrester PowerRankings: 39.62

TD WATERHOUSE

Brokerage Type: Discount brokerage

Mailing Address: TD Waterhouse Group, Inc.
55 Broadway, 20th Floor
New York, NY 10006

Web Address: www.tdwaterhouse.com

Email Address: Available through website.
Telephone Number: 800-934-4448
Fax Number: None.
Market Orders: $12.00 per trade, up to 5,000 shares; over 5,000 shares: additional $0.01 per share on entire order.
Limit Orders: Same as market orders.
Option Trades: $28.13 per trade plus $1.25 per contract; commission goes up with amount of contracts purchased.
Telephone Trading: $45.00 per trade, up to 5,000 shares; over 5,000 shares: additional $0.01 per share on entire order.
After-Hours Trading: 4:30 P.M. to 7:00 P.M. EST. $12.00 per trade up to 5,000 shares; over 5,000 shares: additional $0.01 per share on entire order, limit order only, trades placed over Internet only.
Products Available to Trade Online: Stocks, options, mutual funds, and warrants and rights.
Average Execution Time: Market order: immediate.
Minimum Deposit Required: $1,000 for cash account. $2,000 for margin account.
Additional Fees: Argus research reports: $65.00 a year. Morning Star Reports: $3.00 each. Request physical certificate: $15.00. Returned check: $10.00. Wiring funds out: $15.00.
Free Services and Financial Links: Charts by Quote.com, portfolio tracker, news headlines—current and previous—on over 4,000 companies, S&P stock reports, Zacks, stock screening by Market Guide, Morningstar Data, market commentary by Briefing.com, Market Edge Second Opinion, Email news and stock alerts, earn 10,000 American Airlines AAdvantage miles with a $10,000 new account, earn 1,000 bonus AAdvantage miles per year by maintaining a balance of $25,000, earn one mile for every $10.00 of average monthly (annualized) balance in the American AAdvantage Money Market Mileage Fund, investor education center.
Real-Time Quotes: Unlimited streaming real-time quotes.
States Registered In: All U.S. states.
Mutual Funds Offered: Over 9,000.
Payment for Order Flow: No.
Banking Services Offered: Free Web banking with an online account, which features online bill payment. Clients also have access to an Asset Management Account, which features free check writing and ATM debit card privileges. TD Waterhouse offers a full line of banking services available through TD Waterhouse Bank, N.A.

Company Background: TD Waterhouse Investor Securities, Inc., was originally founded in 1979 and currently has over 2.8 million active accounts, a majority of which are online accounts. TD Waterhouse's clientele consists mainly of individuals. TD Waterhouse is a member of FDIC, which insures clients' accounts up to $150 million: $500,000 is provided by SIPC, of which $100,000 covers cash. The remaining $149.5 million is provided by a private insurance company. TD Waterhouse is a large brokerage firm handling more than $150 billion in customer assets, as of January 31, 2000, and they currently have 160 branches worldwide and plan an additional 40 branches to open by the end of 2000. TD Waterhouse offers customer service 24 hours a day, 7 days a week.

Customer Service Rating: ★★★ Excellent
Gomez Rating: 6.83
Forrester PowerRankings: 55.52

TERRA NOVA TRADING

Brokerage Type: Direct-access brokerage
Mailing Address: Terra Nova Trading, LLC
100 South Wacker Dr. Suite 1550
Chicago, IL 60606
Web Address: www.terranovatrading.com
Email Address: info@terranovatrading.com
Telephone Number: 800-258-5409, 800-228-4216
Fax Number: 312-960-0723
Market Orders: Real-Tick III Software: $14.95 per trade, includes all exchange and ECN fees. Orders routed to Instinet incur a $0.015 per share fee. Web-based Software: 5 free trades, then $11.95 per trade, up to 1,000 shares, and ECN fees that apply thereafter.
Limit Orders: Same as market orders.
Option Trades: $25.00 minimum or $2.50 per contract.
Telephone Trading: $15.00 additional surcharge.
After-Hours Trading: 8:45 A.M. to 9:30 A.M. EST and 4:00 P.M. to 4:45 P.M. EST. Trades placed through Instinet and live broker only.
Products Available to Trade Online: Stocks and options.
Average Execution Time: Market order: less than 5 seconds, depending on line speed being used and whether trade is routed through an ECN.
Minimum Deposit Required: $10,000 for all accounts.
Additional Fees: Real-Tick III software fee: $250.00 per month (Terra

Nova will rebate $125.00 to client with 25 trades per month or waive the entire fee with 50 trades per month). Web-based software fee: $60.00 per month. Optional exchange fees: Options data (OPRA): non-professional fee, $2.50 per month; professional fee, $26.00 per month. CME: nonprofessional fee, $10.00 per month; professional fee, $55.00 per month. CBOT: nonprofessional fee, $30.00 per month; professional fee, $60.00 per month. Comtex: $25.00 per month. Dow Jones Newswire: $95.00 per month. Nasdaq Level II: nonprofessional, $50.00 per month; professional, contact Terra Nova for price. Pass through fees: Instinet, $0.015 per share. Returned check: $15.00. Stop payment within 10 days: $10.00. IRA termination fee: $25.00. Registry and de-livery of certificate: $15.00. Overnight delivery: $16.55. Foreign trans-fer (ACAT): $25.00–50.00. Wire domestic: $15.00. Wire foreign: $35.00.

Free Services and Financial Links: TNT Bookstore, Archipelago, Opti-Mark Technologies, Inc., Nasdaq-Amex, New York Stock Exchange, Chicago Mercantile Exchange, Chicago Board Options Exchange, Quantum Vision Limited, Inc., Southwest Securities Inc.

Real-Time Quotes: Streaming real-time quotes with software package.

States Registered In: All U.S. states.

Mutual Funds Offered: None.

Payment for Order Flow: No.

Banking Services Offered: None.

Company Background: Terra Nova Trading is a registered brokerage/ dealer that was founded in 1994. Terra Nova specializes in electronic trading via private networks and the Internet. Terra Nova's clientele is made up of both institutional and retail investors. Terra Nova of-fers electronic trading and diverse order routing through the following ECNs: Archipelago, Instinet, Island, SOES, SelectNet, and SuperDot. Terra Nova is a member of NASD and SIPC and utilizes Southwest Se-curities as its clearing firm.

Customer Service Rating: ★★★ Excellent

THE EXECUTIONER

Brokerage Type: Direct access
Mailing Address: 7-11 South Broadway Suite 217
White Plains, NY 10601
Web Address: www.executioner.com
Email Address: staff@executioner.com

Telephone Number: 877-453-8352

Fax Number: 415-491-1166

Market Orders: The Executioner I (Nasdaq or listed): $22.50 per trade, unlimited shares. The Executioner II (Nasdaq or listed): 0–19 trades, $22.50 per trade; 20–49 trades, $21.50 per trade; 50–99 trades, $20.95 per trade; 100–149 trades, $19.95 per trade; 150 or more trades, $18.95 per trade (unlimited shares for Nasdaq, NYSE, and Amex issues).

Limit Orders: Same as market orders.

Option Trades: Broker-assisted only at this time. 1–5 contracts: $7.00 per contract. 6–20 contracts: $4.00 per contract. 21–49 contracts: $3.00 per contract. 50 or more contracts: negotiable. $25.00 minimum ticket charge.

Telephone Trading: Same commissions as online schedule.

After-Hours Trading: Island and ARCA: 8:00 A.M. to 9:30 A.M. EST and 4:00 P.M. to 8:00 P.M. EST. SelectNet: 9:00 A.M. to 9:30 A.M. EST and 4:00 P.M. to 6:30 P.M. EST. Instinet: 8:00 A.M. to 9:30 A.M. EST and 4:00 P.M. to 6:30 P.M. EST. Same commissions as online schedule.

Products Available to Trade Online: Stocks.

Average Execution Time: Market order: within 1–7 seconds.

Minimum Deposit Required: $10,000 for all accounts. All accounts opened are considered margin accounts.

Additional Fees: Software fees for The Executioner I: $175.00 per month; exchange fees (Nasdaq, NYSE, Amex), $50.00 per month (fee waived with 25 or more trades per month). The Executioner II: $250.00 per month; exchange fees, $50.00 per month (fee waived with 50 or more trades per month). ECN additional fees: Archipelago, $0.0025 per share; REDI, $0.0055 per share; Island, $0.0025 per share; INCA (Instinet), $0.0150 per share; SOES, $0.5000 per trade; ATTN, $0.0050 per share; Bloomberg, $0.0050 per share with $1.50 minimum; Nexttrade, $0.0150 per share; Strike Technologies, $0.0020 per share; BRUT, $1.50 (0–99 shares), $3.00 (200–299 shares), $4.00 (300 plus shares). SelectNet (preference): $1.00 per trade. SelectNet (broadcast): $2.50 per trade; cancel fee, $0.25 per cancel, applies to SOES orders only. Additional exchange fees: NYSE, $5.25 per month; Amex, $3.25 per month; Nasdaq Level II, $50.00 per month; Level I, $4.00 per month; Options, $5.00 per month; CME, $55.00 per month; CBOT, $60.00 per month. Returned check: $15.00. Stop payment within 10 days: $10.00. Certificate registration: $15.00. Overnight delivery: $16.55. Foreign transfer, ACAT: $35.00–50.00. Wire domestic: $15.00. Dow Jones News Wire: $95.00 per month. Comtex Real-Time News: $25.00 per month.

Free Services and Financial Links: Technical support chat room, live online training room, onsite seminars, online seminars, movies-tutorials, access margin reports, educational corner.

Real-Time Quotes: Streaming real-time quotes with software package.

States Registered In: All U.S. states.

Mutual Funds Offered: Thousands.

Payment for Order Flow: No.

Banking Services Offered: Free check writing with an online account opportunity to apply for a VISA debit card. Clients can also have ATM debit card privileges if they maintain an account balance of $10,000.

Company Background: Terra Nova Trading, LLC, was founded in 1994 and launched online trading through The Executioner in 1997. The Executioner's system is designed for the novice or professional trader; this system is called PCDD for point, click, drag, and drop. The Executioner I consists of a fixed page format with one Level II screen, and The Executioner II program allows clients to have multiple Level II and charting screens. All clients must maintain a minimum balance of $5,000 in their accounts at all times. Clients have access to all ECNs, and Terra Nova is a registered brokerage/dealer with ARCA, ECN, SOES, and SelectNet. The Executioner utilizes Southwest Securities as its clearing firm. Clients' accounts are protected by SIPC up to $500,000, of which $100,000 is for cash coverage. Additional coverage up to $24.5 million is provided by American International Group (AIG).

Customer Service Rating: ★★★ Excellent

THE FINANCIALCAFE.COM

Brokerage Type: Full-service brokerage

Mailing Address: P.O. Box 150
San Francisco, CA 94104-0150

Web Address: www.financialcafe.com

Email Address: customercare@thefinancialcafe.com

Telephone Number: 877-600-6410

Fax Number: 415-217-5030

Market Orders: Free if trade is placed over the Internet.

Limit Orders: $4.75 per trade if account balance is greater than $20,000. $14.75 per trade if account balance is $0–19,999.

Option Trades: Market orders: 0–10 contracts, $14.75 per trade; 10 or more contracts, $14.75 per trade plus $1.50 per contract. Limit orders: $24.75 per trade plus $1.50 per contract.

Telephone Trading: $13.75 additional surcharge.

After-Hours Trading: 6:00 A.M. to 9:00 A.M. EST and 4:00 P.M. to 8:00 P.M. EST. Account balance greater than $20,000: $4.75 per trade plus $0.02 per share. Account balance less than $20,000: $14.75 per trade plus $0.02 per share.

Products Available to Trade Online: Stocks, options, and mutual funds.

Average Execution Time: Market order: From a millisecond to 30–40 seconds, depending on market volatility.

Minimum Deposit Required: None, but sufficient funds must be available to place first trade.

Additional Fees: Returned check: $25.00. Wired funds (outgoing): $20.00. IRA (less than $10,000): $40.00. IRA termination: $50.00. Voluntary tenders: $25.00 per position. Mandatory reorganization: $10.00 per position. Legal transfers: $15.00 per issue. Restricted stock processing (not including legal transfer fee): $50.00. Transfer and ship: $15.00 per certificate. Margin extensions: $5.00 per extension. Copies of statements: $5.00 per statement.

Free Services and Financial Links: Morningstar.com, research (profiles, financials, estimates, and recommendations), insider trading, Streaming Media, market news, IPO news, most actives page, gainers/ losers page, free research from Stox.com (time and sales, interactive charting, market indices, and Marketguide), Freeshop.com, IPO.com, FORM Media Technologies Inc., Echeck Secure (Troy Group), Kana.

Real-Time Quotes: Streaming real-time quotes for a fee of $29.95 per month for 10 symbols or $39.95 a month for 25 symbols.

States Registered In: All U.S. states.

Mutual Funds Offered: Thousands.

Payment for Order Flow: Yes.

Banking Services Offered: Check writing, online bill payment, and ATM debit card privileges with an Asset Management Account.

Company Background: The Financialcafe.com was founded in spring 1999, and the website was launched on May 3, 2000. The Financialcafe.com offers all market orders placed via the Internet or touch-tone telephone commission free. Clients' accounts are protected up to $25 million per account. SIPC provides coverage up to $500,000, of which $100,000 is for cash coverage, and the remaining $24.5 million is provided by AIG Inc. The Financialcafe.com utilizes Penson Financial Services as its clearing firm.

Customer Service Rating: ★★★ Excellent

THE NET INVESTOR

Brokerage Type: Discount brokerage
Mailing Address: 135 South LaSalle St., Suite 1500
Chicago, IL 60603-4398
Web Address: www.netinvestor.com
Email Address: info@netinvestor.com
Telephone Number: 800-638-4250
Fax Number: 312-655-2750
Market Orders: $19.95 per trade plus $0.01 per share. Stocks trading less than $1.00: additional $0.01 per share. Maximum: 4% of the trade amount.
Limit Orders: Same as market orders.
Option Trades: $3.00 or less contract price: $35.00 per trade plus $2.50 per contract. Over $3.00 contract price: $35.00 per trade plus $3.00 per contract.
Telephone Trading: $19.95 per trade.
After-Hours Trading: None.
Products Available to Trade Online: Stocks, options, mutual funds, and bonds.
Average Execution Time: Market order: 5–10 seconds.
Minimum Deposit Required: None.
Additional Fees: Voluntary tenders and redemptions: $25.00 per issue. Mandatory tenders or reorganizations: $10.00. Transfer in noneligible security: $25.00. Foreign security transfer: $75.00 per item. Foreign securities safekeeping: $2.00 per month. Legal transfer: $30.00. Issue physical certificate: $25.00. Transfer out of account: $50.00. Inactive account: $50.00. Check insurance: $0.075 per check. Wire funds transfer (outgoing domestic): $15.00. Returned check: $25.00. Research account information: $25.00 per hour. Reproduce documents (per page): $1.00. Miscellaneous transaction fee: $4.45.
Free Services and Financial Links: Morning News, First Call Earnings Estimates, S&P Reports, Lipper Analytical Mutual Fund Reports, Vickers Insider Trading Reports, free real-time quotes for active traders, online portfolio reporting, historical and intraday price graphs, Argus, stock price watch list, Paw Traks, Reuters, Research on Demand, customer service guaranteed or trade commission is free.
Real-Time Quotes: Free unlimited real-time quotes, although they are not streaming and must be refreshed.
States Registered In: All U.S. states.

Mutual Funds Offered: Over 4,000.

Payment for Order Flow: Not divulged.

Banking Services Offered: Free VISA debit/ATM card and free check writing.

Company Background: The Net Investor is a division of Howe Barnes Investments, Inc., founded in 1915. The Net Investor became an online brokerage firm in 1994. The Net Investor's clientele consists mainly of individuals, and all accounts are protected up to $25 million. Privacy of clients' accounts is possible through the use of encryption technology and nightly audits done on separate computers. The Net Investor automatically updates clients' portfolios to give clients the most current values, taxable gains and losses, dividends, stock splits, and open orders.

Customer Service Rating: ★★★ Excellent

TRADECAST

Brokerage Type: Direct access

Mailing Address: TradeCast Securities, Ltd.
5555 San Felipe Suite 575
Houston, TX 77056

Web Address: www.tradecast.com

Email Address: onlineinfo@tradecast.com

Telephone Number: 877-303-7844, 877-627-6700

Fax Number: 713-331-2793

Market Orders: Elite: $19.95 per trade (under 15 trades per month); $16.95 per trade (15–99 trades per month); $13.95 per trade (100–249 trades per month); $9.95 per trade (250 or more trades per month). Revolution: $14.95 per trade.

Limit Orders: Same as market orders.

Option Trades: Call for commissions.

Telephone Trading: Revolution: $20.00 per trade.

After-Hours Trading: 8:30 A.M. to 9:30 A.M. EST and 4:00 P.M. to 6:40 P.M. EST. Same commissions as online schedule.

Products Available to Trade Online: Stocks and options.

Average Execution Time: Market order: 2–10 seconds.

Minimum Deposit Required: $1,000 for cash account. $2,500 for margin account.

Additional Fees: Elite software fee: $99.00 per month plus exchange fees of $52.00 per month (waived if client executes more than 50 trades per month or maintains a $10,000 minimum cash balance over the course of an entire month). Revolution software fee: none with streaming Level I quotes; upgrade to Level II quotes, $60.00 per month (waived if client executes more than 20 trades per month or maintains a $10,000 minimum cash account balance over the course of an entire month). ECN fees: Attain-ECN, $0.005 per share; The Brass Utility, LLC, $0.004 per share; B-Trade Services, $0.005 per share; Instinet Corp (INCA), $0.015 per share; the Island ECN (ISLD), $0.0015 per share; Speer Leads & Kellogg (REDI), $0.0025 per share; Terra Nova Trading, LLC (ARCA), $0.005 per share; Strike (STRK), $0.005 per share; NexTrade (NTRD), $0.005 per share. Optional fees: OPRA, $2.50 per month; CBOT, $30.00 per month; CME, $10.00 per month.

Free Services and Financial Links: ABC Business, Briefing.com, CBS MarketWatch, CNBC, CNN, CNNfn, Gomez.com, International Trading Institute, Investor Guide, Money.com, MSNBC, OTCBB, USA Today, Yahoo News, articles, investor education, professional training.

Real-Time Quotes: Free streaming real-time Level-I quotes. Streaming real-time Level II quotes are offered for $60.00 per month, waived if 20 or more trades are made within one month or $10,000 minimum cash balance is maintained over the course of an entire month.

States Registered In: All U.S. states except CT and NH.

Mutual Funds Offered: None.

Payment for Order Flow: No.

Banking Services Offered: Check writing and a debit card upon request.

Company Background: TradeCast, a direct-access broker, is a member of NASD and SIPC and was founded in 1996. TradeCast offers software that gives clients efficient access to financial markets and ECNs. TradeCast software currently executes over 40,000 trades per day. TradeCast offers two Windows-based programs, The Elite software and The Revolution software. The Elite caters to analysts, money managers, brokers, professional traders, and serious day traders. The Revolution software caters to the long-term investor, short-term investor, and active investor. Clients' accounts are protected up to $500,000, of which $100,000 is for cash coverage, provided by SIPC. Additional coverage up to $24.5 million is provided by National Union Fire Insurance Company.

Customer Service Rating: ★★★ Excellent

TRADE4LESS

Brokerage Type: Discount brokerage
Mailing Address: Downstate Discount Brokerage, Inc.
259 Indian Rocks Road North
Belleair Bluffs, FL 33770
Web Address: www.trade4less.com
Email Address: trade4less@downstate.com
Telephone Number: 800-780-3543, 813-586-3541
Fax Number: None.
Market Orders: Nasdaq stocks: $19.95 per trade, unlimited shares. Exchange listed stocks and stocks trading under $1.00: additional $0.01 per share to entire order.
Limit Orders: Same as market orders.
Option Trades: Options trading under $1.00: $22.00 per trade plus $1.50 per contract. Options trading $1.00 and over: $22.00 per trade plus $2.00 per contract.
Telephone Trading: Stocks priced $1.00–5.00: up to 1,000 shares, $30.00 per trade plus $0.03 per share; over 1,000 shares, $.015 for each additional share. Stocks priced over $5.00: up to 1,000 shares, $30.00 plus $0.05 per share; over 1,000 shares, $0.015 for each additional share. Stocks priced $1.00 and under: $50.00 minimum ticket charge, $35.00 plus 2.5% of principal.
After-Hours Trading: 8:30 A.M. to 9:30 A.M. EST and 4:00 P.M. to 5:00 P.M. EST. Broker-assisted commission plus $0.05 per share. Broker-assisted trading only.
Products Available to Trade Online: Stocks and options.
Average Execution Time: Market order: within 30 seconds.
Minimum Deposit Required: $2,000 for cash or margin account.
Additional Fees: Returned check: $15.00. Additional fees may apply; contact Trade4Less.
Free Services and Financial Links: Portfolio tracker, Market Snapshot, company news, equity indices, Small Cap—OTC, news, price history, symbol lookup, option chains, option quotes, Zacks, Hot Stocks, company profiles, IPO information, graphs, economic calendar.
Real-Time Quotes: 50 real-time quotes with each trade executed, although they are not streaming and must be refreshed. Clients can also purchase unlimited real-time quotes for a fee of $29.95 a month. Free 20-minute delayed quotes are also available to clients.
States Registered In: AZ, CA, FL, GA, IL, IN, KY.

Mutual Funds Offered: Over 1,500.

Payment for Order Flow: Yes.

Banking Services Offered: Free check writing.

Company Background: Downstate Discount Brokerage, Inc., was founded in 1980 and launched the online trading site Trade4Less in 1998. Clearing services at Trade4Less are provided by U.S. Clearing Corporation, and clients' accounts are protected up to $100 million. SIPC provides coverage up to $500,000, of which $100,000 is for cash coverage. Clientele at Trade4Less is composed mainly of individuals, and the company currently has approximately 500 active online clients.

Customer Service Rating: ★ Poor

TRADEPRO

Brokerage Type: Direct access

Mailing Address: TradePro LLC.
560 Kirts Blvd. Suite 225
Troy, MI 48084

Web Address: www.thetradepros.com

Email Address: mailbox@thetradepros.com

Telephone Number: 248-362-2650, 888-741-8733

Fax Number: 248-362-2678

Market Orders: Trades per month: 1–99, $19.95; 100–199, $18.95; 200–299, $17.95; 300–399, $16.95; 400 or more, $14.95.

Limit Orders: Same as market orders and additional $0.015 per share for all trades over 2,000 shares.

Option Trades: Broker-assisted trading only. 1–5 contracts: $6.00 per contract. Over 6 contracts: $4.00 per contract. $20.00 minimum per trade.

Telephone Trading: Same commissions as online schedule.

After-Hours Trading: 8:00 A.M. to 9:30 A.M. EST and 4:00 P.M. to 8:00 P.M. EST. Same commissions as online schedule.

Products Available to Trade Online: Stocks.

Average Execution Time: TradePro stated that they legally could not give this information.

Minimum Deposit Required: $10,000 for cash or margin account.

Additional Fees: Newswatch: $75.00. Zacks (Newswatch required): $15.00. Software fees for Trade Lite: $100.00 per month; exchange fees: Nasdaq, $4.00. Trade Plus: $175.00 per month; exchange fees: Nasdaq, $50.00. Trade Premier: $250.00 per month; exchange fees: Nasdaq, $50.00.

Free Services and Financial Links: Hamilton Research Chat Room, SEC, Nasdaq, Stock.com, Wall Street Directory, First Call, Stock Smart, Investools, StreetEYE, Zacks, Yahoo, AllStocks, Business Wire, Reuters, PR Newswire, W.S.J., I.B.D., Silicon Investors, Broadwatch, Red Herring, Wired, CMP, Znet, Alert IPO, IPO Online, IPO Central, Right-Line, Jag Notes, The Street.
Real-Time Quotes: Streaming real-time quotes.
States Registered In: All U.S. states except AK.
Mutual Funds Offered: Thousands.
Payment for Order Flow: No.
Banking Services Offered: Free check writing and ATM debit card privileges with a Vision Account.
Company Background: Terra Nova, a registered brokerage/dealer, launched online trading through TradePro in March 1997. TradePro offers a direct access system to eliminate the middleman and give direct routing to clients. TradePro offers multiple order routing systems, including Island, ARCA, SOES, INCA (Instinet), REDI, and SelectNet. TradePro caters to the serious active trader. There are currently around 300 active online clients, 70% of whom are individual clients or joint accounts. TradePro software packages include the following: Trade Elite, which offers RealTick III Level I with electronic execution, position minder, hot keys, board view, tickers, alarms, market minder, and multiquote; Trade Plus, which includes a fixed Nasdaq Level II market maker window, hot keys, technical analysis, alarms, and more; and Trade Premier, which includes customizable multiple Level II windows, time and sales, turbo options, and more. Clients' accounts are protected by SIPC up to $500,000, of which $100,000 is for cash coverage, and Southwest Securities provides additional protection up to $24.5 million.
Customer Service Rating: ★★★ Excellent

TRADESCAPE.COM

Brokerage Type: Direct access
Mailing Address: 135 East 57th Street, 14th Floor
New York, NY 10022
Web Address: www.tradescape.com
Email Address: info@tradescape.com
Telephone Number: 800-467-7065
Fax Number: 212-826-1205
Market Orders: $0.015 per share with a $1.50 minimum per trade fee.
Limit Orders: Same as market orders.

Option Trades: None.

Telephone Trading: Same commissions as online schedule.

After-Hours Trading: 9:00 A.M. to 9:30 A.M. EST and 4:00 P.M. to 5:00 P.M. EST. Same commissions as online schedule.

Products Available to Trade Online: Stocks.

Average Execution Time: Market order: Immediate execution depending on how clients route their order.

Minimum Deposit Required: $10,000. Clients must maintain a minimum daily balance of $5,000 in their accounts in order to receive margin privileges.

Additional Fees: Nasdaq/NYSE fees: SelectNet, $1.14 per trade; SOES, $0.50 per trade; NYSE, $0.02 per share. ECN fees: Archipelago, Brass, Redibook, Bloomberg, and Attain, $0.010–10.00 per 1,000 shares; Nextrade, Strike, and Instinet, $0.015 per 1,000 shares; Island, $0.0025–2.50 per 1,000 shares. Wire transfer: $15.00.

Free Services and Financial Links: Stream Book, bid and ask thermographs, time and sales thermograph, time and sales, ECP book, charts, Market Scan, personal tickers, FYIs, position manager, personal thermographs, TickerAlert, market status bar, risers and fallers, Nasdaq most actives thermographs, latency console, personal statistics, control consoles.

Real-Time Quotes: Streaming Level I and Level II quotes. There is a $79.95 monthly charge for real-time Level II quotes ($29.95 plus the $50.00 exchange fee). Fee is waived if clients maintain a minimum account balance of $25,000 and execute 50 or more trades per calendar month.

States Registered In: AZ, CA, CO, CT, DE, FL, GA, ID, IL, IN, KY, LA, MD, NC, NE, NJ, NV, NY, OK, OR, TN, TX, UT, VA, WA, WI, and WY.

Mutual Funds Offered: None.

Payment for Order Flow: No.

Banking Services Offered: None.

Company Background: Tradescape.com, a division of Momentum Securities LLC, was founded in 1997 and is a direct-access firm. Tradescape currently processes more than 100,000 trades per day and over $27 billion in equity per month. Tradescape.com combines real-time data with its own exclusive Smart Order Communication Portal (EPC) technology. This portal technology provides clients with direct communication to many sources, including Nasdaq, NYSE, and multiple ECNs. The Smart Order Routing System quickly scans these sources for the best possible price. Clients' accounts are protected up to $500,000, of which $100,000 is for cash coverage, provided by SIPC.

Customer Service Rating: ★★★ Excellent

TRADE-WELL

Brokerage Type: Discount brokerage
Mailing Address: Trade-Well Discount Investing, LLC
New Accounts Services
45 Broadway 20th Fl.
New York, NY 10006
Web Address: www.trade-well.com
Email Address: Clientservice@trade-well.com
Telephone Number: 888-907-9797, 212-514-4000
Fax Number: 212-514-4444
Market Orders: U.S. Equities: $19.95 per trade, up to 3,000 shares, and additional $0.01 per share on entire order thereafter. Ordinary shares: $125.00 plus $0.02 per share.
Limit Orders: $19.95 per trade, up to 3,000 shares, and additional $0.01 per share on entire order thereafter.
Option Trades: $19.95 per trade plus $1.50 per contract.
Telephone Trading: $27.00 per trade (OTC and listed), $27.00 per trade up to 3,000 shares, and additional $0.01 per trade on entire order (listed only). Canadian equities: $27.00 per trade plus $0.02 per share.
After-Hours Trading: None.
Products Available to Trade Online: Stocks, options, and mutual funds.
Average Execution Time: Market order: depends on market conditions and size of order.
Minimum Deposit Required: $500.00 for cash account. $5,000 for margin account.
Additional Fees: Postage and handling: $3.50. IRA termination fee: $50.00. Transfer and ship DTC: $25.00. Domestic wires: $20.00. Returned check fee: $25.00. Copies of back statements: $5.00, excluding the current month.
Free Services and Financial Links: Institutional research, news, market updates, research, company profiles, earnings summaries, analyst coverage, Baseline reports, mutual fund reports, calculators, graphs.
Real-Time Quotes: Free real-time quotes. The quotes are not streaming and must be refreshed.
States Registered In: All U.S. states.
Mutual Funds Offered: Thousands.
Payment for Order Flow: No.
Banking Services Offered: Free check writing, VISA debit card, and ATM access through an Asset Management Account (Spectra Vest).

Minimum deposit required to open Asset Management account is $5,000.

Company Background: Trade-Well Discount Investing, Inc., is an affiliate of Josephthal & Co., Inc., which was founded in 1910. Trade-Well went online in 1995 and serves institutions, individuals, and long-term investors. Trade-Well offers a broad range of investment options to its clientele. Trade-Well utilizes Fiserv Securities as its clearing firm. Securities in clients' accounts are protected by SIPC up to $500,000, of which $100,000 is cash protection. An additional $24.5 million is offered through Asset Guaranty Insurance Co.

Customer Service Rating: ★★★ Excellent

TRADING DIRECT

Brokerage Type: Discount brokerage

Mailing Address: 160 Broadway, East Building, 10th Floor
New York, NY 10038

Web Address: www.tradingdirect.com

Email Address: info@tradingdirect.com

Telephone Number: 212-766-0241

Fax Number: 212-766-0914

Market Orders: $9.95 per trade (unlimited shares). Trading Direct will not accept buy orders for stocks under $1.00, but it does allow clients to liquidate stocks under $1.00.

Limit Orders: Same as market orders.

Option Trades: $20.00 per trade plus $1.75 per contract. $25.00 minimum.

Telephone Trading: $29.95 per trade for equity trades and additional $10.00 for option trades.

After-Hours Trading: None.

Products Available to Trade Online: Stocks, options, and mutual funds.

Average Execution Time: Market order: less than one minute, depending on the liquidity of the stock.

Minimum Deposit Required: None.

Additional Fees: Mailgrams: $10.00. Returned checks: $15.00. Additional copies of statements and confirmations: $5.00. Wire transfer of funds outgoing: $15.00. Stock certificate transfer fee: $10.00. IRA termination fee: $50.00. Outgoing transfer: $50.00. Stock certificate issued to third party: $15.00.

Free Services and Financial Links: Market Guide, Market Guide Stock Quest, Marker Edge Second Opinion, Zacks, free postage and handling, free wire transfer of funds incoming, portfolio tracker, Market Snapshot, company news, intraday charts, economic calendar, Currency snapshot, hot stock list, equity indices, small cap—OTC News, IPO information, free IRA setup, Reuters, StockQuest.

Real-Time Quotes: Unlimited real-time quotes are offered for a fee of $29.95 per month. Clients will also receive 50 free real-time quotes per day. The quotes offered are not streaming and must be refreshed.

States Registered In: All U.S. states except AK, AR, ME, MO, ND, NM, and VT.

Mutual Funds Offered: Over 2,000.

Payment for Order Flow: Yes.

Banking Services Offered: None.

Company Background: Trading Direct was founded in 1997 and is the Internet Division of York Securities Inc. Trading Direct designs its online accounts specifically for the individual investor. Trading Direct protects clients' accounts up to $100 million; SIPC provides up to $500,000, of which $100,000 is for cash coverage. All accounts are held at U.S. Clearing Corporation.

Customer Service Rating: ★★★ Excellent

Gomez Rating: 5.47

TREND TRADER LLC

Brokerage Type: Direct access

Mailing Address: 15030 N. Hayden Road Suite 120
                    Scottsdale, AZ 85260

Web Address: www.trendtrader.com

Email Address: GI@trendtrader.com

Telephone Number: 480-948-1146

Fax Number: 480-948-1195

Market Orders: Trend Trader Order Routing System schedule: 1–749 shares (Nasdaq/NYSE/Amex), $10.00 per trade plus $0.02 per share; 750–999 shares (Nasdaq/NYSE/Amex), $21.95 per trade; 1,000–5,000 shares (Nasdaq): $18.95 per trade; 5,000 or more shares (Nasdaq), $18.95 per trade plus $0.01 per share above 5,000; 1,000–2,000 shares (NYSE/Amex), $18.95 per trade; 2,000 or more shares (NYSE/Amex), $18.95 per trade plus $0.01 per share above 2,000; 1–5,000 shares (Bulletin Board), $35.00 per trade; 5,000 or more shares (Bulletin

Board), $35.00 per trade plus $0.01 per share above 5,000. Active traders discount: 200 or more trades per month, 5% discount; 400 or more trades per month, 10% discount; 600 or more trades per month, 15% discount. Trend Trader Easy Trader schedule: Nasdaq stocks, $15.00 per trade, up to 5,000 shares, and additional $0.01 per share thereafter; NYSE/Amex stocks, $15.00 per trade, up to 2,000 shares, and additional $0.01 per share thereafter; Bulletin Board stocks, $35.00 per trade, up to 5,000 shares, and additional $0.01 per share thereafter.

Limit Orders: Same as market orders.

Option Trades: $25.00 per trade plus $3.00 per contract. Minimum charge: $35.00. Discounted commissions with large-volume option trading.

Telephone Trading: OTC (Nasdaq): $25.00 per trade. Listed stocks (Amex, NYSE): $25.00 per trade, up to 5,000 shares, and additional $0.01 per share thereafter.

After-Hours Trading: 8:00 P.M. to 9:30 P.M. EST and 4:00 P.M. to 5:30 P.M. EST. Commissions same as online schedule.

Products Available to Trade Online: Stocks, options, mutual funds, and bonds.

Average Execution Time: Market order: 1–2 seconds.

Minimum Deposit Required: Trend Trader Easy Trader: $5,000. Trend Trader Order Routing System: $15,000.

Additional Fees: Software fees: TORS Elite, $305.00 per month, includes NYSE, ASE, Nasdaq Level II and OPRA exchange fees. Additional news feed fees: Comtex, $25.00. Exchange fees not included in software price: CBOT, $55.00; CME, $10.00. All software fees are waived to clients with 80 or more trades per month (40 round trips). TORS Wall Streeter: $205.00 per month, includes NYSE, ASE, Nasdaq Level II, and OPRA exchange fees. Additional news feed fees: Comtex, $25.00. All software fees are waived to clients with 40 or more trades per month (20 round trips). TORS Express: $103.00 per month, includes NYSE, ASE, Nasdaq Level I, and OPRA exchange fees. Additional news feed fees: Comtex, $25.00. All software fees are waived to clients who trade 20 trades per month (10 round trips). Exchange fee: ARCA, $0.005 per share. Wires outgoing: $15.00. Registry and delivery of certificates: $15.00. Fed call extensions: $10.00. Returned check: $40.00. Bond redemption: $20.00. Overnight delivery (U.S.): $20.00. Transfer charge: $25.00. Stop check fee: $15.00. Legal Items, per CUSIP: $25.00. Early pay of fund: $15.00.

Free Services and Financial Links: Free training and educational services, newsletter archive, Online Investor Expo, Market Analysis,

Stocktalk Live.com, ON24 Video-Audio News, PRARS top 50 Nominee, InvestorLinks, Market Mavens Report.com, IQC.com, Pionline.com, Webmasters, Trend Trader offers free training seminars at their own facilities for a one week time interval.

Real-Time Quotes: Free streaming real-time quotes.

States Registered In: All U.S. states except CT and NH; HI pending.

Mutual Funds Offered: Approximately 3,000.

Payment for Order Flow: No.

Banking Services Offered: Free check writing and ATM debit card privileges.

Company Background: Trend Trader LLC is a brokerage/dealer founded in 1997 that specializes in online trading. Trend Trader offers electronic order routing and execution services geared toward institutions, day traders, and individuals. The clientele base is varied, and there are several hundred online accounts. The Trend Trader offers three different software packages: the TORS Elite, the TORS Wall Streeter, and the TORS Express. The TORS Elite includes flexible page layout; order routing to SOES, ECNs and DOT; unlimited charting; Level II market maker screens; analytics; online P&L, and buying power. The TORS Wall Streeter includes fixed page layout; order routing to SOES, ECNs, and DOT; single chart, Level II market maker screen; analytics; online P&L; and buying power. The TORS Express includes order routing to SOES, ECNs, and DOT; online P&L, and buying power. Accounts are insured up to $25.5 million.

Customer Service Rating: ★★★ Excellent

TRUTRADE

Brokerage Type: Discount brokerage

Mailing Address: 142 North Star West
                       619 Marquette Ave. S.
                       Minneapolis, MN 55402-1701

Web Address: www.trutrade.com

Email Address: info@levitt-levitt.com

Telephone Number: 800-328-8600, 800-671-8505

Fax Number: 612-339-2859

Market Orders: OTC stocks: $12.95 per trade, unlimited shares. Listed stocks: $12.95 per trade, up to 1,999 shares, and additional $0.01 per share thereafter.

Limit Orders for Stocks: OTC stocks: $17.95 per trade, unlimited shares. Listed stocks: $17.95 per trade, up to 1,999 shares, and additional $0.01 per share thereafter.

Option Trades: Under $1.00: $2.00 per contract. $1.00 to $3.99: $3.00 per contract. $4.00 and over: $4.00 per contract. Minimum commission: $29.00.

Telephone Trading: $35.00 minimum, price is determined by number of shares and price of stock.

After-Hours Trading: None.

Products Available to Trade Online: Stocks, options, mutual funds, and corporate bonds.

Average Execution Time: Market order: Within 30 seconds.

Minimum Deposit Required: $5,000 for cash or margin accounts.

Additional Fees: Extensions: $10.00. Wired funds: $20.00. Returned check: $25.00. Accommodation transfer: $25.00 per security. Legal transfer: $35.00 per security. Sell out/buy in mailgrams: $20.00. Duplicate confirmation: $2.50 each. Copies of checks: $20.00 each. IRA termination fee: $50.00. Initial set up fee for qualified retirement plan: $45.00. Annual maintenance for QRP: $60.00. Additional participants for QRP: $35.00 each. Termination fee for QRP: $75.00. Duplicate statements: $5.00 each.

Free Services and Financial Links: No-fee IRA set up, portfolio tracker, Market Snapshot, intraday graphs, indices, statistics, headlines, commentaries, reports, stock charts, ink link stock reports, historical price data, symbol lookup, company news.

Real-Time Quotes: Real-time quotes for a fee of $29.95 per month. The quotes are not streaming and must be refreshed. Clients also have access to free 15-minute delayed quotes.

States Registered In: All U.S. states.

Mutual Funds Offered: Over 1,500.

Payment for Order Flow: Yes.

Banking Services Offered: Free check writing privileges with a money market account.

Company Background: TruTrade is offered through ReCom Securities, Inc., which was founded in 1977. Online trading with TruTrade was launched by ReCom in 1988. TruTrade utilizes U.S. Clearing as its clearing agent. Clients' accounts are protected up to $500,000, of which $100,000 is for cash coverage, provided by SIPC. Additional coverage of $99.5 million is provided by U.S. Clearing. Clientele at TruTrade is composed mainly of individuals and some money managers.

Customer Service Rating: ★★★ Excellent

UNIFIED MANAGEMENT CORPORATION ONLINE

Brokerage Type: Discount brokerage
Mailing Address: Electronic Services
                Unified Management Corporation
                431 N. Pennsylvania St.
                Indianapolis, IN 46204-1806
Web Address: www.umcstock.com
Email Address: customerservice@umcbd.com
Telephone Number: 888-862-7862
Fax Number: 317-266-8756
Market Orders: Listed stocks: $14.95 per trade, up to 2,000 shares, and additional $0.01 per share thereafter. OTC stocks: 1,000 shares or more and above $2.00 per share, trades are commission free. All other OTC/Nasdaq trades: $14.95 per trade.
Limit Orders: Same as market orders.
Option Trades: $19.95 per trade plus $1.75 per contract.
Telephone Trading: $19.95 per trade.
After-Hours Trading: None.
Products Available to Trade Online: Stocks, options, and mutual funds.
Average Execution Time: Market order: less than 5 seconds, depending on market conditions.
Minimum Deposit Required: None for cash account. $2,000 for margin account.
Additional Fees: Return check fee: $15.00. Transfer out: $50.00. Re-organization: $25.00. Inactivity (no trades for 12 months): $35.00.
Free Services and Financial Links: Postage and handling, portfolio tracker and automatic valuation, Bloomberg TV, UFS Financial Search Assistant (requires real audio), Reuters, AP-Online, Business Wire, PR Newswire, Newsbytes, economic calendar, Market Guide, Zacks, monthly earning calendar, symbol and ticker lookup, Lipper Analytics, charts option montage, market statistics, option chains, Meta Stock, Hot Stocks, Earnings Whisper, IPO information.
Real-Time Quotes: Unlimited streaming real-time quotes on a subscription basis: $30.00 per month plus exchange fees. Clients are offered free real-time quotes at time of order entry; one quote is available with each trade being placed. Unlimited delayed quotes are also free to Unified clientele.
States Registered In: All U.S. states.
Mutual Funds Offered: 700 from 317 families.

Payment for Order Flow: Yes.

Banking Services Offered: None.

Company Background: Unified Underwriters was founded in 1952 and changed its name to Unified Management Corporation in 1976. Unified Management began online trading in 1999 and has a client base predominantly composed of individual traders, with some fund managers. UMC Online is designed for traders who prefer to handle their finances online with little or no broker contact. Clients' accounts are protected up to $100 million per account. SIPC provides $500,000, of which $100,000 is for cash. The additional $99.5 million is provided by Asset Guaranty Insurance Co. Unified Management utilizes U.S. Clearing as its clearing firm.

Customer Service Rating: ★★★ Excellent

Gomez Rating: 5.17

U.S. BANCORP

Brokerage Type: Discount brokerage

Mailing Address: U.S. Bank Place
601 Second Ave South
Minneapolis, MN 55402

Web Address: www.usbancorp.com

Email Address: 1800usbank@usbank.com

Telephone Number: 800-872-2657, 800-888-4700

Fax Number: None.

Market Orders: $25.00 per trade, up to 1,000 shares, and additional $0.03 per share thereafter.

Limit Orders: Same as market orders.

Option Trades: 20% discount off telephone trading commission.

Telephone Trading: Stock trades: $0–2,500.99, $38.00 per trade plus .007 times transaction amount; $2,501–6,000.99, $42.00 per trade plus .006 times transaction amount; $6,001–22,000, $62.00 per trade plus .003 times transaction amount; $22,001–50,000, $92.00 per trade plus .002 times transaction amount; $50,001–500,000.99, $132.00 plus .001 times transaction amount; $500,001 and over, $227.00 per trade plus .0008 times transaction amount. Option trades: $0–2,500.99, $38.00 per trade plus .01 times transaction amount; $2,501–10,000.99, $40.00 per trade plus .008 times transaction amount; $10,001 and over, $100.00 per trade plus .003 times transaction amount. Minimum: $30.00 or $2.00 per contract.

After-Hours Trading: None.

Products Available to Trade Online: Stocks, options, and mutual funds.

Average Execution Time: Market order: 15–20 seconds.

Minimum Deposit Required: $1,000 for cash account. $2,000 for margin account.

Additional Fees: Certificate registration: $25.00. IRA termination: $25.00. Wire transfer U.S.: $15.00. Returned check: $20.00. Late payment extension: $15.00. Voluntary tender offer acceptance: $32.00. Account research: $25.00 per hour. Replacements of statements: $5.00 for the first, $2.00 for each additional.

Free Services and Financial Links: Investor Bulletin, Standard & Poor's, Thompson Financial, stock and mutual fund screening, Market Snapshot, financial planning tools, market news and commentary.

Real-Time Quotes: 100 free real-time quotes with every trade executed. The quotes are not streaming and must be refreshed.

States Registered In: All U.S. states.

Mutual Funds Offered: Many.

Payment for Order Flow: No.

Banking Services Offered: None.

Company Background: Bancorp Investments was founded in 1984 and launched its discount online trading in 1998. Clients can request voice or fax confirmations. Clients' accounts are protected up to $500,000, of which $100,000 is for cash coverage, provided by SIPC. Additional coverage up to $24.5 million is provided by a private insurer.

Customer Service Rating: ★★★ Excellent

Gomez Rating: 5.35

US RICA

Brokerage Type: Discount brokerage

Mailing Address: US Rica Financial, Inc.
1630 Oakland Road, Suite A108
San Jose, CA 95131

Web Address: www.usrica.com

Email Address: info@usrica.com

Telephone Number: 408-453-9151

Fax Number: 408-436-1670

Market Orders: 500 shares or more: $4.95 per trade. Under 500 shares (listed or Nasdaq stocks): $9.95 per trade.

Limit Orders: Same as market orders.

Option Trades: None.

Telephone Trading: $34.95 per trade. If US Rica's Internet system goes down, Internet rates will apply.

After-Hours Trading: None.

Products Available to Trade Online: Stocks.

Average Execution Time: Market order: Immediate.

Minimum Deposit Required: None, but sufficient funds must be in account prior to place first trade for a cash account. $5,000 for margin account.

Additional Fees: Service charge on every trade: $2.50. Urgent communication mailgrams: $5.00. Wiring of funds out: $15.00. Personal checks returned fee: $15.00. Galaxy Money Reserve checks returned: $12.00. Special registration of stock certificates: $15.00 per certificate. Duplicate copies of monthly statement: first page $5.00, additional pages $2.00 each. Stop check: $10.00. IRA transfer: $50.00. Duplicate statements of checks issued over 6 months ago: $15.00.

Free Services and Financial Links: Company news, Small Cap—OTC News, economic calendar, Snapshot Report, equity indices, currency rates, hot stocks, company profiles, IPO information, graphs, charts.

Real-Time Quotes: Real-time quotes, although they are not streaming and must be refreshed.

States Registered In: All U.S. states except AS, MT, ND, SD, VT, and WY.

Mutual Funds Offered: Over 400.

Payment for Order Flow: No.

Banking Services Offered: Free unlimited check writing.

Company Background: US RICA is an independent brokerage/dealer that was founded in May 1995. The clientele base consists mainly of individuals. US RICA utilizes U.S. Clearing as its clearing firm. Clients' accounts are protected by SIPC up to $500,000, of which $100,000 is for cash coverage, and the remaining coverage is provided by Asset Guaranty.

Customer Service Rating: ★ Poor

Gomez Rating: 3.67

VANGUARD BROKERAGE SERVICES

Brokerage Type: Discount brokerage

Mailing Address: P.O. Box 2600
Valley Forge, PA 19482-2600

Web Address: www.vanguard.com

Email Address: www.vanguard.com

Telephone Number: 800-992-8327

Fax Number: None.

Market Orders: $20.00 per trade or $0.02 per share, whichever is greater. Stocks priced less than $1.00: the rate is $30.00 per trade plus 3% of principal.

Limit Orders: Same as market orders.

Option Trades: $30.00 per trade plus $1.50 per contract.

Telephone Trading: Stock trades: $45.00 per trade or $0.03 per share, whichever is greater. Option trades: $30.00 per trade plus $2.50 per contract.

After-Hours Trading: 4:15 P.M. to 7:00 P.M. EST. Internet, limit orders, round lots only. Commissions same as online schedule.

Products Available to Trade Online: Stocks, options, and mutual funds.

Average Execution Time: Market order: 10–15 seconds.

Minimum Deposit Required: $3,000 for cash account. None for margin accounts.

Additional Fees: Returned check fee: $20.00. Option exercises and assignments: $45.00 per trade plus $0.03 per share.

Free Services and Financial Links: Free dividend reinvestment, Vickers Insider Trading, Standard & Poor's stock, industry, and news reports, Lipper Fund Analysis, Argus Company Reports, Business Wire, Vanguard University (learn the basics in investing), financial news and commentary, news archive, Newsletters, speeches and interviews, fund finder, symbol/company lookup, fund comparison tool, cost comparison tool/after-tax returns calculator, historical price charts, Trade Winds (VBS's own newsletter).

Real-Time Quotes: 250 real-time quotes with new account and 100 more with each trade placed. The quotes are not streaming and must be refreshed. Clients can also customize a tracker that provides delayed quotes.

States Registered In: All U.S. states.

Mutual Funds Offered: Over 2,600.

Payment for Order Flow: Yes.

Banking Services Offered: Check writing with the Vanguard Money Market Settlement Account for retail clients.

Company Background: Vanguard Marketing Corp. was originally founded in 1974 and launched its online trading under the name Vanguard Brokerage Services in November 1998. Vanguard specializes in mutual funds but also offers its clientele the versatility of trading other financial products online. Vanguard allows clients both access to hand-pick their portfolio of investments in an account that is linked to their money market account and access to most Vanguard funds. Clients' accounts at Vanguard are protected up to $500,000, of which $100,000 is for cash claims. The remaining coverage is offered by Pershing, a division of Donaldson, Lufkin, & Jenrette Securities Corp., its clearing agent.

Customer Service Rating: ★★★ Excellent

Gomez Rating: 5.63

VISION TRADE

Brokerage Type: Discount brokerage

Mailing Address: 310 Central Ave.
Lawrence, NY 11559

Web Address: www.visiontrade.com

Email Address: info@visiontrade.com

Telephone Number: 516-374-2184

Fax Number: 516-374-8443

Market Orders: $14.95 per trade, up to 2,000 shares, and additional $0.01 per share on entire order thereafter.

Limit Orders: Same as market orders.

Option Trades: Options trading under $1.00: $20.00 plus $1.50 per contract, up to 2,000 shares, and additional $0.01 per share thereafter. Options trading $1.00 and over: $20.00 plus $2.00 per contract, up to 2,000 shares, and additional $0.01 per share thereafter. $25.00 minimum.

Telephone Trading: $20.00 additional surcharge.

After-Hours Trading: 8:00 A.M. to 9:30 A.M. EST and 4:00 P.M. to 6:00 P.M. EST. Broker-assisted trading only; broker-assisted commissions apply.

Products Available to Trade Online: Stocks, options, and mutual funds.

Average Execution Time: Market order: within 30 seconds.

Minimum Deposit Required: None, but sufficient funds must be in account to place first trade.

Additional Fees: IRA termination fee: $50.00. Prototype Money Purchace and Profit Sharing (initial setup): $45.00. Annual maintenance: first participant, $60.00; additional participants, $35.00 each; termination charge: $75.00. Legal transfer: $20.00. Extensions: $6.00. Mail-grams: $5.00. Returned checks: $20.00. Additional copies of statements and confirmations: $5.00. Copies of checks: $20.00. Wire transfer of funds outgoing: $20.00.

Free Services and Financial Links: No-fee IRA setup, no-fee IRA annual maintenance, no-fee wire funds incoming, currency rates, hot stock list, Java charts, company news, Zacks, second opinion, portfolio tracker.

Real-Time Quotes: 100 real-time quotes with new account and more quotes with each trade placed. The quotes are not streaming and must be refreshed.

States Registered In: CA, CT, DE, FL, GA, IN, KS, MA, MD, ME, MI, NH, NJ, NY, OH, OK, OR, PA, RI, TN, VA, VT, and WV.

Mutual Funds Offered: Hundreds.

Payment for Order Flow: Yes.

Banking Services Offered: None.

Company Background: Vision Securities was founded in 1993 and launched online trading through Vision Trade in 1998. Vision Trade caters to the active and long-term investor and states that they are not geared for the day trader. Vision Trade assigns its clients their own personal broker and requests that its clients have some knowledge of trading before opening an account. Clientele at Vision Trade consists mainly of individuals. Securities in clients' accounts are protected by SIPC, with coverage up to $500,000, of which $100,000 is for cash coverage. Asset Guaranty Insurance Co. provides clients with additional coverage up to $99.5 million.

Customer Service Rating: ★★★ Excellent

Gomez Rating: 4.56

WACHOVIA

Brokerage Type: Discount brokerage

Mailing Address: Wachovia Investments
101 Greystone Blvd.
Columbia, SC 29202

Web Address: www.wachovia.com

Email Address: onlineinvesting@wachovia.com

Telephone Number: 800-922-9008

Fax Number: 803-988-4044

Market Orders: 1–9 trades per year: $29.95 per trade, up to 1,000 shares, and additional $0.03 per share thereafter. 10–19 trades per year: $24.95 per trade, up to 1,000 shares, and additional $0.025 per share thereafter. 20 or more trades per year: $19.95 per trade, up to 1,000 shares, and additional $0.02 per share thereafter.

Limit Orders: Same as market orders.

Option Trades: 20% discount off broker-assisted commission schedule. Minimum option trade: $32.00.

Telephone Trading: Stock trades: $0–3,000, $29.95 per trade plus 1.7% of principal amount; $3,001–8,000, $54.95 per trade plus 0.7% of principal amount; $8,001–20,000, $69.95 per trade plus 0.4% of principal amount; $20,001–50,000, $99.95 per trade plus 0.2% of principal amount; $50,001–500,000, $149.95 per trade plus 0.1% of principal amount; $500,000 or more, $254.95 per trade; minimum commission, $40.00 per trade; maximum commission, $0.55 per share. Options with premiums of $0.50 or less: 0–49 contracts, $1.80 plus 1.8% of principal amount; 50–149 contracts, $1.10 plus 1.8% of principal amount; 150–499 contracts, $0.75 plus 2.0% of principal amount; 500–1,499 contracts, $0.60 plus 2.0% of principal amount; 1,500 or more contracts, $0.60 plus 1.5% of principal amount. Options with premiums greater than $0.50: $0–2,999, $29.00 per trade plus 1.6% of principal amount; $3,000–9,999, $49.00 per trade plus 0.8% of principal amount; $10,000 or more, $99.00 per trade plus 0.3% of principal amount; minimum commission, $40.00 per trade.

After-Hours Trading: None.

Products Available to Trade Online: Stocks, options, and mutual funds.

Average Execution Time: Market order: Less than 30 seconds, depending on market conditions.

Minimum Deposit Required: $10,000 for Investors Account.

Additional Fees: Safekeeping: $30.00 per year. NSF (returned check): $20.00. Reorganization: $40.00. IRA annual fee: $40.00; if paid by check, $30.00. Annual IRA custodian fee: $20.00. IRA termination: $50.00. Annual Wachovia Investors Account fee: $85.00. Registration of securities: $25.00. Security delivery: $15.00.

Free Services and Financial Links: Investors Education Center, charts, news, analytical information, calculators.

Real-Time Quotes: 1,000 real-time quotes with new account and 100 more with each trade placed. The quotes are not streaming and must be refreshed.

States Registered In: All U.S. states.

Mutual Funds Offered: Several.

Payment for Order Flow: Yes.

Banking Services Offered: Investors Account: access to a money market account, brokerage account, and a checking account.

Company Background: Wachovia Corporation was originally founded in 1888 and is currently a leading interstate financial holding company. Wachovia launched its online trading site, Wachovia.com, in 1998 through Wachovia Investments Direct. As of March 2000, Wachovia reached total assets of $68.8 billion. Wachovia has been providing personal, corporate, and institutional service for over 100 years. Clients' accounts are protected up to $500,000, of which $100,000 is for cash coverage, provided by SIPC. Wachovia Corporation's common shares are traded on the NYSE, under the symbol WB, and is also included in the S&P 500.

Customer Service Rating: ★★★ Excellent

Gomez Rating: 4.88

WALL STREET ACCESS

Brokerage Type: Discount brokerage

Mailing Address: Online Sales Dept.
17 Battery Place
New York, NY 10004

Web Address: www.wsaccess.com

Email Address: info@wsaccess.com

Telephone Number: 800-925-5781

Fax Number: 212-709-9530

Market Orders: $25.00 per trade, up to 5,000 shares, and additional $0.02 per share thereafter.

Limit Orders: Same as market orders.

Option Trades: $25.00 per trade plus $1.50 per contract (less than $1.00); $25.00 per trade plus $2.00 per contract ($1.00 or more).

Telephone Trading: $45.00 per trade, up to 5,000 shares, and additional $0.02 per share thereafter. Broker assisted options trading: $40.00 plus $1.50 per contract (less than $1.00); $40.00 plus $2.00 per contract ($1.00 or more).

After-Hours Trading: 7:00 A.M. to 9:30 A.M. EST and 4:00 P.M. to 9:00 P.M. EST (Monday to Thursday). 7:00 A.M. to 9:30 A.M. EST and 4:00 P.M. to 7:00 P.M. EST (Friday). Trades placed through live broker only. $0.04 a share $80.00 minimum (limit orders only).

Products Available to Trade Online: Stocks, options, and bonds.

Average Execution Time: Market order: 20 seconds under normal market conditions.

Minimum Deposit Required: $10,000 for all accounts.

Additional Fees: Wires: $10.00. Overnight delivery: $10.00. Postage and handling: $1.50 per transaction. Special registration: $17.50 per certificate. Foreign wires: $30.00. Legal rejects: $50.00 per item. Copies of back statements or confirmations: $5.00 per statement (six months or older). IRA termination fee: $50.00.

Free Services and Financial Links: TheStreet.com market commentary, D B Alex Brown Morning Notes, Briefing.com, Zacks, CBS Marketwatch, transfer and shipping, no-fee IRA accounts, CBS Newsroom, Wall Street Access will help pay for Omega Research Software or DBC subscriptions by rebating the fee depending on how high equity or options commissions are each month, portfolio tracking, stock split alerts, Market Guide.

Real-Time Quotes: Free real-time quotes during market hours, although they are not streaming and must be refreshed. New accounts will receive a free one-year subscription to Windows On Wall Street, which will provide streaming real-time quotes to clients.

States Registered In: All U.S. states.

Mutual Funds Offered: Several.

Payment for Order Flow: Yes, but not for every situation.

Banking Services Offered: Check writing privileges through a money market fund. Cash Management Accounts offer VISA debit card privileges, a competitive line of credit, and automated funds transfer.

Company Background: Wall Street Access was founded in 1981 and is an independently owned and operated member of the NYSE. Wall Street Access's clientele consists primarily of sophisticated retail investors and small institutions. Wall Street Access will refund the commission on any trade if a client is not completely satisfied with the service received. Wall Street Access has added something new to their online trading features: Clients can now place sophisticated option trades such as spreads, straddles, and buy-writes online. Preapproved clients can trade the following through their IRA accounts: purchases of puts and calls, covered call writing, and married puts. Clients' accounts are protected up to $500,000, of which $100,000 is for cash coverage, provided by SIPC. Clients also have unlimited protection through the company's clearing firm, Deutsche Banc Alex Brown.

Customer Service Rating: ★★★ Excellent

WALL STREET DISCOUNT CORPORATION

Brokerage Type: Discount brokerage
Mailing Address: 100 Wall Street 7th Floor
New York, NY 10005
Web Address: www.wsdc.com
Email Address: info@wsdc.com
Telephone Number: 888-4WALLST
Fax Number: 212-809-3899
Market Orders: $19.95 per trade, up to 2,500 shares, and additional $0.015 per share thereafter.
Limit Orders: Same as market orders.
Option Trades: Option price: $\frac{1}{16}$ to $\frac{1}{2}$, $1.50 per contract; $\frac{9}{16}$ to $\frac{15}{16}$, $1.75 per contract; 1 to $1\frac{15}{16}$, $2.00 per contract; 2 to $3\frac{7}{8}$, $2.25 per contract; 4 to $7\frac{7}{8}$, $2.75 per contract; 8 to $13\frac{7}{8}$, $3.00 per contract; 14 to $19\frac{7}{8}$, $4.00 per contract; 20 and over, $5.25 per contract. Option trades may not exceed 10 contracts over the web. $29.95 minimum.
Telephone Trading: $29.95 per trade, up to 2,500 shares, and additional $0.015 per share thereafter.
After-Hours Trading: None.
Products Available to Trade Online: Stocks, options, and mutual funds.
Average Execution Time: Market order: 1–2 minutes under normal market conditions.
Minimum Deposit Required: None, but client must have sufficient funds in account to place first trade.
Additional Fees: Late payment on cash account: $4.00 plus late interest charge. Mailgrams: $7.50. Foreign mailgrams: $30.00. Postage and handling: $3.50. Extensions: $5.00. Returned check fee: $35.00. Stop payment fee: $25.00. Wire fee: $20.00.
Free Services and Financial Links: Quote.com, financial web.
Real-Time Quotes: 100 free real-time quotes with new account and 100 free quotes with each executed trade. The quotes are not streaming and must be refreshed.
States Registered In: All U.S. states.
Mutual Funds Offered: Thousands.
Payment for Order Flow: Yes.
Banking Services Offered: None.
Company Background: The Wall Street Discount Corporation was founded in 1978. It began its online trading at wsdc.com at the end of 1997. WSDC caters to individual traders as well as day traders and cur-

rently services approximately 1,000 online accounts. WSDC utilizes Ernst & Co. as its clearing firm. Clients' securities are protected by SIPC up to $500,000, of which $100,000 is for cash coverage. An additional $49.5 million is provided by a private insurer.

Customer Service Rating: ★★★ Excellent

WALL STREET ELECTRONICA ONLINE TRADING INC.

Brokerage Type: Full-service/discount brokerage
Mailing Address: 7242 SW 42 Terr.
Miami, FL 33155
Web Address: www.wallstreete.com
Email Address: info@wallstreete.com
Telephone Number: 305-669-3026, 888-925-5783
Fax Number: 305-661-7402
Market Orders: Nasdaq (OTC): $24.95 per trade, up to 1,000 shares, and additional $0.02 per share thereafter. NYSE listed: $29.95 per trade plus $0.02 per share.
Limit Orders: $29.95 per trade plus $0.02 per share.
Option Trades: $25.00 per trade plus $2.50 per contract.
Telephone Trading: $20.00 additional surcharge per trade plus $0.01 per share.
After-Hours Trading: 4:30 P.M. to 6:00 P.M. EST. $29.95 plus $0.02 per share; limit orders only; trades placed through live broker only.
Products Available to Trade Online: Stocks, options, mutual funds, and bonds.
Average Execution Time: Market order: 15–25 seconds under constant market conditions.
Minimum Deposit Required: $2,500 for cash or margin account.
Additional Fees: IRA annual fee: $25.00. Accommodation transfer: $40.00. Domestic money wire outgoing: $35.00. Foreign money wire outgoing: $35.00. Overnight check request: $15.00. ACAT transfer out: $100.00. DTC transfer: $25.00. Closing of account: $50.00. Fed call extension: $15.00. Buy in/sell out: $15.00. Yearly inactivity fee: $75.00. Returned check: $25.00. Stop payment: $25.00. Certificate insurance: $25.00. Double ticket charge: $20.00. Restricted securities processing fee: $150.00. Extensions: $25.00. Physical DVP: $15.00. IRA setup: $25.00. Service charge for postage and handling: pending electronic confirmations. Cancel corrects: $20.00. Options exercise and assignments: $25.00. Request for noncurrent statement: $15.00 annual fee.

Miscellaneous service rendered: $25.00. Stock certificate handling fee: $25.00. Cash (margin call letters): $5.00. Transaction of restricted account: $20.00 per trade.

Free Services and Financial Links: Charts, news from Reuters, PR Newswire, Business Wire, CBS Marketwatch, Zacks, detailed profile of mutual funds, Edgar Reports, personal profile, criteria searches, bond quotes, investment newsletters.

Real-Time Quotes: 100 free real-time quotes per day, although they are not streaming and must be refreshed. Streaming real-time quotes will be offered in the near future.

States Registered In: All U.S. states.

Mutual Funds Offered: Over 200.

Payment for Order Flow: No.

Banking Services Offered: Free check writing and ATM debit card privileges with an online account. Wall Street Electronica offers an "all-in-one" bank account with a minimum deposit of $5,000. This account is accessible 24 hours a day, 7 days a week. All balances in the account will earn 4.625% interest.

Company Background: Wall Street Electronica Online Trading Inc. was founded in 1992 and services global investors, independent financial advisors, brokers, and banks. Client securities are held by Herzog Heine Geduld and protected up to $25 million per account. Wall Street Electronica also specializes in supporting investors, brokers, investment advisors, money managers, and financial institutions needing efficient handling of their transactions over the Internet. Wall Street Electronica is a member of the NASD, SIA, and SIPC, and is registered with the SEC. Wall Street Electronica offers clients who generate more than $1,000 in commissions per month a 15% discount on commissions over $1,000. Clients who are charged $2,000 in commission will receive a 20% discount.

Customer Service Rating: ★★★ Excellent

Gomez Rating: 6.14

WANG INVESTMENTS

Brokerage Type: Discount brokerage
Mailing Address: 41-60 Main St. Suite 209
Flushing, NY 11355
Web Address: www.wangvest.com
Email Address: info@wangvest.com

Telephone Number: 800-353-9264, 718-353-9264 outside U.S.

Fax Number: 718-353-9711

Market Orders: $8.00 per trade (stocks $1.00 or less per share); $5.00 per trade (stocks at $5.00 or more and 1,000 shares or more).

Limit Orders: $8.00 per trade (stocks $1.00 or less per share).

Option Trades: $15.00 per trade plus $1.75 per contract. $25.00 minimum per option order.

Telephone Trading: $22.00 per trade, $37.00 round trip. Canadian equities: $22.00 per trade plus $0.02 per share. Foreign equities: $125.00 per trade plus $0.02 per share. Options trades: $20.00 per trade plus $2.00 per contract. $30.00 minimum per option order.

After-Hours Trading: 4:00 P.M. to 8:00 P.M. EST. Broker-assisted trades only. $25.00 per trade.

Products Available to Trade Online: Stocks, options, and mutual funds.

Average Execution Time: Market order: within 10 minutes.

Minimum Deposit Required: None, but a fee of $20.00 will be charged on accounts opened with less than $5,000.

Additional Fees: Special handling fee to direct Wang Investments where and how to execute trades. Postage and handling for all trades: $3.00. Account opening fees: $20.00 (one time fee, waived if equity in account is greater than $5,000). Late payment charges: $0.25 per day, per $1,000 of principal from settlement date. Duplicate monthly statements: free if notified in advance, otherwise $5.00 per month. Transfer and ship: $20.00 per certificate. Margin extensions: $10.00. Mailgrams: $5.00. Bank wiring of funds: $25.00. IRA annual maintenance fee: $30.00, waived if equity is less than $10,000. IRA termination: distribution fees, $50.00. Processing ACAT termination: $30.00. Inactive custodian fees: $25.00. Voluntary or mandatory reorganization: $25.00. Returned checks: $25.00. Stop payment: $25.00. Option exercise and assignment: $20.00 per transaction. Legal returns: $30.00. Wang-DTN.IQ (real-time news & data): $95.00 signup fee plus $89.00 per month service fee.

Free Services and Financial Links: Barrons Online, Bloomberg, Briefing.com, New York Times Business, TheStreet.com, Wall Street Journal, CNBC, Finance.com, SmartMoney.com, Thomson Investors Network, Money.com, Stock Master, Yahoo Finance Industry Research, Nelson's Company Profiles, NYSE-Amex-Nasdaq market statistics, stock screener, Morningstar Mutual Fund Screener, fund profiles, news, options lookup, charts, calculators.

Real-Time Quotes: 400 free real-time quotes, $0.005 per quote thereafter. The quotes are not streaming and must be refreshed. Free unlimited 20-minute delayed quotes are also available.

States Registered In: AK, CA, CO, CT, DC, DE, FL, GA, IA, ID, IN, KS, KY, LA, MA, MD, ME, MI, MN, MT, NB, NH, NJ, NV, NY, OH, OK, OR, PA, RI, SC, SD, TN, TX, UT, VA, WA, WI, WV, WY.

Mutual Funds Offered: Approximately 1,000.

Payment for Order Flow: No.

Banking Services Offered: Check writing and a VISA debit card for a $60 annual fee. Clients who are only interested in check writing privileges can receive free check writing through a Brokerage Access Account.

Company Background: Wang Investments was founded in 1986 and caters to individuals as well as institutional clients. The firm appeals to Chinese investors also, offering its website in Chinese as well as English. Wang does not provide investment advice or guidance to its clientele; it only supplies the tools and services that investors need to trade as effectively as possible. Clients' accounts are protected by SIPC up to $500,000, of which $100,000 is for cash coverage, and additional coverage up to $99.5 million provided by Asset Guaranty Insurance Company.

Customer Service Rating: ★★ Average

Gomez Rating: 5.90

WEB STREET

Brokerage Type: Discount brokerage

Mailing Address: 510 Lake Cook Road 4th Floor
Deerfield, IL 60015

Web Address: www.webstreetsecurities.com

Email Address: customerservice@webstreetsecurities.com

Telephone Number: 800-932-8723, 312-775-6700 (outside U.S.)

Fax Number: 312-258-9103

Market Orders: $14.95 per trade, up to 1,000 Nasdaq shares. Commission is free with trade of 1,000 or more shares of Nasdaq stocks and with stock trading above $2.00.

Limit Orders: Same as market orders.

Option Trades: $14.95 per trade plus $1.75 per contract.

Telephone Trading: Stock trades: $24.95 per trade. Option trades: $24.95 plus $1.75 per contract.

After-Hours Trading: 4:00 P.M. to 6:00 P.M. EST. $24.95 per trade, broker-assisted only.

Products Available to Trade Online: Stocks, options, and mutual funds.

Average Execution Time: Market order: 6–10 seconds.

Minimum Deposit Required: None for cash account. $2,000 for margin account.

Additional Fees: Nasdaq Level II Market Maker information: $79.95 a month (includes streaming real-time quotes). One-Click Trading, including streaming real-time quotes: $49.95 per month; with Nasdaq Level II Market Maker information, additional $50.00 per month. Wire transfer out: $20.00. Delivery of certificates: $25.00. Legal transfers: $15.00. Regulation T extensions: $25.00. Returned check fee: $25.00. IRA termination: $50.00.

Free Services and Financial Links: Baseline company and industry files, customers trading 25 trades per month or possessing account balance of $250,000 will receive watchlists and one-click trading free (excluding the Nasdaq level II Market Maker information, customers trading 45 trades per month or possessing account balance of $500,000 will receive both the watchlists and one-click trading plus the Nasdaq level II Market Maker information free, Morning Stars Equity Research, company news, OCT News, economic calendar, Market Snapshots, Java charting, equity indices, category news, intraday charts, global market briefs.

Real-Time Quotes: Free real-time quotes, although they are not streaming and must be refreshed. For $29.95 per month clients can receive streaming real-time quotes.

States Registered In: All U.S. states.

Mutual Funds Offered: Over 4,000 from more than 250 families.

Payment for Order Flow: Yes.

Banking Services Offered: Free unlimited check writing through a Global Asset Manager Account.

Company Background: Web Street was founded in September 1996 and has approximately 87,500 online clients. Web Street protects clients' accounts up to $100 million. The company's share trades on Nasdaq under the symbol WEBS. The SIPC provides insurance coverage of $500,000 ($100,000 in cash and $400,000 in securities) per account. Web Street also provides extended coverage up to $99,500,000 for each account. Web Street offers customer service 24 hours a day, 7 days a week.

Customer Service Rating: ★★★ Excellent
Gomez Rating: 6.40

WILSHIRE CAPITAL MANAGEMENT, LLC

Brokerage Type: Direct access
Mailing Address: 120 Broadway, Suite 960
New York, NY 10271
Web Address: www.wilshirecm.com
Email Address: info@wilshirecm.com
Telephone Number: 800-926-9991, 888-777-4330
Fax Number: 212-433-6024
Market Orders: Nasdaq or NYSE: 0–50 trades per month, $20.00;
51–100 trades per month, $18.00; 101–150 trades per month, $17.00;
151–200 trades per month, $16.00; 200 or more trades per month,
$15.00.
Limit Orders: Same as market orders.
Option Trades: $3.00 per contract plus exchange fees; $25.00 minimum. Broker-assisted trades only.
Telephone Trading: 100 shares of any priced stock: $15.00. 200 shares of any priced stock: $17.50. 300 shares of any priced stock: $20.00. 400 shares of any priced stock: $22.50. 500 or more shares of any priced stock: $0.03 a share; $25.00 minimum. Instinet orders: $0.045 a share; $30.00 minimum.
After-Hours Trading: Island or ARCA: 8:00 A.M. to 9:30 A.M. EST and 4:00 P.M. to 6:30 P.M. EST.
Products Available to Trade Online: Stocks, S&P futures, and treasury bond futures.
Average Execution Time: Depends on volatility of stock.
Minimum Deposit Required: $10,000 for cash or margin account.
Additional Fees and Financial Links: Execution charges (pass-through fees) for market or limit order are as follows. SOES: $0.50 per execution. ISLD (Island): $1.00 per execution. NYSE/Amex (nonbillable): $0.005 per share. NYSE/Amex (billable): over 90 seconds, $0.012 per share. ARCA/ARCA (Archipelago): $0.0005 per share ($0.50 minimum). ARCA/SelectNet Market Maker: $1.50 plus $1.00 per execution. ARCA/ISLD (Island): $1.50 plus $0.0025 per share. ARCA/INCA (Instinet): $1.50 plus $0.015 per share. ARCA/ATTN (Attain): $1.50

plus $0.005 per share. ARCA/REDI: $1.50 plus $0.0025 per share. ARCA/BRUT (BRASS): $1.50 plus $0.005 per share ($1.50 minimum). ARCA/BTRD (Bloomberg): $1.50 plus variable ($4.00 max). ARCA/STRK (Strike): $1.50 plus $0.002 per share. ARCA/NTRD (Pim): $1.50 plus $0.015 per share. Access and exchange fees: 0–50 trades per month, $300.00; 51–100 trades per month, $150.00. Wires out: $20.00. Returned check: $15–20.00. SEC charge 0.1% of market value of each stock. Software fee: $0–300.00 per month based on volume of trading. Dow Jones News Wire: $125.00, waived after 150 trades per month. CME—S&P futures: $10.00, waived after 50 trades per month. CBOT—T-bond futures: $30.00, waived after 50 trades per month.

Free Services and Financial Links: Bloomberg Online, Briefing.com, Big Charts, CBS Marketwatch, CNBC, CNNfn, the Daily Rocket Company, DBC Online, Day Traders USA, Earnings Whisper.com, Individual Investor, investor links, Investools, IPO Central.com, IQC.com, JagNotes.com, Market Guide, the Motley Fool, Market Guide Inc., Microsoft Investor, news alert, ON24, Pristine Day Trader, Quote.com, Silicon Investor, Stock Master, Stock Point, TheStreet.com, Wall Street City, Wall St. Journal Interactive Edition, Zacks, Stockpickers. net, Coast Investments Software, Inc., Gibbons Burke, Epic Investments, P Davies.com, Ajaxo.com, Wall Street Courier, Sapphire Bay, Daytradingstocks.com, The Power House Systems Group, Inc., Doh.com stock picks, historical charts, intraday charts.

Real-Time Quotes: Real-time Level II quotes with software package. Software costs range from $0–300.00, and the fee is based on the amount of trades placed.

States Registered In: All U.S. states excluding AK, AL, AR, CO, DE, IA, KS, KY, ME, MN, MO, MT, ND, NH, OR, PR, SD, UT, WI, WV, WY.

Mutual Funds Offered: At client's request.

Payment for Order Flow: No.

Banking Services Offered: None.

Company Background: Wilshire Capital Management was founded in 1993 and launched online trading in September 1997. Wilshire caters to the serious day trader and the online investor. Clients consist of retail investors, smaller broker/dealers, and hedge funds. Wilshire utilizes Spear, Leeds, and Kellogg as its clearing firm. Clients' accounts are protected up to $24.5 million. The website is offered in Spanish as well as English.

Customer Service Rating: ★★★ Excellent

WINGSPAN INVESTMENT SERVICES, INC.

Brokerage Type: Discount brokerage

Mailing Address: 125 South Wacker Drive, Suite 300
Chicago, IL 60606

Web Address: www.wingspan.com

Email Address: customerservice@wingspanbank.com

Telephone Number: 800-977-9464

Fax Number: 312-954-0672

Market Orders: $19.95 per trade, up to 1,000 shares, and additional $0.02 per share thereafter. Stocks trading at less than $1.00: minimum commission of $20.00 and a maximum of 5% of the principal amount. Wingspan Premier Accounts: $14.95 per trade, up to 1,000 shares, and additional $0.015 per share thereafter. Wingspan Ultimate Account (statement net worth): $100,000–250,000, $500.00 minimum and 0.50%; $250,001–500,000, 0.35%; $500,001–1,000,000, 0.25%; $1,000,001–2,000,000, 0.15%; $2,000,001–5,000,000, 0.10%; $5,000,001–6,000,000, 0.07%; $6,000,001–10,000,000, 0.05%; Over $10 million, negotiable.

Limit Orders: Same as market orders.

Option Trades: $35.00 per trade plus $1.75 per contract.

Telephone Trading: Commissions ranging from $26.25 plus 1.3% of transaction amount to $82.50 plus 0.18% of transaction amount. Options: $40.00 plus $2.50 per contract.

After-Hours Trading: 8:00 A.M. to 9:15 A.M. EST and 4:15 P.M. to 7:00 P.M. EST. Commissions same as online schedule. Trades can be placed through internet or live broker. Limit orders only.

Products Available to Trade Online: Stocks, options, and mutual funds.

Average Execution Time: Market order: Within one minute.

Minimum Deposit Required: $2,000 for cash or margin account.

Additional Fees: Voluntary reorganization: $25.00. Mandatory reorganization: $10.00. Mandatory non-DTC eligible: $25.00. Accommodation transfers: $30.00. Physical redemption: $20.00. Legal transfer: $20.00. Annual custody fee: $40.00. Retrieval of account information: $30.00. Returned check fee: $20.00. Extension fee: $20.00. Wire transfer: $20.00. Custom name change: $15.00.

Free Services and Financial Links: Morning Market Comment, Market Wrapup, credit and interest report, economic and market indicators, week in review, individual stock reports on over 40 stocks, S&P Marketscope, S&P Three Page Reports, online annual reports, automatic sweep money market funds, transaction history up to 120 days, portfolio balances automatically updated, online messaging, mutual fund profiler, real-time quotes, real-time online order status.

Real-Time Quotes: 100 free real-time quotes with each trade placed, although they are not streaming and must be refreshed. Unlimited free delayed quotes are also available.

States Registered In: All U.S. states.

Mutual Funds Offered: Over 7,000.

Payment for Order Flow: Information unavailable.

Banking Services Offered: Wingspan Investment Gold Account: clients must keep a minimum account balance of $10,000 to access check writing and debit card privileges.

Company Background: Wingspan Investment Services, Inc., is a subsidiary of Bank One Corporation and was founded on June 26, 1999. The clientele at Wingspan consists mainly of individuals. Clients' accounts at Wingspan are protected by SIPC up to $500,000, of which $100,000 is for cash coverage, and additional unlimited coverage is provided by Pershing. Wingspan offers a variety of investment accounts. The Wingspan Investment Account caters to the new investor and to the investor who is looking to open a second online brokerage account. The Wingspan Investment Gold Account caters to investors looking for banking services with their online account, and the minimum balance for this account is $10,000. The Wingspan Investment Premier Account caters to investors looking not only for banking services with their account but also for free IRAs and free alerts to email and wireless devices; this account requires a minimum balance of $50,000. The Wingspan Investment Ultimate Account caters to investors who are looking for the convenience of a low asset-based account fee, free trades, and a Platinum debit card. This account requires a $100,000 minimum balance.

Customer Service Rating: ★★★ Excellent

Gomez Rating: 6.07

██████ WORLD TRADE FINANCIAL CORPORATION ██████

Company Name: World Trade Financial Corporation
Brokerage Type: Discount brokerage
Mailing Address: 888 Prospect Street Suite 330
                      La Jolla, CA 92037
Web Address: www.worldtradefinancial.com
Email Address: wtrade1@san.rr.com

Telephone Number: 888-459-8883, 858-459-8883

Fax Number: 858-459-8811

Market Orders: Nasdaq/NYSE/Amex: $29.00 per trade, up to 3,000 shares, and additional $0.02 per share thereafter.

Limit Orders: Same as market orders.

Option Trades: None.

Telephone Trading: Commissions depend on exchange used.

After-Hours Trading: 4:00 P.M. to 5:30 P.M. EST. Same commissions as online schedule.

Products Available to Trade Online: Stocks.

Average Execution Time: Market order: 10–15 seconds depending on stock being traded.

Minimum Deposit Required: $2,500 for cash or margin account.

Additional Fees: Postage and handling: $3.50 per trade. Overnight delivery: $11.00. Check returned: $25.00. Additional fees are charged through clearing firm Emmett A. Larkin Company.

Free Services and Financial Links: Financial research, finance search engine, financial news (Asia), financial news (U.S. and world), futures and option links, U.S. markets and regulators links, money chat, Taxes for Traders.

Real-Time Quotes: Free unlimited streaming real-time quotes.

States Registered In: All U.S. states.

Mutual Funds Offered: None.

Payment for Order Flow: No.

Banking Services Offered: Free check writing privileges.

Company Background: World Trade offers online technology that provides overseas investors with a link to online trading. World Trade's automated system provides routing of clients' trades to all U.S. stock exchanges, market makers, and specialists. World Trade utilizes Emmett A. Larkin Company as its clearing firm. World Trade is a member of NASD and SIPC. Clients' accounts are protected up to $500,000, of which $100,000 is for cash coverage, provided by SIPC. Additional coverage up to $2 million is provided by Emmett A. Larkin Company.

Customer Service Rating: ★★★ Excellent

WR HAMBRECHT

Brokerage Type: Discount brokerage

Mailing Address: WR Hambrecht & Co., LLC
539 Bryant Street Suite 100
San Francisco, CA 94107

Web Address: www.wrhambrecht.com

Email Address: wrhco@wrhambrecht.com

Telephone Number: 877-673-6476, 415-551-8600

Fax Number: 610-725-1167

Market Orders: $19.95 per trade, up to 3,000 shares, and additional $0.02 per share thereafter. Stocks trading less than $1.00: 3% of the total trade value, with an overriding minimum of $19.95 per trade.

Limit Orders: Same as market orders.

Option Trades: $30.00 per trade plus $1.75 per contract.

Telephone Trading: Stock trades: $24.95 per trade, up to 3,000 shares, and additional $0.02 per trade thereafter. Stocks trading less than $1.00: 3% of the total trade, with an overriding minimum of $24.95 per trade. Option trades: $40.00 per trade plus $1.75 per contract.

After-Hours Trading: None.

Products Available to Trade Online: Stocks, mutual funds, IPOs, and options.

Average Execution Time: Not divulged.

Minimum Deposit Required: $2,000 for cash or margin account.

Additional Fees: Late payment: $15.00. Returned check fee: $15.00. Transfer of securities into name other than name on account: $25.00. Account transfer: $12.50. Wire transfer: $15.00. Annual safekeeping: $20.00 per year (waived upon one transaction per year).

Free Services and Financial Links: Radio Wallstreet, eNetwork Research, Red Herring Charts, WRH & Co. research, Marketwatch, sector updates, financial news, IPO center recent filings, IPO calendar.

Real-Time Quotes: Free real-time quotes, although they are not streaming and must be refreshed.

States Registered In: All U.S. states.

Mutual Funds Offered: Over 4,000 from 160 families.

Payment for Order Flow: No.

Banking Services Offered: Free check writing and ATM debit card privileges.

Company Background: WR Hambrecht & Co. was founded in 1998, and its online trading began in 1999. Clients are protected by SIPC for up to $500,000, of which $100,000 covers cash. Excess protection is available from WR Hambrecht up to $99.5 million. WR Hambrecht uses Gainskeeper for its automated gain/loss portfolio valuation. WR Hambrecht offers a range of financial services, including electronic underwriting, retail brokerage, private equity, research, and mergers and acquisitions advisory services.

Customer Service Rating: ★★★ Excellent
Gomez Rating: 4.95

WYSE SECURITIES

Brokerage Type: Discount brokerage
Mailing Address: 20735 Stevens Creek Blvd. Suite C
Cupertino, CA 95014
Web Address: www.wyse-sec.com
Email Address: customerrelation@wysemail.com
Telephone Number: 800-640-8668, 408-343-2900
Fax Number: 408-252-4538
Market Orders: $7.95 per trade. Round lot share price $1.00 and up.
Stocks under $1.00 per share: $25.00 per trade, plus 2.75% of principal amount.
Limit Orders: Same as market orders.
Option Trades: $0–2,500: $17.00 plus 1.7% of principal. $2,501–10,000: $36.00 plus 0.8% of principal. $10,001 and up: $59.00 plus 0.3% of principal. Minimum charge: $5.75 per contract for first 5 contracts; $3.50 per contract for next 3 contracts; and $1.95 per contract thereafter. Minimum: $34.00 per execution. Maximum: $23.00 per contract.
Telephone Trading: $19.95 flat rate, round lot stocks over $1.00.
After-Hours Trading: 4:30 P.M. to 7:00 P.M. EST. Limit: $34.00 per trade. Round lots and broker-assisted trading only.
Products Available to Trade Online: Stocks and options.
Average Execution Time: Market order: immediate.
Minimum Deposit Required: $2,000 for cash or margin account.
Additional Fees: Duplicate statements: $5.00 first page plus $2.00 each additional page. Postage and handling: $4.50 (applies to all trades). IRA termination: $50.00. Returned checks: $15.00. Open order: $3.00.
Free Services and Financial Links: Portfolio tracker, quotes and symbol lookup, option quotes, option chains, price history, Market Snapshot, company news, intraday graphs, currency rates, economy calendar, Zacks, Briefing.com, investment newsletter, CNNfn, options symbols directory, Learn It Online, Digital Think.com, Gartner.com, Download.com, American Leasing.
Real-Time Quotes: 100 real-time quotes with each trade completed, although they are not streaming and must be refreshed.
States Registered In: All U.S. states.

Mutual Funds Offered: Over 317 families.

Payment for Order Flow: Yes.

Banking Services Offered: Free check writing privileges through a money market account (cash account only).

Company Background: Wyse Securities, a division of Pyramid Financial Corporation, was founded in 1989. It started providing online service in 1994. All Wyse clients are offered its website in English, Spanish, and Chinese. Clients' accounts are protected up to $100 million: SIPC covers $500,00 and Asset Guaranty Insurance Co. covers $99.5 million. Wyse Securities utilizes U.S. Clearing as its clearing firm. Wyse Securities consists mainly of individual traders and currently has a client base of approximately 9,000 online accounts.

Customer Service Rating: ★★ Average

Gomez Rating: 5.14

YOURTRADE.COM

Brokerage Type: Direct access

Mailing Address: 7997 West Sahara Ave. Suite 101
Las Vegas, Nevada 89117

Web Address: www.yourtrade.com

Email Address: info@yourtrade.com

Telephone Number: 877-999-5809, 702-214-7500

Fax Number: 702-214-7510

Market Orders: $14.95 per trade, up to 1,000 shares. Active traders can receive discounted commissions as low as $9.95 per trade.

Limit Orders: Same as market orders.

Option Trades: $25.00 per trade plus $1.75 per contract. Minimum: $30.00 per trade.

Telephone Trading: $24.95 per trade, up to 1,000 shares, and additional $0.01 per share thereafter.

After-Hours Trading: 9:00 A.M. to 9:30 A.M. EST and 4:00 P.M. to 6:30 P.M. EST. Same commissions as online schedule.

Products Available to Trade Online: Stocks and options.

Average Execution Time: Market order: approximately 5 seconds.

Minimum Deposit Required: $10,000 for all accounts. All trading accounts are considered margin accounts.

Additional Fees: Software fees: Remote Traders, $240.00 per month (fee waived with 100 trades per month). ECN fees: Island (Nasdaq), $1.00 per trade; Island (NYSE listed), $1.00 per trade; ARCA, $1.00 per trade; SOES, $0.50 per trade; SelectNet (preferenced), $1.00 per trade; SelectNet (broadcast), $2.50 per trade; NYSE listed, $0.008 per share; INCA, $1.00 per trade or $0.015 per share; BTRD, $1.00 per trade or $0.015 per share; TNTO, $1.00 per trade or $0.005 per share; REDI, $1.00 per trade or $0.015 per share; BRUT, $6.50 per trade; ATTN, $1.00 per trade base or $0.015 per share; STRK, $1.00 per trade base or $0.0066 per share; NTRD, $1.00 per trade base or $0.015 per share; SOES/SelectNet cancels, $0.25 per trade. Options exercise: $19.95. Wiring funds: $20.00. Outgoing account transfers: $25.00. Stop payments on checks: $15.00. Returned checks: $40.00. Transfer fee per certificate: $15.00. Legal transfers: $25.00. Regulation T extensions: $5.00. Reorganization items: $5.00. Overnight mail: $15.00. Copies of back statements: $5.00. Boot Camp Training (two weeks): $1,495.

Free Services and Financial Links: Company research, charts, Nasdaq and NYSE gainers, news.

Real-Time Quotes: Streaming real-time quotes with software package.

States Registered In: All U.S. states.

Mutual Funds Offered: Approximately 75–80.

Payment for Order Flow: No.

Banking Services Offered: Free check writing with discount brokerage account.

Company Background: YourTrade.com, a branch of InvestIN.com, was founded in June 1999 and went online in October 1999. YourTrade.com caters to active traders and online investors. Your-Trade's trading platform bypasses Web servers and executes clients' order directly with the exchanges. Clients' accounts are protected up to $25 million. SIPC provides coverage up to $500,000, of which $100,000 is for cash coverage, and the remaining $24.5 million is provided by a private insurer.

Customer Service Rating: ★★★ Excellent

Glossary

ACATS.   Automated Customer Account Transfer Service.

Account statement.   A periodic report giving the status of a client's transactions, debits, and credits.

Accredited investor.   To acquire this status, an investor must have a net worth of no less than $1 million or an annual income of no less than $250,000 or must invest a minimum of $150,000 per investment.

All or none (AON).   The buying or selling of a security, stipulating that a partial transaction is not to be executed.

American depository receipts (ADR).   Receipt for shares of a foreign-based corporation, being held in a U.S. bank vault so that the shareholder is entitled to all dividends and capital gains.

American Stock Exchange (Amex).   The second largest securities and commodities exchange, located at 86 Trinity Place in lower Manhattan, New York, NY.

Analyst.   A professional in the investment industry who evaluates the nature, features, and relationships of companies and industries, a process that, in turn, provides sound buying and selling recommendations to a brokerage firm or an individual client.

At or better.   An order given by a client to buy or sell a security at a specific price. The client will accept at or below the specific price if buying, or at or above the price if selling.

Asked price.   The lowest price at which a security is offered to sell on an exchange or market.

Bear market.   Term used to describe the atmosphere of the stock market when prices decline over a long period of time.

Bid.   The price a buyer is willing to pay for a security on an exchange or market.

Bond.   A debt security that is interest bearing and requires the issuer to pay the bondholder on a fixed due date.

Breakout.   A rise in a security price above its previous high price, or a drop below its previous low price. The breakout indicates that the price will continue in that direction for some time.

Brokerage. An intermediary between a buyer and a seller of securities that works on a commission basis.

Brokerage account. Official business relationship with a client in which all transactions are recorded.

Brokerage dealer. A firm that acts both as a brokerage, handling customer transactions, and as principal, acquiring securities for its own inventory and selling those securities for a profit.

Buy order. A client's order to buy a security at a specific price.

Canceled order. A transaction that is terminated before the order is executed.

Chicago Board of Options Exchange (CBOE). A U.S. marketplace that deals exclusively in options trading.

Chicago Board of Trade (CBOT). The largest U.S. futures exchange.

Cash account. A brokerage customer account in which all transactions are completed in cash.

Certificate. A formal document stating ownership and terms of a securities transaction.

Chicago Mercantile Exchange (CME). The second-largest U.S. futures exchange.

Clearing house. An organization that facilitates the validation, delivery, and settlement of securities transactions between member firms.

Commission. Fees paid to a broker for executing a trade.

Common stock. A security issued in shares of a public corporation. Stockholders have voting privileges and receive dividends on their holdings.

Confirmation. A formal trade notice to customers detailing their securities transaction.

Correction. A reversal movement, common in any long-term price trend, in the price of a stock, bond, or commodity.

Day order. A buy or sell order that will expire at the close of a day if it is not executed on the same day it was entered.

Day trade. To buy or sell a security during market hours on the same day.

Discount brokerage. A brokerage firm that executes trades at a lower commission rate but does not provide investment advice or full brokerage services.

Discretionary account.   A client account that allows a firm to buy or sell securities on the client's behalf but without the client's prior permission.

Dow Jones Industrial Average.   The oldest market indicator. The price movement of 30 actively traded industrial stocks provides a gauge that indicates the health and direction of the stock market.

Electronic Communication Network (ECN).   An electronic limit order book that allows investors to bypass a market maker and trade directly with one another. All participants can directly execute trades and place orders.

Extended-hours trading.   Trading time allowed before and after a stock market's normal trading hours.

Federal Deposit Insurance Corporation (FDIC).   A fund that insures all commercial and savings bank member accounts up to $100,000.

Fill or kill order (FOK).   A term that instructs a broker to trade an order completely as soon as it is requested. If the trade is not executed immediately, it is automatically cancelled.

Full-service brokerage.   A brokerage firm that offers its clients a wide variety of services, such as trading advice and account management.

Gain.   The profit acquired when a security is sold for more than its purchase price.

Individual Retirement Account (IRA).   A U.S. government tax-deferred retirement plan.

Limit order.   To buy or sell a security at a specific price or better.

Lipper Mutual Fund Industry Average.   The average performance level of all mutual funds, as reported by Lipper Analytical Services of New York.

Liquidity.   When company assets can be converted into cash or sold easily.

Margin account.   The amount of money a client deposits with his or her brokerage, against which the client can borrow when he or she wants to buy securities.

Market order.   An order to buy or sell a security at the best available price.

Mutual fund.   An investment firm that utilizes the shareholder's money by investing it in stocks, bonds, options, currencies, and money market securities for a fee.

National Association of Securities Dealers Automated Quotations (Nas-

daq).   A nationally computerized system for bid and ask quotations on over-the-counter stocks and NYSE listed stocks.

National Association of Securities Dealers (NASD).   A nonprofit organization comprised of brokers and dealers who trade in over-the-counter U.S. securities. NASD provides and enforces regulations to all its members. The NASD is supervised by the Securities and Exchange Commission.

New York Stock Exchange (NYSE).   The oldest and largest stock exchange in the United States, located at 11 Wall Street, New York, NY.

Option.   A contract that allows an investor to buy or sell a predetermined quantity of securities at a specific price and in a specific amount of time. If the transaction does not occur during the specific time period, the option expires.

Over-the-counter (OTC) securities.   Securities not listed on any of the major exchanges. Securities are traded over the telephone or a computerized network that connects the dealers.

Partial execution.   When the investor accepts that only part of a round-lot order is executed.

Penny stock.   Low-priced securities that trade over-the-counter for less than $1.00 per share.

Portfolio.   All the securities in a client's account.

Quotation.   A security's current bid or ask price.

Regulation T.   A federal regulation that states the amount of credit a brokerage firm may extend to its customer.

Round lot.   100 shares of stock.

Retail investor.   An individual investor.

Round-trip trade.   Buying and selling a security within a short period of time.

Securities.   Term used to describe bonds, stocks, and shares of all types.

Securities and Exchange Commission (SEC).   A federal agency that regulates and supervises the laws governing the securities industry.

Securities Investor Protection Corporation (SIPC).   A private nonprofit organization that provides insurance protection for brokerage accounts at a maximum of $500,000 per customer with a limit of $100,000 in cash.

Sell order.   A client's request to sell a security at a specific price.

Settlement date.   The date in which executed securities must be settled to complete a transaction.

Small cap. Small capitalization stocks.

Standard & Poors Index (S&P 500). A measure of the average performance of 500 of the most commonly held stocks used to predict potential movements and market volatility.

Stop order. An order given to a broker to buy or sell a security when a specific price is reached or passed.

SuperDot (Designated Order Turnaround). An automated NYSE order entry system.

Tick. The movement in a security's trade up or down.

Trade confirmation. A customer's written transaction verification.

Unit investment trust (UIT). A fixed portfolio of securities sold to investors as units.

Volatility. The sharp rise or fall in the price of a security within a short period of time.

Volume. The total number of shares traded by a single security or by the entire market within a specific period.

Index